English & Grammar
MASTER

영어 시험에 꼭 필요한
영문법 6코스

박연우 지음

English&북스

English&
Grammar
MASTER

초판 1쇄 발행 2023년 9월 15일
초판 2쇄 발행 2023년 12월 15일

지은이 박연우
펴낸이 박성호
펴낸곳 잉글리쉬앤(주)

편　집 장서원
영업마케팅 여주형, 김성윤, 방성출, 박훈효, 조민형, 이달님, 강정구, 이진희, 조병운, 변중구, 정노을, 조예선, 조광민, 이현정, 김정민, 최희성, 최인태, 윤종철, 엄주아, 윤지원, 우민지, 이가은

주　소 서울 특별시 관악구 쑥고개로 67-1
대표전화 (02) 878-1945
출판등록 2002년 3월 3일 제 320-2002-00045호

ISBN 978-89-6715-168-3　13740

저작권자 2023 잉글리쉬앤(주)
이 책은 잉글리쉬앤(주)에 의해 출간되었으므로
저자와 출판사의 서면에 의한 허락 없이 글과 그림의 인용, 복제, 발췌를 금합니다.

* 가격은 뒤표지에 있습니다. 파본은 바꾸어 드립니다.
www.english.co.kr

서문

현대 사회에서 영어의 중요성은 아무리 강조해도 지나치지 않습니다. 취업, 진학, 승진 등 모든 분야에서 활용되고 있고, 개인의 능력을 평가하는 잣대가 되기도 하니 국내의 수험생 대부분이 영어에 열중 하는 것은 어찌 보면 당연한 일일 수도 있습니다.

영어를 강의하면서 제가 가장 많이 받는 질문은 "어떻게 하면 영어를 잘 할 수 있습니까? 고득점 비결은 무엇인가요?"입니다. 저는 그때마다 '최고의 비결은 꾸준함'이라고 답변을 합니다.

어학 공부는 다이어트를 하는 과정과 같습니다. 독한 마음을 먹고 처음부터 강하게 밀고 나가야 나중에 습관으로 굳어져 저절로 공부하게 된다는 점을 강조하고 싶습니다. 또 '무엇을 위해 공부하는가?'에 대한 명확한 목표 의식과 하루 학습 일과 등 구체적인 로드맵 설정도 필요합니다.

모든 언어를 습득하는 과정은 듣고, 말하고, 읽고, 쓰는 일련의 과정을 거치게 됩니다. 이때, 문법은 효율적으로 언어를 습득하고 정확한 표현을 위한 도구라고 생각하면 됩니다. 영문법을 공부하는 가장 좋은 방법은 제대로 된 교재와 방법으로 이론부터 차근차근 익히고, 실전문제를 통해 반복 연습을 하는 것입니다.

'잉글리쉬앤 그래머 MASTER'는 영문법을 체계적으로 학습하여 실전 시험에 적용할 수 있도록 하는데 초점을 맞췄습니다. GRAMMAR POINT에서 학습한 이론을 GRAMMAR PRACTICE로 문제를 풀며 확인하고, GRAMMAR IN SENTENCE를 통해 독해력을 향상시킬 수 있습니다. 또한 공인 영어 시험을 준비를 하는 수험생들에게는 ACTUAL TEST, MINI TEST, FINAL TEST 등을 통해 체계적으로 정리할 수 있는 기회를 갖도록 구성했습니다. '잉글리쉬앤그래머 MASTER'로 여러분이 원하는 영어 문법의 실력을 쌓고, 이를 바탕으로 더 큰 세상으로 도약할 수 있기를 바랍니다.

마지막으로 '잉글리쉬앤그래머 MASTER'를 집필할 수 있도록 해주신 박성호 대표님, 여주형 이사님, 변중구 과장님 그리고 장서원 편집자님께 진심으로 감사드립니다.

저자 **박연우**

차 례

서문 ··· 8
이 책의 구성과 특징 ··· 10

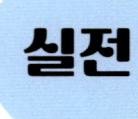

1코스

Unit 1 | 명사 ··· 12
Unit 2 | 대명사 ·· 22
Unit 3 | 동사 ··· 32
Actual Test 1 ·· 42

2코스

Unit 4 | 형용사 ·· 46
Unit 5 | 부사 ··· 56
Unit 6 | 전치사 ·· 66
Actual Test 2 ·· 76
Mini Test 1 ·· 78

3코스

Unit 7 | 수일치 ·· 84
Unit 8 | 시제 ··· 90
Unit 9 | 태 ·· 100
Actual Test 3 ·· 110

4코스

Unit 10 │ 부정사	114
Unit 11 │ 동명사	124
Unit 12 │ 분사	134
Actual Test 4	144
Mini Test 2	146

5코스

Unit 13 │ 접속사 I	152
Unit 14 │ 접속사 II	162
Unit 15 │ 관계사	170
Actual Test 5	180

6코스

Unit 16 │ 가정법	184
Unit 17 │ 비교	192
Unit 18 │ 강조와 도치	198
Actual Test 6	204
Mini Test 3	206
Final Test	210

정답 및 해설 · 217

문법 개념 학습과 문제 풀이 적용을 한번에!

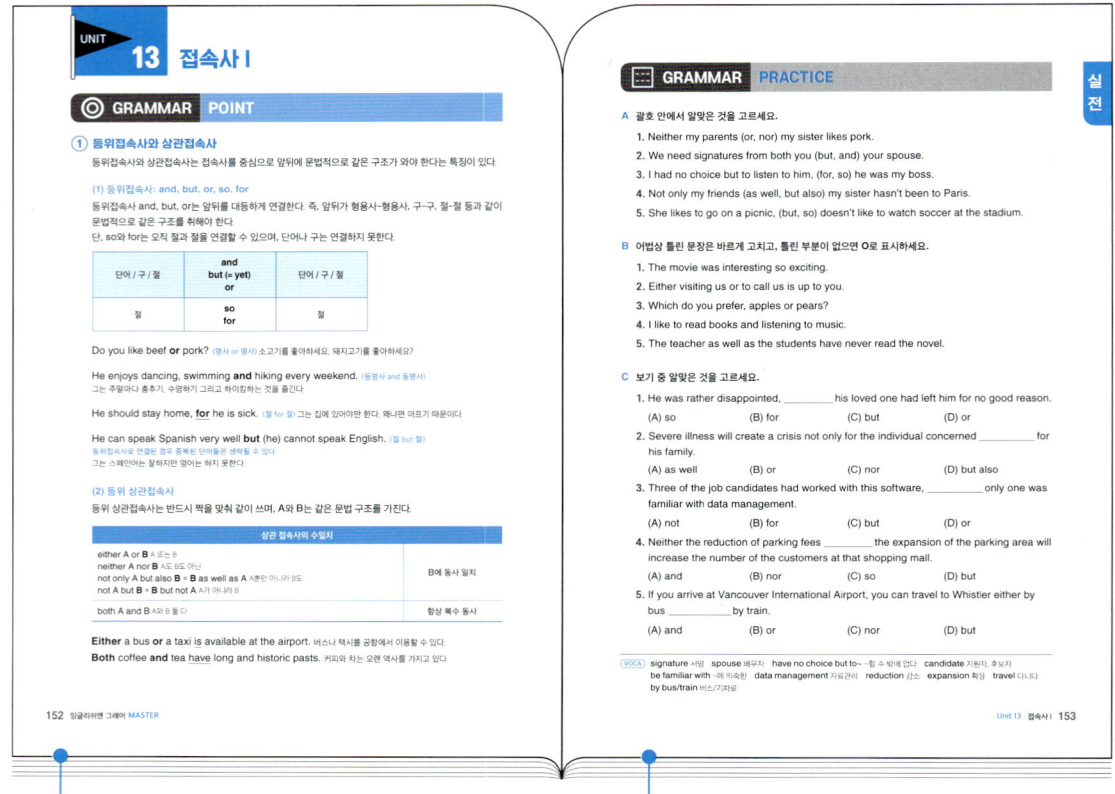

**쉽고 상세한 문법 설명
천천히 읽고 개념에 익숙해지세요.**

방대한 문법 체계 안에서 무엇부터 공부해야 할지부터 막막하지 않았나요?
가장 암기하기 쉬운 개념부터 심화 개념까지 효율적인 순서대로 학습합니다.

**방금 배운 알게 된 문법 개념을
오픈북 방식으로 문제를 풀어보세요.**

처음부터 외우려고 부담 갖지 마세요!
처음에는 문법 개념에 익숙해지고 이해하고 정리된 내용을 보고 문제에 적용하는 연습을 해봅니다.

문장 안에서 학습한 문법 개념을 독해까지 적용하기

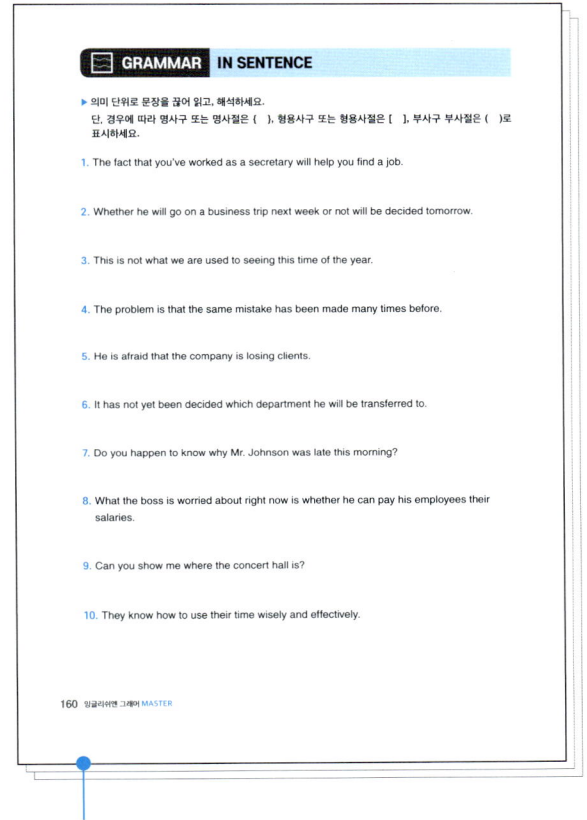

유닛별로 문장 안에 문법 개념을 적용해서 해석해보세요.

문법 개념을 배울 때는 이해가 됐는데 막상 문장이나 지문을 봤을 때 해석이 막혀서 답답한 적 없었나요? 문법을 문장 안에서 다시 적용해보고 나면, 학습한 문법 개념이 독해에 적용되어 어느새 끊어 읽기를 자연스럽게 하고 있는 자신을 발견하게 됩니다.

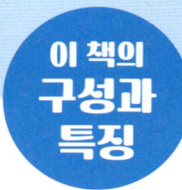

이 책의 구성과 특징

Unit과 Unit 사이 핵심 개념 요약으로 다시 또 정리!

요약된 중요 개념 포인트를 보며 단번에 전체 내용을 정리해볼 수 있습니다.

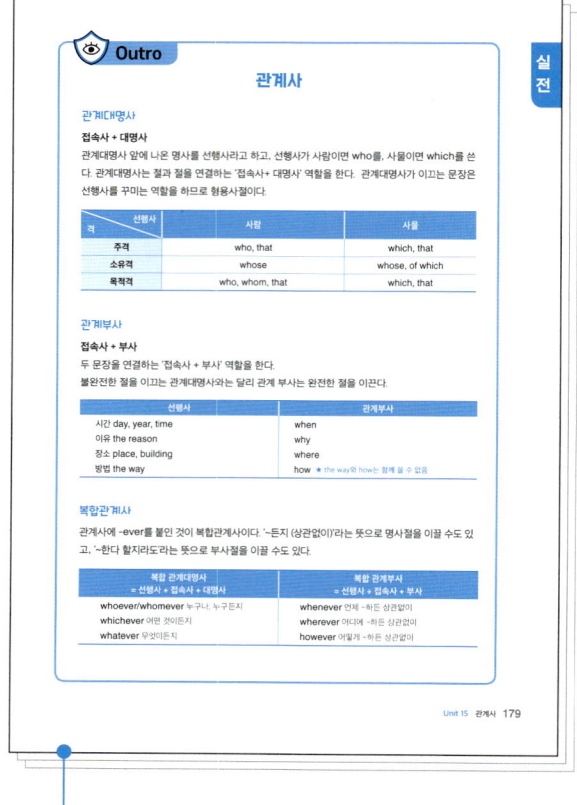

새로운 문법 개념을 공부하기 전, 바로 직전에 배웠던 문법 개념을 짧게 훑어보세요.

문법은 서로 서로 개념이 연결되어 있어 중요한 포인트를 암기하고 있지 않으면 다른 개념 학습에도 어려움이 있습니다.
그 많은 양을 언제 다 복습하지? 머리가 아파오는 순간, 그때 Outro 한 페이지를 활용해보세요.

* OUTRO 요약본 PDF 무료 제공!

코스와 코스 사이 TEST로 마무리!

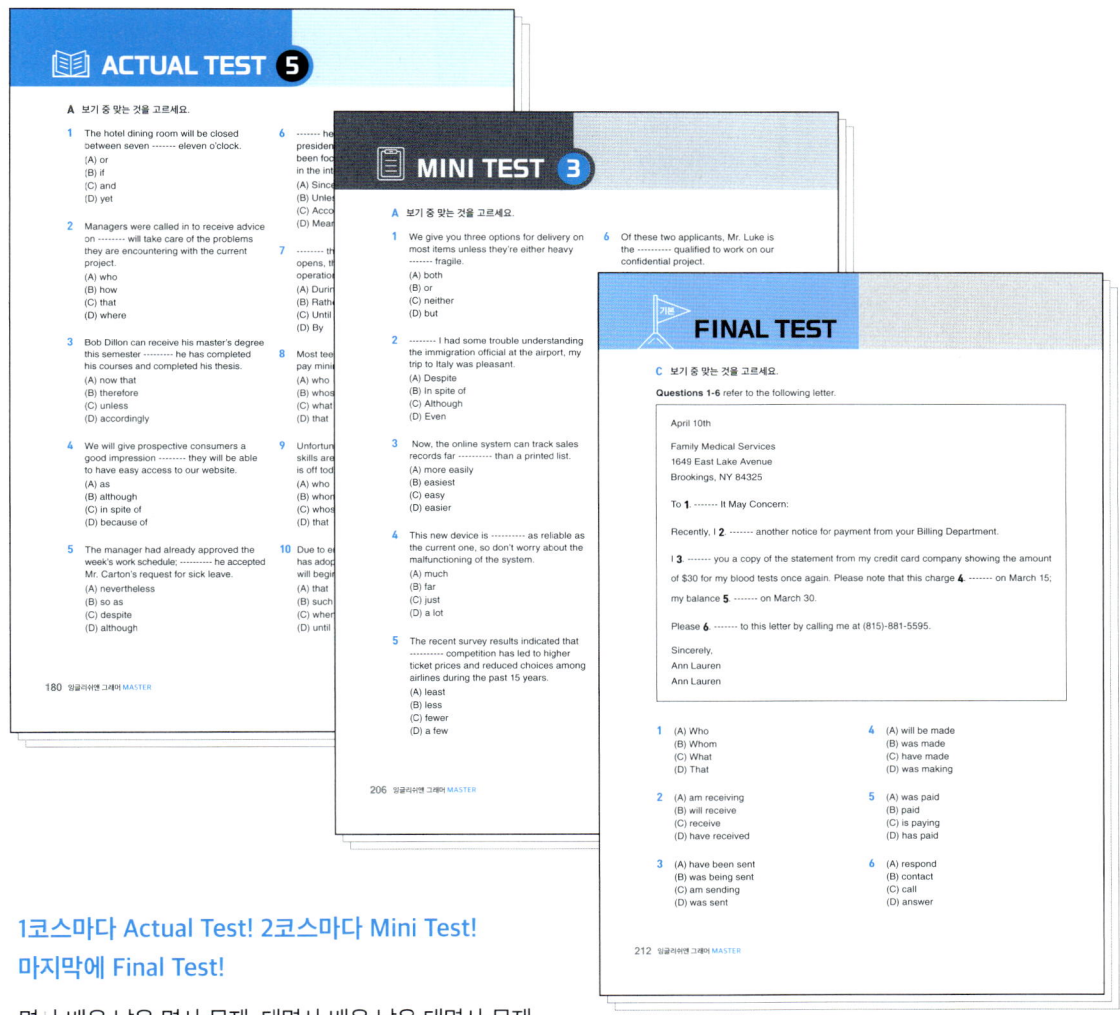

**1코스마다 Actual Test! 2코스마다 Mini Test!
마지막에 Final Test!**

명사 배운 날은 명사 문제, 대명사 배운 날은 대명사 문제. 문법서에서 문제는 잘 풀렸는데 막상 시험장에서 문제는 안 풀리지 않았나요? 학습 범위가 누적될수록 Test의 범위도 넓어집니다. 전체 범위에서 학습한 문법 개념을 적용하여 시험까지 준비할 수 있어요.

잉글리쉬앤 그래머 MASTER

실전편

 코스

Unit 1 명사
Unit 2 대명사
Unit 3 동사

6코스

5코스

4코스

UNIT 01 명사

◎ GRAMMAR POINT

명사는 사람, 사물을 지칭하는 girl, book, David 와 같은 단어이다. 문장에서 주어, 보어, 타동사의 목적어, 전치사의 목적어 등 여러 가지 중요한 역할을 한다.

① 명사의 역할과 위치

명사는 문장에서 주어, 보어, 타동사의 목적어, 전치사의 목적어 등 여러 가지 중요한 역할을 한다.

(1) 주어 + 동사

The manager came up with a highly competitive marketing campaign.
매니저가 매우 경쟁력 있는 마케팅 캠페인을 생각해냈다.

(2) 타동사 + 목적어

They have not been able to reach **an agreement**. 그들은 합의점을 찾지 못했다.

(3) 전치사 + 목적어

We were surprised by **the news**. 우리는 그 소식에 놀랐다.

(4) 자동사 + 주격보어

James became **an actor**. James 는 배우가 되었다.

(5) 타동사 + 목적어 + 목적격보어

Teachers thought David **a genius**. 모든 사람들은 David를 천재라고 생각했다.

② 명사가 쓰이는 형태

(1) 한정사 (관사, 소유격) + 명사

Mr. Davidson reserved the right to give his **opinion** to the committee.
Davidson 씨는 위원회에 그의 의견을 말할 권리가 있었다.

(2) 형용사 + 명사

Tom Jefferson is one of the competitive **applicants** for the position.
Tom Jefferson 씨는 경쟁력 있는 지원자들 중의 한 명이다.

(3) 한정사 + 부사 + 형용사 + 명사

Sara is looking at the newly purchased **computer** in her room.
Sara는 그녀의 방에 새로 구입한 컴퓨터를 바라보는 중이다.

GRAMMAR PRACTICE

A 괄호 안에서 알맞은 것을 고르시오.

1. The (manager, managing) came up with a competitive marketing campaign.
2. All proceeds will be used to acquire more (proper, property).
3. There is no cost or obligation to register in (advance, advancement).
4. People elected Mr. Anderson a (presidential, president).
5. The (construct, construction) of City Hall has been canceled.
6. Our team made a (decision, decisive) about a marketing proposal last week.
7. Mr. Tylor will deliver a short speech to express his (appreciation, appreciate) for the retirement gift.
8. Ms. Johns led the team to double-digit revenue growth and received a (promote, promotion) to new business director.
9. The exhibition area will be closed at night but please don't leave any (valuables, value) unattended.
10. This position needs to be filled due to the (resign, resignation) of the present vice president.

B 어법상 틀린 문장은 바르게 고치고, 틀린 부분이 없으면 O로 표시하세요.

1. In spite of his deny that he robbed the bank, the man was found guilty.
2. These results suggest that dogs have the capacity to empathize with humans.
3. Company officials have taken steps to obtain approve from the U.S. Food and Drug Administration.
4. Our special is creating multilevel work arrangements by widening floor spaces.
5. It is a matter of regret that the long continued negotiate have finally proved a failure.

VOCA come up with ~을 생각해내다 proceeds 수입금 acquire 취득하다 property 재산, 자산, 소유물 obligation 의무, 책임 in advance 미리, 사전에 advancement 전진, 발달 presidential 대통령의, 주재하는 deliver a speech 연설하다 express one's appreciation 감사를 표하다 retirement gift 은퇴 선물 receive a promotion 승진하다 exhibition 전시 valuables 귀중품 guilty 유죄의 capacity 수용 능력 empathize 공감하다 U.S. Food and Drug Administration. 미국 식품 의약국 create 디자인하다 arrangement 배열 widen 넓히다 floor 바닥 space 공간 It is a matter of regret ~이 아쉬운 점이다 failure 실패

◎ GRAMMAR POINT

③ 가산명사와 불가산명사

명사는 셀 수 있는 가산명사와 셀 수 없는 불가산명사로 나뉜다.
가산명사는 단수와 복수가 있고, 불가산명사는 셀 수 없는 명사이고, 언제나 단수취급을 한다.

(1) 가산 명사의 특징

① 단수 가산 명사 앞에는 항상 한정사(관사, 소유격, 지시 형용사)가 온다.
I read book. (X) → I read **a** book / **the** book / **this** book. (O) 나는 책을 읽었다.

② 가산 명사의 복수 형태는 주로 뒤에 **-(e)s**를 붙이며, 한정사 없이 쓸 수 있다.
I like reading **books**. 나는 책 읽기를 좋아한다.

③ 가산 명사는 **many, a few, few, several** 등의 수량 형용사의 수식을 받는다.
A few students passed the exam. 몇 명의 학생들이 시험을 통과했다.
There are **many** students on the ground. 운동장에 많은 학생들이 있다.

☑ 셀 수 없는 것처럼 보이지만 가산 명사인 것(앞에 a, the, 소유격 등의 한정사가 없으면 반드시 복수 형태로 쓸 것)

a discount 할인	a price 가격	a refund 환불	a relation 관계
an approach 접근법	a statement 내역서, 진술	a source 근원, 출처	a description 설명
an account 설명	an issue 발행물	a purpose 목적	a delay 연기

(2) 불가산 명사의 특징

① 항상 단수 취급하며, 부정관사(**a/an**)가 올 수 없고, 복수형도 없다.
a furniture (X), furnitures (X) → furniture (O)

② 특정 단위를 이용하여 셀 수 있다.
two pieces of furniture 가구 두 점   **three cups of** coffee 석 잔의 커피

③ **much, a little, little** 등 양을 나타내는 수식어와 쓰인다.
We don't need too **much** information. 우리는 너무 많은 정보가 필요한 것은 아니다.

☑ 기억해야 할 불가산 명사

access 접근, 출입	advice 조언, 충고	information 정보	news 소식
equipment 기구, 장비	machinery 기계류	stationery 문구류	weaponry 무기류
scenery 장면	furniture 가구	progress 진보	baggage = luggage 수하물

☑ 가산 명사 vs. 불가산 명사

가산 명사	불가산 명사	가산 명사	불가산 명사
an account 계좌	accounting 회계	an advertisement 광고	advertising 광고하기
clothes 옷	clothing 의류	a fund 자금	funding 자금 제공
furnishings 가구	furniture 가구류	goods 상품	merchandise 상품류
a lender 대출 기관	lending 대출, 대부	a process 과정 procedures 절차	processing 처리하기
a letter 편지	mail 우편물	a seat 좌석	seating 앉히기

GRAMMAR PRACTICE

A 괄호 안에서 알맞은 것을 고르시오.

1. People are waiting to claim their (baggage, baggages) at the airport.
2. This is (a great news, great news) for Lucas Construction.
3. No invoices has been found for any of the (good, goods).
4. Happy Mart is offering big (discount, discounts) on some of our most popular items.
5. (Advertisement, Advertising) through TV commercials is impossible for some smaller businesses.
6. The new manger requested (access, approach) to the sales report for the last three years.
7. We need a lot of (information, informations) about our competitor.
8. We recommend purchasing some office (furnitures, furniture) such as desks and chairs.
9. Professional and cultural organizations can be (source, sources) of information about scholarships.
10. If your claim is approved, we will issue (refund, a refund) in the same form that your original payment was made.

B 어법상 틀린 문장은 바르게 고치고, 틀린 부분이 없으면 O로 표시하세요.

1. Jane should ask our parents and teachers for good advices.
2. Starting next month, you will receive monthly issue of *New Scientist journal*.
3. The woman is looking for a restaurant with outdoor seat.
4. The investment includes product development, machinery and new equipment.
5. The luggages had never been used before and was in perfect condition.

VOCA claim (기탁물을) 찾다 invoice 송장 popular 인기 있는 commercial 광고 competitor 경쟁자, 경쟁 상대
professional 직업의, 전문직의, 직업적인, 프로의 source 출처, 근원, 원천 scholarship 장학금, 학문 claim 요구
approve 승인하다 issue 지급하다 issue 발행(물) investment 투자 product development 제품 개발
machinery 기계류

◎ GRAMMAR POINT

④ 한정사의 개념

명사의 뜻을 한정하는 말을 한정사라고 한다. 한정사에는 관사 (a, an, the), 지시형용사 (this, that, these, those 등), 대명사의 소유격 (my, your, his, her 등)이 있다.

한정사 뒤에는 반드시 명사가 와야 하며, 한정사의 종류에 따라 명사의 단수와 복수가 결정된다는 것에 주의해야 한다. 특히, 앞에 a, the, 소유격 등의 한정사가 없으면 반드시 복수 형태로 써야 한다.

한정사	가산명사		불가산명사
	단수	복수	
부정관사 a (an)	a suggestion (O)	X	X
정관사 the	the suggestion (O)	the suggestions (O)	the advice (O)
무관사 (한정사 없음)	X	suggestions (O)	advice (O)
소유격 (my, your)	my suggestion (O)	my suggestions (O)	my advice (O)
지시형용사 (this, that)	this suggestion	X	this advice (O)
지시형용사 (these, those)	X	these suggestions	X

⑤ 관사의 용법

(1) 부정관사(a, an)의 용법

가산 명사의 단수 앞에만 쓸 수 있으며, 명사의 발음이 자음으로 시작되면 a, 모음으로 시작되면 an을 사용한다.

one (하나)	I have **an** American friend here. 나는 이곳에 미국인 친구가 한 명 있다.
a certain (어떤)	In **a** sense, it is true. 어떤 의미로는 사실이다.
the same (같은)	We are of **an** age. 우리는 동갑이다.
per (마다)	I write a letter to her twice **a** week. 나는 그녀에게 일주일에 두 번씩 편지를 쓴다.
some (어느 정도, 약간)	He was speechless for **a** time. 그는 잠시 말이 없었다.

(2) 정관사 the의 용법

가산 명사의 단수와 복수 앞에 모두 쓰일 수 있으며, 불가산 명사 앞에도 나올 수 있다. 앞에 나온 명사가 반복될 때, 수식어 구에 의해 한정이 될 때, 문맥상 전후 관계로 보아 무엇을 가리키는지를 누구나 알 수 있는 경우, 일반적으로 유일무이한 것과 최상급 및 서수(first, second …), last, same 앞에서 사용된다.

Water is changed into steam by heat. (물질명사) 물은 열에 의하여 수증기로 변한다.
The water in this cup is hot. 이 컵에 있는 물은 뜨겁다.

(3) 관사에 주의해야 할 관용표현

at the beginning/end of the month 이 달 초/말에
as a result of ~의 결과로
as a whole 전체적으로
reach an agreement 합의점에 도달하다
take advantage of ~을 이용하다
in error 실수로

in an effort to ~의 노력의 일환으로
all of a sudden 갑자기
come to an end ~으로 끝나다
take care of ~을 돌보다
until further notice 추후 통보가 있을 때까지
in detail 자세히

GRAMMAR PRACTICE

A 괄호 안에서 알맞은 것을 고르세요.

1. All the planets travel in (same, the same) direction.
2. This is (best, the best) movie that I have ever seen.
3. Don't forget to send (report, the report) about the sales figures.
4. The company has increased its incentives in (an effort, effort) to encourage employees.
5. You should finish the report by (an end, the end) of this month.

B 다음 밑줄 친 부분 a(n)의 의미를 찾아 번호를 쓰시오.

> ① one (하나) ② a certain (어떤) ③ the same (같은) ④ per (마다) ⑤ some (어느 정도, 약간)

1. Ms. Kimberly stays at **a** small hotel.
2. The students in the classroom are all of **an** age.
3. **A** year has 12 months.
4. We have a meeting three times **a** week.
5. David was seated on the bench for **a** while.

C 다음 밑줄 친 부분 the의 쓰임을 찾아 번호를 쓰시오.

> ① 앞에 나온 명사가 반복될 때
> ② 수식어구(형용사구, 형용사절)에 의해 한정이 될 때
> ③ 문맥상 전후 관계로 보아 무엇을 가리키는지를 누구나 알 수 있는 경우
> ④ 일반적으로 유일무이한 것에 사용
> ⑤ 최상급, 서수(first, second ...), last, same 앞에서 사용

1. The water in this well is not good to drink.
2. I met a man, and the man showed me the way.
3. The sun is much larger than the moon.
4. The post office is near the station.
5. Seoul is the largest city in Korea.

VOCA planet 행성 direction 방향 sales figures 판매 수치 in an effort to ~의 노력의 일환으로 encourage 촉진하다, 장려하다, 격려하다

◎ GRAMMAR POINT

⑥ 복합명사

둘 이상의 명사가 결합하여 이루어져 하나의 명사와 같은 구실을 하는 것을 복합명사라고 한다.

account number 계좌 번호	attendance record 출석 기록
assembly line 조립 라인	application form 지원서
accounting certification 회계 증명서	apartment complex 아파트 단지
construction site 건설 현장	consumer awareness 소비자 인식
consumer loan 소비자 대출	customer satisfaction 소비자 만족
delivery schedule 배송 일정	expiration date 만기일
employee satisfaction 직원 만족	grocery store 식료품점
identification card 신분증	insurance coverage 보험 보상 범위
media coverage 언론 보도	production schedule 생산 일정
product availability 제품 이용	pay raise = pay increase 급여 인상
precipitation data 강수량 자료	research program 연구 프로그램
safety precaution 안전 예방 수칙	marketing strategy 마케팅 전략
-s형 명사 + 명사	
customs officer 세관원	customs clearance 세관 수속
customs declaration 세관 신고	earnings growth 수익 성장
savings account 저축 예금	sales strategy 판매 전략
sports complex 종합 경기장	Human Resources Department 인사부, 인사과

⑦ 형태는 비슷하지만 의미가 다른 명사

cover 표지, 덮개 coverage (취재, 보상적용) 범위	chairs under **covers** 덮개를 씌운 의자 a pension fund and healthcare **coverage** 연금과 의료 혜택
delivery 배달 deliverance 구조, 해방	overseas **delivery** 해외 배송 **deliverance** from sin 죄로부터의 해방
entry 참가등록 entrance 입구	gain **entry** into a club 클럽에의 가입이 허가되다 at the **entrance** to a city 도시의 입구에서
object 물체 objection 반대 objective 목적, 목표 objectivity 객관성	an unidentified **object** 미확인 물체 **Objection**, your honor. 재판장님, 이의 있습니다. the **objective** of the president's visit 사장님 방문의 목적 a matter of personal **objectivity** 개인적인 객관성의 문제
permit 허가증 permission 허가	a parking **permit** 주차 허가증 written **permission** 서면상의 허가
remainder 나머지 remains 유물	the **remainder** of the property 잔여 재산 fossils or other **remains** 화석과 다른 유해들
responsibility 책임 response 응답	the government's primary **responsibility** 정부의 주요한 책임 a good **response** from fans 팬들의 좋은 반응
produce 농산물, 농작물 product 제품 production 생산, 제작 productivity 생산성, 생산능력	a lot of **produce** 많은 농작물 a lot of food **products** 많은 식품 higher **production** efficiency 더 높은 생산 효율성 raise **productivity** 생산성을 높이다

GRAMMAR PRACTICE

A 괄호 안에서 알맞은 것을 고르시오.

1. There are a lot of (products, produce) in the field.
2. The price seldom directly reflects the cost of (delivery, deliverance).
3. Ms. Kimberly said music raised (production, productivity) in her classroom.
4. This is lower in cost and has higher (produce, production) efficiency.
5. Anybody who visits our company should contact the (informative, information) desk for identification.
6. All the employees already have their own savings (accounting, account).
7. Please send copies of academic transcripts and certificates and a letter of reference along with a completed (applying, application) form.
8. The bank branch will open once inspectors verify that we have complied with all (safe, safety) regulations.
9. This year, a lot of (products, produces) have come in pink and red from lipsticks to high heels.
10. The company's first five-year plan requires a steady increase in employee (production, productivity)

B 어법상 틀린 문장은 바르게 고치고, 틀린 부분이 없으면 **O**로 표시하세요.

1. The visitors are in the underground park lot.
2. They have reformed their business regulations to promote foreign investment.
3. Our goal is to provide customer satisfactory and to ensure that customers return over and over again.
4. The Account Department has paid all of the monthly invoices.
5. The emphasis of this annual contest is a part of the government's promotion strategy.

VOCA deliverance 구출, 구조, 해방 informative 유익한, 정보를 제공하는 along with ~와 함께, ~와 같이 complete (형용사) 완전한, 완비된 academic transcript 성적표 certificate (학위 없는 과정의) 수료증 inspector 시찰 자 verify 확인하다 comply with ~을 따르다 lipstick 립스틱 require 요구하다 steady 지속적인, 꾸준한 underground 지하의 ensure 책임지다 invoice 송장 emphasis 강조

GRAMMAR IN SENTENCE

▶ 의미 단위로 문장을 끊어 읽고, 해석하세요.
단, 경우에 따라 명사구 또는 명사절은 { }, 형용사구 또는 형용사절은 [ ], 부사 부사구 부사절은 ( )로 표시하세요.

1. These results suggest that dogs have the capacity to empathize with humans.

2. Our specialty is creating multilevel work arrangements by widening floor spaces.

3. Anybody who visits our company should contact the information desk for identification.

4. The company has increased its incentives in an effort to encourage employees.

5. You should finish the report by the end of the month.

6. Please send copies of academic transcripts or certificates and a letter of reference along with a completed application form.

7. The bank branch will open once inspectors verify that we have complied with all safety regulations.

8. They have reformed their business regulations to promote foreign investment.

9. Our goal is to provide customer satisfaction and to ensure that consumers return over and over again.

10. The emphasis of this annual contest is a part of the government's promotion strategy.

명사

사람, 사물을 지칭하는 단어인 명사는 문장에서 주어, 보어, 타동사의 목적어, 전치사의 목적어 등 여러 가지 중요한 역할을 하며, 가산명사와 불가산 명사가 있다. 가산명사는 단수와 복수가 있고, 불가산명사는 셀 수 없는 명사이고 언제나 단수취급을 한다.

명사의 역할

주어 역할	**Employees** rejected the proposal. 직원들은 그 제안을 거절했다.
목적어 역할	Intel, Inc. submitted **a proposal**. Intel 사는 제안서를 제출했다.
보어 역할	Tom became **a chemist**. Tom은 화학자가 되었다.

명사의 형태

명사를 나타내는 접미사는 주로 -ion [-tion, -sion], -ty [-ity], -ance [ence], -ment, -ness, -age, -al 등이 있다.

-ion [-tion, -sion]	-ty [-ity]	-al
cancellation 취소	authority 권위(자)	appeal 호소
confirmation 확인	flexibility 융통성, 유연성	arrival 도착(지)
decision 결정	possibility 가능성	appraisal 평가
expansion 확장	responsibility 책임, 의무	potential 잠재력
identification 신분증	creativity 독창성	approval 승인, 허가
relation 관계	maturity 성숙(기)	proposal 제안(서)

-ance [ence]	-ment	-age
advance 진보, 향상	agreement 일치, 합의	age 나이, 연령
evidence 증거	development 발달, 개발	damage 피해
performance 수행	investment 투자	**-ness**
observance 준수, 연주	commitment 위탁, 공약	illness 병
difference 차이	disappointment 실망	effectiveness 효율성

UNIT 02 대명사

GRAMMAR POINT

대명사란 이미 언급된 특정 명사가 반복되어 사용되는 것을 피하기 위해 명사를 대신해서 쓰이는 것으로서 문장 안에서 명사와 마찬가지로 주어, 목적어, 보어로 쓰인다. 대명사는 사람이나 사물을 대신해서 쓰이는 인칭대명사와 특정한 것을 나타내는(이것, 저것) 지시대명사, 막연한 명사를 나타낼 때 쓰이는 부정대명사 (some, any, one 등)가 있다.

① 인칭대명사의 종류

	인칭	주격	소유격	목적격	소유대명사	재귀대명사
단수	1인칭	I	my	me	mine	myself
	2인칭	you	your	you	yours	yourself
	3인칭	he	his	him	his	himself
		she	her	her	hers	herself
복수	1인칭	we	our	us	ours	ourselves
	2인칭	you	your	you	yours	yourselves
	3인칭	they	their	them	theirs	themselves

② 인칭 대명사의 격

(1) 주격 : 주격 + 동사

I **believe** that **she is** a good professor. 나는 그녀가 훌륭한 교수라고 생각한다.

(2) 소유격 : 소유격 + 명사

Please give **your business card** to everybody. (business card를 수식)
사람들에게 모두 당신의 명함을 주세요.

(3) 목적격

① 타동사 + 목적격

Please fill out this form and **submit it** to us. 이 양식에 기입해 주세요. 그리고 우리에게 그것을 제출하세요.

② 전치사 + 목적격

Our team bought some flowers **for her**. 우리 팀은 그녀를 위해 꽃을 좀 샀다.

(4) 소유대명사

<소유 + 명사>의 의미를 띠는 것이 소유대명사이다. 주로 be동사 뒤에 나온다.

The photos in the envelope **are** my sister's and **mine**.
봉투 안에 있는 사진들은 나의 여동생과 나의 것이다.

■ 소유격과 소유대명사의 구분

소유격 형용사 뒤에는 명사가 와서 대명사가 명사를 수식하는 '형용사' 역할을 하지만, 소유대명사는 뒤에 명사가 올 수 없고, 스스로 '~의 것'이라는 의미를 갖는다.

This is **her book** = This book is **hers**.

GRAMMAR PRACTICE

A 괄호 안에서 알맞은 것을 고르시오.

1. We believe that (her, she) is a good manager.
2. All customers are free to use (our, us) swimming pool.
3. I can't go there because of (him, his).
4. (She, Her) first novel won a prestigious literary prize.
5. Ms. Lee submitted her report this morning, but I haven't finished (mine, myself) yet.

B 주어진 표현을 활용하여 문장을 완성하시오.

1. Her hair is long, but _____ is short. (he)
2. I'll transfer _____ call to the Human Resources division. (you)
3. The journal was sent to _____ yesterday. (she)
4. This white car in the parking lot is _____. (he)
5. The film _____ isn't good, but I like the music. (it)

C 다음 글을 읽고 어법상 틀린 문장은 바르게 고치고, 틀린 부분이 없으면 O로 표시하세요.

From:	Phillip Fantone
To:	Melody Choi
Subject:	Job openings
Date:	July 15th

1. Hello, Ms. Choi. When our last talked in February, you were waiting to hear back about a job you had applied for.
2. If you didn't take that job, I thought you might like to know that we are in need of a trainer here.
3. Our trainer, Mr. Lee, will be transferring to us new Singapore office in August, and I think you would be the perfect person to replace him.
4. Please give my an e-mail or give me a call to let me know if you're available.
5. I look forward to talking with you again. Thanks.

VOCA prestigious 명성 있는　literary 문학의　prize 상　available 가능한, 시간이 되는

◎ GRAMMAR POINT

③ 재귀대명사

(1) 재귀적 용법
문장의 주어와 목적어가 같은 경우에 목적어 자리에 재귀대명사를 쓴다. 생략 불가능.

I would like to introduce **myself** to you. 제 자신을 소개하겠습니다.

(2) 강조적 용법
주어나 목적어를 강조하기 위해 강조하는 말 바로 뒤나, 문장 맨 뒤에 온다. 생략 가능.

The president himself shook hands with each employee.
= **The president** shook hands with each employee **himself**.
= **The president** shook hands with each employee.
사장이 직접 개별적으로 직원들과 악수를 했다.

(3) 관용표현

by oneself 혼자서	for oneself 스스로	beside oneself 제정신이 아닌
of itself 저절로	in itself 본래	

I will leave her to solve the problem **for herself**. 나는 그녀가 스스로 그 문제를 풀도록 내버려 두겠다.

☑ **by oneself = on one's own = alone**

Austin was able to finish the project on time **by himself**.
= Austin was able to finish the project on time **on his own**.
Austin은 혼자서 제 시간에 그 프로젝트를 마칠 수 있었다.

④ 지시대명사 that 과 those

비교하는 문장에서 앞에 나온 명사를 반복해서 쓰는 대신 단수일 때는 that을, 복수일 때는 those를 쓴다. 'those who + 복수 동사'는 ~하는 사람들이라는 의미이다. anyone who ~도 같은 의미인데, 단 이때 who 뒤에 오는 동사는 단수라는 점에 주의한다.
those와 anyone은 '주격관계대명사 who + be 동사'가 생략된 형태로 현재분사나 과거분사의 수식을 받을 수 있다. 관계대명사가 which인 경우에는 anyone이 아니라 anything을 쓴다.

The population of Seoul is much bigger than **that** of Vancouver.
서울의 인구는 밴쿠버의 인구(that)보다 훨씬 많다.

Those who apply for the positions **need** to fill out a form.
Anyone who applies for the positions **needs** to fill out a form.
그 직책에 지원하는 사람들은 양식을 작성하셔야 합니다.

GRAMMAR PRACTICE

A 괄호 안에서 알맞은 것을 고르시오.

1. The dog looks at (its, itself) in the mirror.

2. Is this (anything, those) which you want to have?

3. Mr. Taylor cannot perform his duties all by (him, himself).

4. I'll deliver these documents (myself, mine).

5. Your presence (yourself, itself) is my happiness.

B **that** 과 **those** 중 빈칸에 알맞은 것을 넣으시오.

1. The temperature here is higher than _____ of Paris.

2. _____ who are responsible for the conference will arrive here at 10 o'clock.

3. The legs of Tim are longer than _____ of David.

4. We invited _____ who are interested in movies last week.

5. _____ interested in the musical will be invited to the party.

C 다음 문장의 대명사 중에서 어법상 틀린 부분을 찾아서 바르게 고치시오.

1. We are finally going to post pictures of all of our employees participating in the past year's various company events on us company website.

2. If you have pictures of you and fellow staff members at an outside activity, please forward them to me.

3. Otherwise, I will hire a professional photographer and have his come around in the next few weeks.

VOCA presence 존재 temperature 온도 기온 participate in 참가하다 activity 활동 professional 전문적인

Unit 02 | 대명사   25

GRAMMAR POINT

⑤ 부정대명사

부정대명사는 말 그대로 어떤 사물이나 사람 또는 수량을 막연하게 나타내는 명사이다.

(1) 부정대명사 + of the + 명사

<부정대명사 + of the + 명사>의 형태로 쓰이는 경우는 다음과 같다. 이때 of the는 생략할 수 있다.

most (of the) some (of the)	+ 가산 명사(복수)/불가산 명사	most of the books/equipment some of the books/equipment
many (of the) (a) few (of the) fewer (of the) several (of the)	+ 가산 명사(복수)	many of the books a few of the books fewer of the books several of the books
much (of the) (a) little (of the) less (of the)	+ 불가산 명사	much of the equipment a little of the equipment less of the equipment

> **참고** Most of **the** books/equipment = most of **my** books/equipment
> of the의 the 자리에는 소유격 대명사를 쓸 수 있다.
>
> **Many of the analysts** expect that the economy will improve next year.
> 많은 분석가들이 내년에는 경기가 좋아질 거라고 예상한다.

(2) some, any

some(약간, 몇몇)은 긍정 평서문에, any(몇몇, 조금도)는 부정문과 의문문, 조건문에 쓸 수 있다.
둘 다 대명사와 형용사로 쓰일 수 있으며 뒤에 가산, 불가산 명사가 모두 올 수 있다.

I have **some** books. 나는 책이 좀 있다 (긍정 평서문)
I **don't** have **any** money now. 나는 지금 돈이 없다. (부정문)
If you have **any** trouble, let us know. 어떤 문제라도 있으시면 알려주십시오. (조건문)

some은 권유나 부탁의 의문문에서 쓸 수 있다.
any는 '어떤 ~라도, 누구라도'의 의미일 경우 평서문에서도 쓴다.

Would you like **some** coffee? 커피 한 잔 하실래요? (권유)
Could you please lend me **some** money? 돈 좀 꿔줄래? (부탁)
Any of those reports should be reviewed. 그것들 중 어떤 보고서라도 다 검토되어야 한다. (긍정평서문)

GRAMMAR PRACTICE

A 괄호 안에서 알맞은 것을 고르시오.

1. The board has shown (few, little) interest in funding for the facility expansion.

2. (Much, Some) bosses are nastier than others.

3. Some of our employees (is, are) more capable than others.

4. All of the books on the desk (is, are) mine.

5. (Any, Many) information that RBC receives through its website will be deemed to be nonconfidential.

6. Fortunately, we got (much, most) of the products earlier than scheduled.

7. Many of the applicants (possess, possesses) a junior college degree at a minimum.

8. (A little, A few) of the airlines have already begun to sell food on board.

9. I have all of the (document, documents) on my computer.

10. Our company did all of the architectural (design, designs) for this restaurant.

B some 과 any 중 빈칸에 알맞은 것을 넣으시오.

1. Ann has _____ friends.

2. I don't have _____ money with me.

3. Are there _____ students in the classroom?

4. If you have _____ coins, please lend me _____.

5. Do you want _____ milk?

VOCA fund 자금을 제공하다 facility 시설 expansion 확장, 확대 nasty 거친 deem 간주하다 architectural 건축학의

GRAMMAR POINT

⑥ 부정대명사 One, another, the other, others

one은 '사람/것, 하나'의 의미를 지닌 대명사로 쓰이고, another는 <an + other (+ 가산 명사의 단수)>를 의미한다고 기억하자. 불특정한 '또 하나의 다른 것/사람'을 나타내기도 한다. the other는 특정한 나머지 하나를 나타낸다. the others는 <the other + 복수 명사>의 의미로 '나머지 모두'를 가리킨다.

	대명사 역할	형용사 역할
one	'사람/것, 하나'의 의미를 지닌 대명사.	one + 가산명사(단수)
another	an + other (+ 가산 명사의 단수), 불특정한 '또 하나의 다른 것/사람'	another + 가산명사(단수)
the other	특정한 나머지 하나	the other + 모든 명사
the others	<the other + 복수 명사>의 의미. '나머지 모두'	X

- **one, the other** (둘 중에서) 하나는, 다른 하나는

  There are two pens. **One** is black. **The other** is blue.
  펜이 두 자루 있다. 하나는 검정색이고, 다른 하나는 파랑색이다.

- **one, the others** (정해진 다수에서) 하나는, 나머지 전부는

  There are many pens. **One** is black. **The others** are blue.
  펜이 많이 있다. 하나는 검정색이다. 나머지는 모두 파랑색이다.

- **one, another, the other** (셋 중에서) 하나는, 또 하나는, 나머지 하나는

  There are three pens. **One** is black. **Another** is blue. **The other** is red.
  펜이 세 자루 있다. 하나는 검정색이고, 또 다른 하나는 파랑색이고, 나머지 하나는 빨강색이다.

- **some, others** (다수 중에서) 일부는, 다른 일부는

  There are many pens. **Some** are black. **Others** are blue.
  펜이 많이 있다. 일부는 검정색이고, 일부는 파랑색이다.

- **some, the others** (특정 다수 중에서) 일부는, 나머지 전부는

  There are 100 pens. **Some** are black. **The others** are blue.
  펜이 100자루 있다. 일부는 검정색이고, 나머지는 모두 파랑색이다.

- **each other** (둘 사이에) 서로서로 **vs. one another** (셋 이상 사이에) 서로서로

  Both parties should show respect for **each other**'s opinion.
  양당은 서로의 의견에 대해 존중하는 모습을 보여야 한다.

  They sat for two hours without talking to **one another**.
  그 사람들은 서로 아무 말도 하지 않은 채 2시간 동안 앉아 있었다.

- **other:** 오로지 형용사로만 쓰이며, 단독으로는 대명사로 쓸 수 없다.

GRAMMAR PRACTICE

A one, another, the other 중 빈칸에 알맞은 것을 넣으시오.

1. There are a lot of balls.

   _____ is black, and _____ is blue.

2. There are two shirts.

   _____ is black, and _____ is white.

3. There are three cars.

   _____ is black. _____ is white. _____ is gray.

4. There are four students. Three are from Japan, and _____ is from China.

5. Let me check my calendar and come up with _____ day.

B the others, others, other 중 빈칸에 알맞은 것을 넣으시오.

1. Some people say American beef is safe, but _____ say it could cause some disease.

2. We have twelve students in class. Five are from Japan, and _____ are from Korea.

3. A few _____ airlines have already begun to sell food on board.

4. Thanks to my special experience in Tokyo, I understand the Japanese and their working style better than _____.

5. Your smiling face will make a good impression on _____ people.

C each other 과 one another 중 빈칸에 알맞은 것을 넣으시오.

1. How did Jane and Tom know _____?

2. The two teams will compete against _____.

3. We have ten students in class. We helped _____ with our projects.

4. Our team members always listen to and respect _____'s opinion.

5. The gentleman and the lady have been in love with _____ since childhood.

VOCA calendar 달력   disease 질병   airline 항공사   impression 인상

GRAMMAR IN SENTENCE

▶ 의미 단위로 문장을 끊어 읽고, 해석하세요.
단, 경우에 따라 명사구 또는 명사절은 { }, 형용사구 또는 형용사절은 [ ], 부사 부사구 부사절은 ( )로 표시하세요.

1. When we last talked in February, you were waiting to hear back about a job you had applied for.

2. If you didn't take that job, I thought you might like to know that we are in need of a trainer here.

3. Our trainer, Mr. Lee, will be transferring to our new Singapore office in August, and I think you would be the perfect person to replace him.

4. Those who are responsible for the conference will arrive here at 10 o'clock.

5. The board has shown little interest in funding for facility expansion.

6. Any information that RBC receives through its website will be deemed to be nonconfidential.

7. Our company did all of the architectural designs for this restaurant.

8. Some people say American beef is safe, but others say it could cause some diseases.

9. We have 12 students in class. Five are from Japan, and the others are from Korea.

10. Thanks to my special experience in Tokyo, I understand the Japanese and their working style better than others.

Outro

대명사

인칭대명사

사람이나 사물을 대신해서 쓰이는 대명사

인칭, 성, 수에 따라 다양하며, 주격, 소유격, 목적격등이 있다.

재귀대명사

인칭대명사의 목적격이나 소유격에 단수는 -self, 복수는 -selves를 붙인 것

	인칭	주격	소유격	목적격	소유대명사	재귀대명사
단수	1인칭	I	my	me	mine	myself
	2인칭	you	your	you	yours	yourself
	3인칭	he	his	him	his	himself
		she	her	her	hers	herself
복수	1인칭	we	our	us	ours	ourselves
	2인칭	you	your	you	yours	yourselves
	3인칭	they	their	them	theirs	themselves

지시대명사

특정한 대상을 지칭하는 대명사. this, that, these, those

부정대명사

정해지지 않는 사람이나 사물을 가리키는 대명사

단수	one another the other none	everything something anything nothing	everybody, everyone somebody, someone anybody, anyone nobody,	each either neither
복수	others the others	many several	a few few	both
단/복수	all	some, any	most	

UNIT 03 동사

◎ GRAMMAR POINT

동사는 주어가 하는 동작이나 상태를 나타내는 말이다. 한 문장 안에는 반드시 하나의 동사가 있어야 하고, 또한 접속사 없이는 하나의 동사만이 쓰여야 한다. 자동사는 스스로 자립할 수 있는 동사로 뒤에 목적어를 갖지 않는다. <자동사 + 전치사 + 목적어(전치사에 대한 목적어임)>가 기본적인 형태이다.

반면, 타동사는 목적어에 의지하는 동사이며, 능동태의 경우 타동사는 반드시 목적어가 있어야 한다. 타동사의 경우, 목적어 없이 쓰려면 수동태로 전환이 되어야 한다. 주어보다는 목적어가 중요한 동사가 타동사이다.

① 1형식 (완전 자동사) : 주어(S) + 동사(V)

말하다	speak (to/with) 말하다 respond (to) 응답하다	talk (to/with) 말하다 react (to) 반응하다	reply (to) 대답하다 agree (with/on) 동의하다
이동	go (to) 가다 proceed (to) 진행하다	come (to) 오다 move (to) 이동하다	arrive (at) 도착하다 transfer (to) 옮기다
증감	rise 오르다 decline 감소하다	grow 성장하다 culminate 정점에 이르다	fall 떨어지다 soar 급등하다
기타	happen (to) 발생하다 function 기능을 하다	occur (to) 발생하다 live 살다	wait (for) 기다리다 work 일하다

<u>A bird</u> <u>is flying</u> in the sky. 새 한 마리가 하늘을 날고 있다.
　S　　　V

<u>My brother</u> <u>lives</u> in Seattle. 우리 오빠는 Seattle에 살고 있다.
　　S　　　　V

② 2형식 (불완전 자동사) : 주어(S) + 동사(V) + 주격 보어(C)

주격 보어 자리에는 명사와 형용사 역할을 하는 것이 올 수 있는데, 명사가 올 때는 주어와 보어가 동격일 때만 가능하다.

주어	불완전 자동사	보어
	be / become / get feel / smell / sound / taste look / seem / appear remain / stay prove / turn out	형용사 명사 (S = C) to부정사 / that절

If you **become** a good listener, communicating with others will **become** easier.
만약 여러분이 남의 말에 귀를 기울여 주는 사람이 된다면, 다른 사람들과 의사소통하는 것이 쉬워질 것이다.

GRAMMAR PRACTICE

A 괄호 안에서 알맞은 것을 고르세요.

1. I am sorry that I haven't been able to (respond, respond to) you sooner.
2. I would be honored to (speak, tell) at the event.
3. You may think some traditions in other countries seem (strange, strangely).
4. Would it be (possible, possibly) to take your vacation another day?
5. Your suggestion is (worthy, worth) considering.
6. All the students are (capability, capable) of achieving their goals.
7. More information will be (available, availability) on the company website.
8. Saturday and Sunday will be (perfect, perfectly) for outdoor activities.
9. I wondered what (happened, happened to) him.
10. We (agreed, agreed with) the qualification that there should be adequate compensation.

B 보기 중 맞는 것을 고르세요.

1. Experts predict that the unemployment rate will ---------- next year.
   (A) raise   (B) fell   (C) fall   (D) rose

2. Some of the participants actually ---------- very famous and even make appearances on TV shows.
   (A) become   (B) allow   (C) require   (D) take

3. The secretary at the law firm ---------- telephones and schedules clients' appointments.
   (A) replies   (B) reacts   (C) answers   (D) responds

4. Interest rates were expected to ---------- high for the remainder of the year.
   (A) make   (B) take   (C) have   (D) remain

5. The American diplomat will ---------- in Seoul next week to hold talks with the president.
   (A) attend   (B) arrive   (C) send   (D) make

VOCA adequate 적절한　compensation 보상　participant 참석자　appearance 출연, 나타남　secretary 비서　law firm 법률 사무소　client 고객　appointment 약속　reply to ~에 대답하다　react to ~에 반응하다　respond to ~에 응답하다　diplomat 외교관　talks 회담

GRAMMAR POINT

③ 3형식(완전 타동사): 주어(S) + 동사(V) + 목적어(O)

목적어 자리에는 명사 및 명사 역할을 할 수 있는 명사 상당 어구(명사구, 대명사, to부정사, 동명사, 명사절)가 올 수 있다.

자동사로 착각하기 쉬운 타동사	
access 접근[접속]하다, 사용하다	damage 손상시키다
accompany 동반하다	disclose 폭로하다
alert 주의를 끌다	discuss 토론하다
approve 승인하다	enter 들어가다
approach 접근하다, 다가가다	exceed 능가하다
arrange 정돈하다, 처리하다	join 합석하다, 합류하다
attend 참석하다	regret 후회하다
check 확인하다	reach 도착하다, 도달하다
contact 연락하다	resemble 닮다
coordinate 조정, 관리하다	request 요청하다

The board of the directors will **discuss** the problem at the weekly meeting.
이사회는 그 문제를 주간 회의에서 의논할 것이다.

전치사와 함께 기억해야 하는 타동사	
사람에게 사물을 제공하다	provide, supply, furnish someone with something
목적어가 ~하는 것을 막다	prevent, discourage, prohibit 목적어 from ~ing
A를 B로 바꾸다(대체하다)	exchange A for B, replace A with B, substitute A with B

It will gradually **substitute** all of the shuttle buses **with** eco-friendly electric buses.
모든 셔틀 버스를 점차 친환경적인 전기 버스로 교체할 계획이라고 말했다.

④ 4형식(수여 동사): 주어(S) + 동사(V) + 간접 목적어(IO) + 직접 목적어(DO)

give, send, show, lend, offer, award, grand, forward

4형식에서 직접 목적어와 간접 목적어가 같이 있을 때, 직접 목적어는 '~을(를)'에 해당하는 목적어이며, 간접 목적어는 '~에게'에 해당하는 목적어이다.

The company **will give** every employee a $500 Christmas bonus next week.
                    수여 동사   간접 목적어   직접 목적어

= The company **will gave** a $500 Christmas bonus to every employee next week.
회사는 다음주에 모든 직원들에게 500달러의 크리스마스 보너스를 줄 것이다.

GRAMMAR PRACTICE

A 괄호 안에서 알맞은 것을 고르시오.

1. During repairs, patrons will not be able to (access, access to) the main entrance.
2. The company (offers, provides) its employees with paid vacation.
3. You'd better replace saturated fats such as butter (to, with) olive oil.
4. Mr. Johnson is able to (discuss, deal) with the problem.
5. Many people say that Jennifer closely (takes, resembles) her older sister.
6. A spokesperson decided to (disclose, talk) details of the merger to the media.
7. If you have any problems, please (speak, contact) our customer service center immediately.
8. Ms. Smith (approached, went) the financial institution for a loan.
9. The company (provided, gave) him the employee of the year award.
10. The local government prevented any damage (for, from) the heavy rain.

B 빈칸을 완성하여 같은 의미의 문장으로 만드세요.

1. Governments should give farmers adequate compensation.
   = Governments should give _____.
2. Our hospital is dedicated to providing the best service to our patients.
   = Our hospital is dedicated to providing _____.
3. Please forward all mail coming to us to the new address.
   = Please forward _____.

C 보기 중 맞는 것을 고르세요.

1. The Wendy's restaurant will ---------- customers special discounts next month if they make a reservation online.
   (A) travels   (B) tells   (C) buys   (D) offer
2. To prepare them for the test, the college board will ---------- students with free test preparation materials online.
   (A) give   (B) send   (C) offer   (D) provide

VOCA main entrance 주 출입구 paid vacation 유급 휴가 spokesperson 대변인 merger 합병
financial institution 금융 기관 adequate 충분한

GRAMMAR POINT

⑤ 5형식(불완전 타동사): 주어(S) + 동사(V) + 목적어(O) + 목적격 보어(OC)

(1) 상태, 판단, 동격의 동사

상태	make, keep, leave
판단	find, think, deem, consider
동격	call, name, elect, appoint

목적격 보어 자리에는 명사와 형용사 역할을 하는 것이 올 수 있는데, 명사가 올 때는 목적어와 목적격 보어가 동격(Asher = a famous actor)일 때만 가능하다.

The movie director **made** Asher **a famous actor**. 그 영화감독은 Asher를 유명한 배우로 만들었다.

(2) to 부정사를 목적보어로 취하는 동사

희망	expect, want, would, like
권유	enable, encourage, persuade, advise, instruct
요청	ask, require, request
허락	allow, permit

Ms. William **asked** me **to pick** her daughter up at her school.
William 씨는 나에게 그녀의 아들을 학교에서 데려오도록 요청했다.

(3) 사역동사

'시키다'라는 사역의 의미를 가진 let, make, have는 목적어와 목적격 보어가 능동 관계이면 목적 보어 자리에 동사원형을, 수동 관계이면 과거 분사를 쓴다. 단, 준사역동사인 help는 목적보어 자리에 to 부정사를 써도 되고 동사원형을 써도 된다.

사역동사	let, make, have
준사역동사	help

The supervisor **made** his employees **follow** his order. (his employees와 follow가 능동 관계)
감독관은 직원들이 자신의 명령을 따르도록 했다.

I **made** the pizza **delivered**. 나는 피자를 배달 시켰다. (the pizza 와 delivered가 수동 관계)

Ms. Kimberly **helped** her son **(to) go** to school. Kimberly씨는 그녀의 아들이 학교 가는 것을 도와주었다.

(4) 지각동사

보고, 듣고, 느끼고, 맛보고, 냄새를 맡는 5가지 감각과 관련된 동사를 지각동사라고 한다. 목적보어 자리에는 동사원형이 온다. 목적어와 목적보어의 관계가 능동일 때는 현재분사, 수동일 때는 과거분사가 올 수도 있다.

지각동사	see, watch, hear

I **heard** my sister **sing** a song. 나는 나의 여동생이 노래하는 것을 들었다. (my sister과 sing이 능동 관계)
I **saw** the glass **broken**. 나는 유리가 깨진 것을 보았다. (the glass와 broken이 수동 관계)

GRAMMAR PRACTICE

A 괄호 안에서 알맞은 것을 고르시오.

1. The boring books make me (sleep, slept).

2. Mr. Tyler let his son (throw, throwing) a party.

3. Austin had his old car (repair, repaired).

4. I will have the groceries (deliver, delivered) by tomorrow morning.

5. I asked the laundry (to deliver, delivered) the clothes.

6. My supervisor (advised, let) me to go to work early.

7. I (made, helped) my colleague to organize the warehouse.

8. The teacher watched the students (crossed, cross) the street.

9. The security guards (make, require) visitors to present identification.

10. David helped the old man (carry, carrying) the heavy load.

B 어법상 틀린 문장은 바르게 고치고, 틀린 부분이 없으면 O로 표시하세요.

1. Mr. Jackson is a music teacher, and likes to hear the students sung happily.

2. He made the students to bring their instruments yesterday.

3. He taught the students how to play the instrument.

4. They are planning to hold a small concert in the park next month.

5. Therefore, the teacher encouraged the students practice after school.

VOCA boring 지루한   throw a party 파티를 열다

GRAMMAR POINT

⑥ 조동사

조동사 will, may, can, must, should 다음에는 반드시 동사원형이 와야 한다. 조동사와 동사원형 사이에 not이나 부사가 있을 경우 혼동을 줄 수 있으므로 주의한다.

(1) 주어 + 조동사+(부사) + 동사원형(본동사)

The system **will** (**eventually**) **need** to be modernized.
그 시스템은 (궁극적으로) 근대화될 필요가 있다.

High prices **do not** (**necessarily**) **lead** to a better quality.
가격이 높다고 반드시 질이 더 좋아지는 것은 아니다.

(2) 조동사 대용어구

be able to + 동사원형 ~할 수 있다	have to + 동사원형 ~해야만 한다
be going to + 동사원형 ~할 것이다	used to + 동사원형 ~하곤 했다
had better + 동사원형 ~하는 것이 더 낫다	cannot but + 동사원형 ~하지 않을 수 없다
ought to + 동사원형 ~해야 한다	would like to + 동사원형 ~하고 싶다

Our team **used to have** meetings on Mondays.
우리 팀은 월요일마다 회의를 했었다. (지금은 더 이상 안한다.)

(3) 조동사의 부정문

주어 + 조동사 + not + 본동사	It **will not rain** tomorrow. 내일 비가 내리지 않을 것이다.
do not 주어 + does not + 동사원형 did not	Sometimes, Tom **doesn't arrive** on time. 가끔 Tom은 정시에 도착하지 않는다. Tom **didn't arrive** on time yesterday. Tom은 어제 정시에 도착하지 않았다.

⑦ 명령문

(1) 주어 you 가 생략된 형태로 주어 없이 동사 원형으로 시작한다.

Look at the tall gentleman over there. 저기 있는 키 큰 신사를 봐라.
동사원형

(2) 명령문은 주절에만 위치할 수 있다.

When **making** a speech, **discuss** interesting and impressive topics.
　　　현재분사 (종속절)　　　　　　동사원형 (주절)
연설을 할 때는, 흥미진진하고 감동적인 주제를 논의하라.

GRAMMAR PRACTICE

A 괄호 안에서 알맞은 것을 고르시오.

1. We will (discontinue, discontinued) pursuing potential clients aggressively.
2. You can (running, run) the program directly from the CD.
3. A résumé should adequately (show, showing) your personal history.
4. Don't (pressed, press) the red button and the yellow button simultaneously.
5. We'll see how their decision will (affect, affection) the outcome in one week.
6. You'd better (go, to go) home now and take a rest.
7. I used to (go, going) shopping on Sundays.
8. Don't (use, used) your mobile phone during the show.
9. All the people could not but (admire, admiring) her courage.
10. Children should (have to, be able to) read and write by the age of eight.

B 빈칸을 완성하여 같은 의미의 문장으로 만드세요.

1. Parents should take care of their children.
   = Parents _____ take care of their children.
2. Albert can't help falling in love with Anna.
   = Albert _____ fall in love with Anna.

C 보기 중 맞는 것을 고르세요.

1. Please ---------- the application form in as much detail as possible and return it to the address shown above.
   (A) completion   (B) completed   (C) complete   (D) completely

2. Next week, Mike will ---------- his e-mail to a professor of the Chemistry department to get related information directly.
   (A) forwarding   (B) forwarded   (C) to forward   (D) forward

3. This warranty does not ---------- any damage incurred due to alternations, modifications, accidents, or damage resulting from excess power.
   (A) covered   (B) covers   (C) covering   (D) cover

VOCA pursue 뒤쫓다, 따라다니다, ~를 추구하다   aggressively 공격적으로   personal history 경력, 이력   simultaneously 동시에, 일제히   outcome 결과   application form 신청서   related 관련된   warranty 보증, 보증서   cover ~에 대해 보상하다   damage 손상   alternation 변경, 개조   modification 수정, 변경   excess power 과전압

GRAMMAR IN SENTENCE

▶ 의미 단위로 문장을 끊어 읽고, 해석하세요.
단, 경우에 따라 명사구 또는 명사절은 { }, 형용사구 또는 형용사절은 [ ], 부사 부사구 부사절은 ( )로 표시하세요.

1. Experts predict that the unemployment rate will fall next year.

2. Some of the participants actually become very famous and even make appearances on TV shows.

3. The secretary at the law firm answers telephones and schedules clients' appointments.

4. Interest rates were expected to remain high for the remainder of the year.

5. The American diplomat will arrive in Seoul next week to hold talks with the president.

6. The Wendy's restaurant will offer customers special discounts next month if they make a reservation online

7. To prepare them for the test, the college board will provide students with free test preparation materials online.

8. Please complete the application form in as much detail as possible and return it to the address shown above.

9. Next week, Mike will forward his e-mail to a professor in the Chemistry Department to get related information directly.

10. This warranty does not cover any damage incurred due to alternations, modifications, accidents, or damage resulting from excess power.

 **Outro**

동사

동사
주어가 하는 동작이나 상태를 나타내는 말

문장의 형식	문장의 형태
1형식	주어(S) + 동사(V) Tom is sleeping now. Tom은 지금 자고 있다.
2형식	주어(S) + 동사(V) + 주격 보어(C) Linda is a doctor. Linda는 의사이다.
3형식	주어(S) + 동사(V) + 목적어(O) I bought a book. 나는 책 한권을 샀다.
4형식	주어(S) + 동사(V) + 간접 목적어(IO) + 직접 목적어(DO) He sent me a letter. 그는 나에게 편지를 보냈다.
5형식	주어(S) + 동사(V) + 목적어(O) + 목적격 보어(OC) You make me happy. 너는 나를 행복하게 해 준다.

자동사 (+ 전치사 + 목적어)

agree with ~에 동의하다
comply with ~에 따르다
interfere with ~를 방해하다
look into ~을 조사하다

speak to ~와 이야기하다
deal with ~를 다루다
enroll in ~에 등록하다
participate in ~에 참석하다

타동사 + 목적어

contact ~에 연락하다
attend ~에 참석하다
access ~에 접근[접속]하다, 사용하다
disclose ~를 폭로하다

exceed ~를 능가하다
approach ~에 접근하다, 다가가다
arrange ~를 정돈하다, 처리하다
join ~에 합석하다, 합류하다

ACTUAL TEST 1

A 보기 중 맞는 것을 고르세요.

1. The excutives kept on arguing about the difficult problem for many hours, and then they finally made a ----------.
   (A) decide
   (B) decisions
   (C) decisive
   (D) decision

2. This scientific journal will provide a very persuasive ---------- to all readers interested in the field.
   (A) argue
   (B) arguing
   (C) argument
   (D) arguments

3. The device will come on the market within the next year as an -------- to existing computer systems.
   (A) attachments
   (B) attach
   (C) attaching
   (D) attachment

4. Our ---------- at World Architects is designing and building homes to your exact specifications, tastes, and needs.
   (A) special
   (B) specialty
   (C) specialize
   (D) especially

5. Although she is having hard time working on the project, Stacy can also feel a sense of accomplishment once she finishes -------.
   (A) she
   (B) her
   (C) hers
   (D) herself

6. People who took the exam are not permitted to sell exam information of any sort, nor should they share their answers with --------.
   (A) other
   (B) others
   (C) some
   (D) any

7. To prepare for the annual report, Ashley Newhall is gathering design materials by -------.
   (A) she
   (B) her
   (C) herself
   (D) hers

8. Either the city council or the city administration will have to declare ---------- support for the proposed park.
   (A) it
   (B) it's
   (C) its
   (D) itself

9. Some of the participants actually ------- very famous and even make appearances on TV shows.
   (A) become
   (B) allow
   (C) require
   (D) take

10. To prepare them for the test, the college board will -------- students with free test preparation materials online, starting in spring 2025.
    (A) give
    (B) send
    (C) offer
    (D) provide

B 보기 중 맞는 것을 고르세요.

Questions 11-16 refer to the following email.

Dear Tom Johns,

Hello. my name is Lisa Hudson and I made a **11** ------- at your bed and breakfast for three nights next week. I **12** ------- fly to Chicago next week, but unfortunately, my flight was canceled. I still want to stay at **13** ------- place when I get to Chicago. Could you let **14** ------- know if there is a room available from the 20th to the 22nd? Also, I still need the pick-up service. My flight will **15** ------- there at 1 pm next Thursday. I am sorry to cause you trouble. Please **16** ------- me when you get this email. Thank you.

11 (A) reserve
 (B) reserved
 (C) reserving
 (D) reservation

12 (A) was supposed to
 (B) was supposing to
 (C) supposed to
 (D) suppose

13 (A) you
 (B) your
 (C) yours
 (D) yourself

14 (A) I
 (B) my
 (C) me
 (D) myself

15 (A) visit
 (B) arrive
 (C) contact
 (D) take

16 (A) reply
 (B) respond
 (C) react
 (D) call

잉글리쉬앤 그래머 MASTER

실전편

 코스

Unit 4 형용사
Unit 5 부사
Unit 6 전치사

4코스 5코스 6코스

UNIT 04 형용사

◎ GRAMMAR POINT

형용사는 명사의 앞이나 뒤에서 명사를 수식하며, 주어나 목적어를 설명해주는 보어로서 쓰인다.
형용사 중 수량을 나타내는 수량형용사의 경우 수식을 받는 명사가 가산명사 또는 불가산명사인가에 따라 다르게 쓰인다. 형용사는 -ous, -ful, -able, -tive, -ic, -cal 등의 형태를 갖는 경우가 많다.

① 명사를 수식하는 형용사

(1) 관사 + 형용사 + 명사

the **important** information 중요한 정보
a **complimentary** coupon 공짜 쿠폰

(2) 관사 + 형용사 + 명사 + 명사 (복합명사)

the **strengthened** customs clearance 강화된 세금 수속

(3) 후치 수식

① all, every, any 최상급 + 명사 + -ible/-able로 끝나는 형용사

The grocery store will take **every** measure **possible** to meet customer needs.
그 식료품점은 손님들의 욕구를 충족시키기 위해 가능한 모든 조치를 취할 것이다.

② 대명사 (-thing, -body, -one) +형용사

I met **someone nice** yesterday. 나는 어제 친절한 사람을 만났다.

③ 명사 + (분사형) 형용사구

명사 뒤에 (주격관계대명사 + be 동사) 가 생략된 형태이다.

The people (who are) **responsible** for the seminar have already arrived here.
세미나에 책임이 있는 사람들이 이곳에 이미 도착했다.

분사의 경우 전치사와 같이 자주 어울려 특정한 의미를 구성하는 어구가 있으면 뒤에서 수식하는 것이 보통이다. left(남은), attached(첨부된), involved(포함된) 등의 형용사들도 주로 명사의 뒤에서 수식한다.

That was the only choice **left** for the company.
그것만이 회사에 남겨진 유일한 선택이었다.

GRAMMAR PRACTICE

A 괄호 안에서 알맞은 것을 고르세요.

1. Youth violence is a (serious, seriously) problem that needs to be eradicated.
2. Please return the supply room keys to their (proper, properly) place.
3. Ms. Kimberly has (broad, broaden) knowledge of medicine.
4. The hotel offers all guests a (compliment, complimentary) continental breakfast.
5. Ms. kimberly is a person (considerable, considerably) in the company.
6. This is the most advanced type of engine (available, availably).
7. Our company has produced goods (compare, comparable) to those of foreign nations in both quality and quantity.
8. Wickham was not the only city (affect, affected) by the heavy snow.

B 어법상 틀린 문장은 바르게 고치고, 틀린 부분이 없으면 O로 표시하세요.

1. The reviews turned out to be something helpful for his writing career.
2. This book will provide very persuasively argument.
3. He didn't have any plans to come back in the foreseeable future.
4. The properly safety precautions were not taken.
5. He is responsibility for all the legal affairs at the company.

C 보기 중 맞는 것을 고르세요.

1. Management mentioned that everything ---------- should be done to protect the workers from accidents.

   (A) possible   (B) possibly   (C) possibility   (D) possibilities

2. The Sales Department needed to conduct an ---------- survey on the financial damage.

   (A) extend   (B) extensive   (C) extensions   (D) extending

---

(VOCA) eradicate 근절하다 safety precaution 안전 조치 legal affairs 법무 관련 일 management 경영진 mention 언급하다 protect 보호하다 Sales Department 판매부서 conduct a survey 조사를 실시하다 extensive 광범위한 financial 재정의 damage 손실

◎ GRAMMAR POINT

② 보어로 쓰이는 형용사

(1) 주격보어

주어 + 자동사 + **주격보어**

■ 주격보어를 취하는 대표적인 자동사

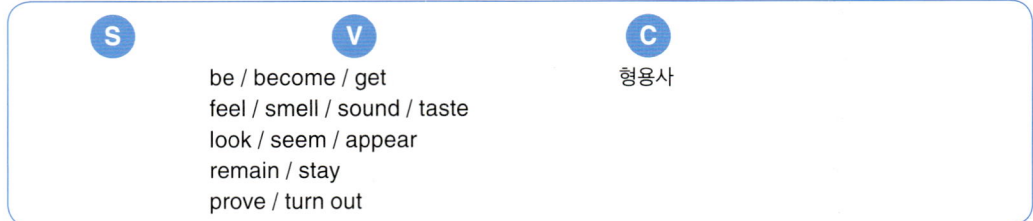

The conference room is **available**. 회의실이 이용 가능하다.
　　　　S　　　　　V　　C

The damage to his reputation was **severe**. 그의 명성에 대한 손상은 심각했다.
　　　　　S　　　　　　　V　　C

(2) 목적보어

주어 + 타동사 + 목적어 + **목적보어**

■ 목적보어를 취하는 대표적인 타동사 (5형식 동사)

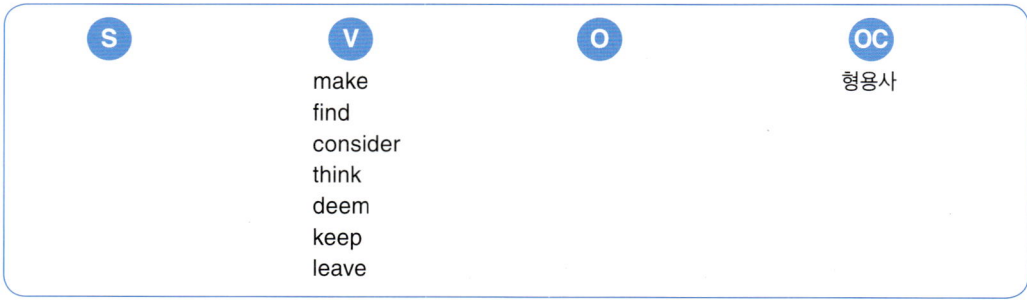

I found my car **stolen**. 차가 도난당한 것을 알게 되었다.
S　V　　O　　OC

Subscribers found the magazine **interesting**. 구독자들은 그 잡지가 흥미롭다는 것을 알게 되었다.
　　S　　　　V　　　　O

특히, 목적 보어가 excite, bore, tire, impress, satisfy 등과 같은 감정동사에서 파생된 경우에는 목적어와의 능동, 수동 관계에 주의한다.

GRAMMAR PRACTICE

A 괄호 안에서 알맞은 것을 고르세요.

1. This river is not very (depth, deep), so even children can swim in it.
2. The plan sounds (great, greatly) and will be discussed at the meeting.
3. The ladder leaning against the wall doesn't look (safe, safely).
4. To remain (competitive, competitively), the company needs a new strategy.
5. A new contract with a pharmaceutical company made made all of the employees (happy, happily).
6. Judy was in a hurry, so she rushed out, leaving the door (open. openly).
7. The president found the sales strategy (impractical, impracticality).
8. All the students found their test results (satisfy, satisfactory).
9. The results of last month's study made the researchers (happily, happy).
10. In both America and Europe, the fast food market has become increasingly (full, fully).

B 보기 중 맞는 것을 고르세요.

1. Most of the workers at the plant find the new machines ----------.
   (A) efficient   (B) efficiency   (C) efficiently   (D) effect
2. The whole audience in the auditorium thought Dr. William's address was very ----------.
   (A) impress   (B) impressive   (C) impression   (D) impressed
3. The mediator said that the woman had not been ---------- throughout the meeting.
   (A) cooperate   (B) cooperatively   (C) cooperated   (D) cooperative
4. Sprints, Inc. offers full medical coverage as well as a retirement plan and paid vacations, which makes its employees ----------.
   (A) satisfaction   (B) satisfactory   (C) satisfied   (D) satisfying
5. Ace Movers is not ---------- for any claim due to loss, damage, non-delivery, or missed delivery in excess of $1,000.
   (A) response   (B) responsible   (C) responsibility   (D) responsibly

---

VOCA strategy 전략 pharmaceutical 제약의 auditorium 강당 audience 청중 address 연설 mediator 중재자 throughout ~하는 동안 내내 be responsible for~ ~에 대한 책임을 지다 claim 요구, 주장, 청구액 in excess of ~을 초과하여

◎ GRAMMAR POINT

③ 혼동하기 쉬운 형용사

(1) 형태가 비슷하지만 의미가 달라 혼동하기 쉬운 형용사

beneficial 유익한	**beneficent** 인정 많은
considerable 상당한, 중요한	**considerate** 사려 깊은
comprehensible 이해할 수 있는	**comprehensive** 포괄적인, 종합적인
confident 확신하는	**confidential** 기밀의
economic 경제의	**economical** 경제적인, 절약하는
impressive 인상적인	**impressed** 감명 받은
industrial 공업상의	**industrious** 근면한, 부지런한
informed 정통한, 알고 있는	**informative** 유익한
numerous 다수의, 수많은	**numerical** 수의, 숫자상의
persuasive 설득력 있는	**persuaded** 확신하고 있는
profitable 유리한, 이익이 많은	**proficient** 능숙한
prospective 장래의	**prosperous** 번영하는
reliable 믿을 수 있는	**reliant** 의지하는
respectable 존경할 만한	**respective** 각자의
responsible 책임이 있는, 믿을 수 있는	**responsive** 민감하게 반응하는
successful 성공한	**successive** 연속의, 상속의

(2) 부사로 혼동하기 쉬운 형용사: 명사 + -ly형

friendly 친근한, 우호적인	**lovely** 사랑스러운	**lively** 활기찬
costly 값비싼	**timely** 시기적절한	**likely** 가능성 있는

a **friendly** match 친선 경기
a **timely** remark 시기적절한 발언

(3) 형용사와 동사의 모양이 같은 단어

complete 완전한, 완성시키다	**correct** 정확한, 고치다	**secure** 안전한, 지키다
separate 별개의, 분리하다	**present** 현재의, 출석한, 발표하다 (*present에는 명사로 '선물'이란 뜻도 있음)	

(4) 형용사와 명사의 모양이 같은 단어

alternative 대안, 대안이 되는	**objective** 목표, 객관적인	**professional** 전문가, 전문적인
representative 대표자, 대표적인	**executive** 간부, 행정상의	**original** 원물의, 원물

(4) 형용사와 부사가 모양이 같은 단어

daily, weekly, monthly, quarterly, yearly, fast, early, fine, low, right, straight, wide

quarterly 연 4회의, 4분의 1의
straight 곧은, 일직선의

GRAMMAR PRACTICE

A 괄호 안에서 알맞은 것을 고르세요.

1. He is always polite and (considerate, considerable) to his fellow workers.
2. It is natural that he should succeed, for he is so (industrious, industrial).
3. (Industrious, Industrial) production tailed off at the end of the year.
4. The magazine has (numerous, numerical) spelling errors.
5. The snow made a (time, timely) appearance for the winter festival.
6. He put (considerate, considerable) effort into passing the test.
7. The company should buy a document shredder for (confident, confidential) materials.
8. (Industrial, Industrious) pollution is derived principally from plants that refine and manufacture basic metals.
9. The architecture is a (successive, successful) combination of old and new.
10. Most (economic, economical) growth in the U.S. can be traced to innovations in science and technology.

B 다음 밑줄 친 단어의 쓰임을 찾아 번호를 쓰고, 전체 문장을 한글로 해석을 하세요.

> ① 명사   ② 동사   ③ 형용사   ④ 부사

1. Alex subscribes to a **daily** newspaper.
   The escalators in this building are inspected three times **daily**.
2. My supervisor gave a **correct** answer.
   My supervisor **corrected** the errors.
3. **Quarterly** earnings are seldom reported to shareholders.
   Sales earnings are reported to shareholders **quarterly**.
4. He made an **objective** observation.
   Mr. Lucas achieved his **objective.**
5. The **original** is kept in an art museum.
   The construction project will proceed according to the **original** plan.

VOCA polite 예의바른 tail off 감소하다 error 오류 put an effort 노력을 기울이다 document shredder 문서 분쇄기
be derived from ~에서 비롯되다 refine 정제하다 be traced to ~에서 비롯되다 innovation 혁신

◎ GRAMMAR POINT

④ 수량 형용사

(1) 수량 형용사

가산 명사를 수식하는 형용사	* many * (a) few, several a number of, a variety of, a range of	복수 명사	복수 동사
	* each every, another	단수 명사	단수 동사
불가산 명사를 수식하는 형용사	* much, (a) little a large/small amount of a great deal of	단수 명사	단수 동사
가산, 불가산 명사를 모두 나타낼 수 있는 형용사	* some, any * all, most a lot of = lots of plenty of	가산 명사(복수)	복수 동사
		불가산 명사(단수)	단수 동사

위 표에서 *로 표시된 형용사들은 대명사로 쓰일 때 <~ of + the (소유격) + 복수 명사 / 불가산 명사>의 구조를 취한다.

(2) Every vs. Each

each와 every가 이끄는 주어 뒤에는 단수 동사가 오며, 각각의 용법 차이는 다음과 같다.

each	대명사	각각, 각자	each of the[소유격] + 복수 명사
	형용사	각각의, 각자의	each + 단수 명사
every	형용사	모든	every + 단수 명사 * every + 숫자 + 가산 명사(복수) ex. every three days 3일마다

every는 형용사 기능만 하기 때문에 <every + of the + 명사>의 형태가 불가능하다.

(3) 막연한 수 vs. 정확한 수를 나타내는 말

수량 형용사 가운데 백, 천, 만 등의 큰 단위 수를 나타내는 hundred, thousand 등과 같은 형용사는 명사로도 쓰인다. 단, 명사로 쓸 경우에는 hundreds of와 같이 관용적으로 쓰여 막연한 수량을 나타낸다.

① 형용사로 쓰인 경우

다음과 같은 형태로 쓰여 정확하고 구체적인 수를 나타낸다.

> 수사(a, one, three 등) + hundred, thousand, million, billion + 복수 명사

five **hundred** people 500명의 사람들

② 명사로 쓰인 경우 : 다음과 같이 관용표현으로 쓰여 막연한 수를 나타낸다.

> hundreds of 수백의
> thousands of 수천의   + 복수 명사
> millions of 수백만의

hundreds of people 수백 명의 사람들

GRAMMAR PRACTICE

A 다음 셋 중에서 괄호 안에서 알맞은 것을 고르세요.

1. (A number, Most, Much) products displayed on the second floor are refundable.
2. (A large amount of, A lot, Many) experts expect that the economy will improve next year.
3. (A few, Little, The number) employees who attended the company event are under 30.
4. There is (a lot, a large amount, little) furniture in the office.
5. (All, Many, Several) the equipment was moved to the basement.

B 괄호 안에서 알맞은 것을 고르세요.

1. You have to read (many, much) books and newspapers.
2. You should inform each (division, divisions) of his arrival at the airport.
3. We can see (thousand, thousands) of people in the square.
4. Most (employee, employees) didn't attend the meeting.
5. There is a (number, great deal) of information on the Internet.

C 어법상 틀린 문장은 바르게 고치고, 틀린 부분이 없으면 O로 표시하세요.

1. Three hundreds people applied for the position.
2. The keynote speaker has a diverse range of interests and experience.
3. About three thousands people gathered for the rally.
4. Thousands of people gathered for the rally.
5. All of the employees had gone home by that time.

VOCA refundable 환불되는   expert 전문가   equipment 장비, 설비   square 광장   keynote speaker 기조 연설자   rally 집회

GRAMMAR IN SENTENCE

▶ 의미 단위로 문장을 끊어 읽고, 해석하세요.
단, 경우에 따라 명사구 또는 명사절은 { }, 형용사구 또는 형용사절은 [ ], 부사 부사구 부사절은 ( )로 표시하세요.

1. Wickham was not the only city affected by the heavy snow.

2. The review turned out to be something helpful to his writing career.

3. He didn't have any plans to come back in the foreseeable future.

4. Management mentioned that everything possible should be done to protect the workers from accidents.

5. The new contract with a pharmaceutical company made all employees happy.

6. The entire audience in the auditorium thought Dr. William's address very impressive.

7. The mediator said that the woman had not been cooperative throughout the meeting.

8. Industrial pollution is derived principally from plants that refine and manufacture basic metals.

9. The results of last month's study made the researchers happy.

10. In both America and Europe, the fast food market has become increasingly full.

 **Outro**

형용사

형용사는 명사의 앞이나 뒤에서 명사를 수식하며, 주어나 목적어를 설명해 주는 보어로도 쓰인다.

형용사의 형태

-able[-ble]	-ive[-tive]	-ic[-ical]
accessible 이용할 수 있는	attractive 마음을 끄는	emphatic 단호한
affordable 알맞은	competitive 경쟁력 있는	optimistic 낙관적인
available 이용 가능한	effective 효과적인, 유효한	realistic 실제적인, 현실적인
eligible 자격이 있는	expansive 광대한	specific 명확한, 구체적인
foreseeble 미리 알 수 있는	creative 창조적인	strategic 전략의
probable 유망한, 있음직한	protective 보호하는	sympathetic 공감하는

-al	-ent [-ant]	-ful
additional 부가적인	confident 확신하는	careful 조심성 있는, 주의하는
environmental 환경의	dependent 의지하는	powerful 강력한
exceptional 뛰어난	different 다른	**-ous**
formal 공식적인	efficient 효율적인, 능률적인	conscious 알고 있는
international 국제(상)의	significant 상당한, 중요한	courteous 예의바른
substantial 상당한	vacant 공식의, 빈	famous 유명한

수량형용사

명사 앞에서 명사의 수나 양을 나타내는 형용사
ex) many, much, few, little, several

UNIT 05 부사

◎ GRAMMAR POINT

① 부사의 역할과 위치

부사는 문장에서 동사, 형용사 그리고 또 다른 부사를 수식하여 상태나 정도를 나타내거나 강조한다.

(1) 조동사 + 부사 + 본동사(동사원형)

The museum building will **eventually** need to be demolished.
그 박물관 건물은 결국에는 철거되어야 할 것이다. ▶ demolish (건물을) 철거하다

(2) have + 부사 + p.p.

Dell, Inc. has **voluntarily** recalled some of the products.
Dell 사는 자발적으로 상품의 일부를 회수했다. ▶ voluntarily 자발적으로 recall (제품을) 회수하다

(3) be + 부사 + -ing/p.p.

I am **currently** looking for a new job. 나는 지금 새 직업을 찾고 있다.

(4) to + 동사원형 (+ 목적어/보어) + 부사

Interest rates began to climb **dramatically.** 금리가 극적으로 오르기 시작하였다.
▶ interest rates 이자율, 금리 dramatically 극적으로

(5) 부사 + 형용사 + 명사

To survive in an **increasingly** competitive global market, we will do our best.
점점 더 경쟁이 심해지는 국제 시장에서 살아남기 위하여, 우리는 최선을 다할 것이다.

(6) 타동사+목적어+부사

We need to clean the recycling bin **periodically**.
우리는 재활용 통을 주기적으로 청소할 필요가 있다.

(7) 문장의 맨 앞

Fortunately, no one was in the plant when the fire broke out.
다행히 불이 났을 때 공장에는 아무도 없었다.
▶ fortunately 다행히 plant 공장 break out (불, 사건 등이) 터지다, 일어나다

(8) 명령문 앞

명령문에 simply나 just가 종종 사용되어 '~하기만 하면 된다'라는 의미를 만든다.

If you have any questions, **just** give us a call at 1-800-887-8282.
만약 질문이 있다면, 1-800-887-8282로 전화하면 됩니다.

GRAMMAR PRACTICE

A 괄호 안에서 알맞은 것을 고르세요.

1. High prices do not (necessary, necessarily) lead to better quality.
2. A résumé should (adequate, adequately) show your personal history.
3. Customers were (complete, completely) satisfied with our service.
4. GE has (consistent, consistently) provided high-quality goods.
5. The advice of a professional can (significant, significantly) improve your chances of success.
6. The Happy Library was designed (exclusively, exclusive) for children.
7. To (accurately, accurate) account for the increase in revenue, we deducted all the taxes.
8. The advertisement for the new product was (extremely, extremes) successful.
9. (Simple, Simply) cut the cake in half and give some to the people in the next office.
10. Due to a lack of manpower, we will discontinue pursuing potential clients (aggressive, aggressively).

B 어법상 틀린 문장은 바르게 고치고, 틀린 부분이 없으면 O로 표시하세요.

1. The director conducted an extreme successful on-site training session.
2. The construction was temporary suspended.
3. The items that we ordered a day ago arrived promptly at 1:00.
4. Flight attendants are trained to react calm to any emergency.
5. Make sure your seatbelt is secure fastened.

VOCA account for ~를 설명하다　revenue 수입　deduct 공제하다　manpower 인적자원, 노동력　suspend 일시정지하다
emergency 비상, 위급　fasten 묶다

◎ GRAMMAR POINT

② 빈도부사

'얼마나 자주'를 나타내며, be동사 뒤 일반 동사의 앞, 조동사와 일반 동사의 사이에 위치한다. sometimes, usually 등은 문장의 앞에서도 자주 쓰인다.

sometimes 가끔, 이따금	often 종종, 자주	almost 거의
always 항상	usually 대개, 보통	frequently 자주
rarely, hardly, seldom, barely, scarcely 거의 ~않는		

My son **hardly** ever calls me. 나의 아들은 나에게 거의 전화를 하지 않는다.

📝 시험에 자주 출제되는 **almost**

> almost = approximately = nearly = around = about 거의

Profits has increased by **nearly[almost]** ten percent. 이익이 거의 10퍼센트 증가했다.

③ 시간부사 already, still, yet

	already	still		yet
의미	이미, 벌써	아직도, 여전히		아직
시제	주로 현재 완료, 과거 완료	주로 현재, 현재 진행		주로 현재 완료
문장	긍정문	긍정문	부정문	부정문

(1) already 이미, 벌써 (긍정문에 쓰임)

She has **already** finished the report. 그녀는 이미 보고서를 마쳤다.

(2) still 아직도, 여전히 (긍정문, 부정문, 의문문에 모두 쓰임)

> **still의 위치**
> ① still + 일반 동사 ② be동사 + still ③ 조동사 + still + 본동사 ④ still + 부정 조동사

He is **still** standing. 그는 아직도 서 있다.
He **still** doesn't like her. 그는 여전히 그녀를 좋아하지 않는다.
I **still** don't understand the theory. 나는 아직도 그 이론을 이해하지 못한다.

(3) yet 아직까지 (부정문에 쓰임)

부정문에서 still과 yet은 동일한 의미로 모두 '아직'을 의미하지만, 위치는 비교하여 기억해야 한다.

> still ~ not = not ~ yet

They **haven't** finished the report **yet.** 그들은 아직 보고서를 끝내지 못했다.
= They **still haven't** finished the report.
= They **have yet to** finish the report.
* have yet to do 아직 ~하지 못하다

GRAMMAR PRACTICE

A 주어진 단어들을 하나씩 사용하여 문장을 완성하세요.

1. often / the man / fishing / goes

   = _____

2. always / makes / my puppy / me / smile

   = _____

3. never / David / cries

   = _____

4. sometimes / Susan / the piano / plays / on Saturdays

   = _____

   = _____

5. they / made of / usually / are / plastic

   = _____

B 괄호 안에서 알맞은 것을 고르세요.

1. They (usually, since) have milk delivered before 5:00 every morning.
2. The funds for the events are (yet, still) not sufficient.
3. It costs (approximate, approximately) 50 dollars.
4. I can (hard, hardly) hear what he is talking about.
5. He joined the company (near, nearly) twenty years ago.

C 어법상 틀린 문장은 바르게 고치고, 틀린 부분이 없으면 **O**로 표시하세요.

1. We are busy at this time of the year always.
2. Because it is the most durable model, it hard ever needs repairs.
3. The hotel can accomodate approximately 5,000 guests.
4. Austin has opened three new offices in California in near six months.
5. Although she spent many months researching, Julia didn't still finished the project.

VOCA　fund 자금, 기금　sufficient 충분한　durable 내구성이 강한

GRAMMAR POINT

④ 정도부사 very, much, too

	very	much
형용사, 부사	원급 수식	비교급, 최상급 수식
동사	수식 X	수식 O
현재 분사	형용사화된 현재 분사 수식 (주로 감정동사)	수식 X
과거분사	형용사화된 과거 분사 수식 (주로 감정동사)	수식 O (형용사화된 과거 분사 제외)

(1) very: 형용사와 부사의 원급이나 현재 분사를 수식한다.

He was **very** kind to me. (형용사 kind 수식) 그는 나에게 매우 친절했다.

(2) much: 비교급, 과거 분사, 동사, 구, 절 등을 수식한다.

This is **much** better than that. (비교급 better 수식) 이것이 저것보다 훨씬 낫다.

(3) too: 정도가 '너무 ~하게, 지나치게'란 뜻으로 형용사나 부사를 수식한다.

The book was **too** complicated to understand. (형용사 complicated 수식)
그 책은 너무 복잡해서 이해할 수 없었다. ▶ complicated 복잡한

⑤ 강조부사

(1) enough + 명사 vs. 형용사/부사 + enough

명사를 수식하는 enough는 수식하는 말 앞에 놓이고, 형용사나 부사를 수식하는 enough는 수식하는 말 뒤에 놓인다.

I need **enough** eggs. (명사 eggs를 수식) 달걀이 충분히 있어야 한다.

He is not old **enough** to go to school. (형용사 old를 수식) 그는 학교에 갈 만한 나이가 되지 않는다.

(2) just 다만, 단지, 바로, 금방, 막

Our tuition fee is **just** $50.00 a month. 우리의 수업료는 고작 한 달에 50달러이다.

(3) even 심지어, ~조차, 비교급 강조/ even so 그렇다 하더라도, 그렇게 해도

Even moderate exercise is good for your health. 가벼운 운동조차도 너의 건강에 좋다.

We worked for 20 hours, but **even so**, we couldn't finish the report.
우리는 20시간이나 일했지만, 그래도 그 보고서를 끝낼 수가 없었다.

(4) right 바로, 틀림없이 (before나 after 앞에서 강조의 역할을 함)

Interview schedules will be set **right** after we review the applicants.
지원서를 검토하는 즉시 인터뷰 스케줄이 잡힐 것이다.

(5) so 형용사/부사 that ~: 매우 ~해서 ~하다

Anna is **so** young **that** she **can't** go to school. = Anna is **too** young **to go** to school.
Anna 는 너무 어려서 학교에 갈 수 없다.

Anna is **so** old **that** she **can** go to school. = Anna is **old enough to go** to school.
Anna 는 학교에 갈 수 있을 만큼 충분히 나이가 들었다.

GRAMMAR PRACTICE

A 괄호 안에서 알맞은 것을 고르세요.

1. This novel is (too, very) interesting for everyone.
2. To meet the deadline, we have to work (too, even) quicker than planned.
3. The delegates have (enough, too) time to go on a tour of the city.
4. She was (just, very) about to leave the room.
5. I was (even, much) interested in that opera.
6. Alex was (enough kind, kind enough) to take me to the station.
7. We don't have (enough money, money enough) to buy a new car.
8. It is (so, too) cold that we cannot swim in the sea.
9. The tent is (too, much) small for my whole family to sleep in.
10. The fire alarms are so (sense, sensitive) that they're always being set off by cigarette smoke.

B 다음 대화 내용에서 어법상 틀린 부분을 찾아서 바르게 고치시오.

Ann 11:09 a.m.	1. I had justly gotten in town when I realized it was a national holiday. 2. I want to try lunch at the new restaurant nearly the ice cream shop.
Bob 11:11 a.m.	3. Oh, I went there last week and I wasn't very impressed. 4. There were many too people and there wasn't enough space between the tables.
Ann 11:12 a.m.	Really? That's too bad. What do you want to do?
Bob 11:14 a.m.	5. Well, let's order sandwiches and take them to the park since it's a beautiful day to sit outside.

VOCA delegate 대표, 사절   be about to + 동사원형 막 ~하려고 하다   fire alarm 화재경보기   affordable 구입할 여유가 있는
set off (알람 등이) 울리다

◎ GRAMMAR POINT

⑥ 형용사와 부사의 형태가 같은 단어

형용사와 부사의 형태가 같은 단어	hard, late, fine, high, wide, close, fast, early, free, low, right, straight, wrong
형용사, 부사의 형태가 같은 단어에 -ly를 붙여서 다른 뜻이 되는 부사	**hardly**(거의 ~않는), **lately**(최근에), **finely**(잘게), **highly**(매우), **widely**(널리), **closely**(면밀히, 상세히)

Put some **finely** chopped onions in the saucepan. 소스 팬에 잘게 썬 양파를 조금 넣으세요.
She is a **highly** respected professor. 그녀는 매우 존경 받는 교수다.

⑦ 접속 부사 : 문법적으로 부사이고 해석상으로만 접속사이다.

접속사는 문장을 연결하는 역할을 하지만, 접속 부사는 문장을 연결할 수 없다.
접속 부사는 하나의 문장 앞에 쓰던가, 문장 사이의 세미콜론(;)과 콤마(,) 사이에 쓴다.

- **첨가**: besides, moreover, furthermore, in addition
- **원인, 결과**: therefore, thus, hence, consequently
- **역접**: however, nevertheless, nonetheless
- **만약 그렇지 않으면**: otherwise
- **그러면**: then
- **그동안에, 그사이에**: meantime = meanwhile

The national budget will increase next year. **Otherwise,** the problem will continue.
The national budget will increase next year; **otherwise,** the problem will continue.
내년에 국가 예산이 증가할 것이다. 그렇지 않으면, 문제는 계속될 것이다.

⑧ 전치사 vs 접속사 vs 접속부사

	전치사	접속사	접속 부사
~에도 불구하고	despite, in spite of	although, even though even if, whereas	however, nevertheless nonetheless
~하는 동안	during, over	while	meantime, meanwhile
만약 ~ 않다면	without	if ~ not, unless	otherwise

In spite of their distinct culture, the four countries are united in harmony.
= **Although** each country has a distinct culture, the four countries are united in harmony.
= Each country has a distinct culture. **Nevertheless,** the four countries are united in harmony.
= Each country has a distinct culture; **nevertheless,** the four countries are united in harmony.
비록 각 국은 독특한 문화를 가지고 있을지라도, 네 나라는 조화롭게 연합하고 있습니다.

GRAMMAR PRACTICE

A 괄호 안에서 알맞은 것을 고르세요.

1. Educational TV programs like these must be viewed (wide, widely).

2. Ms. Simpson has served her neighbors all her life and is (high, highly) respected by people.

3. As the yen has weakened (late, lately), many people have traveled to Japan.

4. It was cold yesterday; (however, moreover), it suddenly started to rain.

5. Richard is rich; (however, furthermore), he is not generous.

6. Mr. Johnson had a high fever and was sick; (therefore, nonetheless), he attended the meeting.

7. They were so full that they (hard, hardly) touched their food.

8. David is interested in politics. (However, Thus), he does not have the right to vote because he is only 16.

9. Recent investigations have found that the two incidents are (close, closely) related.

10. The weather is mild from (late, lately) fall to early spring.

B 빈칸에 알맞은 접속부사를 넣어 연결하세요.

> otherwise, consequently, however, therefore, meantime

1. People are moving into this area; _____, housing is becoming scarce.

2. All items in the exhibition are for sale unless _____ marked.

3. Austin caught a cold; _____, he went to work to finish the report.

4. I haven't received the details of your order yet; _____, send me an email as soon as possible.

5. I will be in touch with her soon; _____, don't let her know I'm here.

VOCA neighbor 이웃 generous 관대한 fever 열 investigation 조사 scarce 부족한

GRAMMAR IN SENTENCE

▶ 의미 단위로 문장을 끊어 읽고, 해석하세요.
단, 경우에 따라 명사구 또는 명사절은 { }, 형용사구 또는 형용사절은 [ ], 부사 부사구 부사절은 ( )로 표시하세요.

1. Because it is the most durable model, it hardly ever needs repairs.

2. Austin has opened three new offices in California for nearly six months.

3. Although she spent many months researching, Julia still hasn't finished the project.

4. People are moving into this area; consequently, housing is becoming scarce.

5. All items in the exhibition are for sale unless otherwise marked.

6. I haven't received the details of your order yet; therefore, send me an email as soon as possible.

7. I will be in touch with her soon; meantime, don't let her know I'm here.

8. Ms. Simpson has served her neighbors all her life and is highly respected by people.

9. The fire alarms are so sensitive that they're always being set off by cigarette smoke.

10. Flight attendants are trained to react calmly to any emergency.

 **Outro**

부사

부사
문장에서 동사, 형용사 그리고 또 다른 부사를 수식하여 상태나 정도를 나타내거나 강조한다.

- **부사의 형태** : 고유한 형태 또는 형용사 + ly
  - **고유한 형태** : well(잘), very(잘), still(아직도). already(이미, 벌써) always(항상)
  - **형용사 + -ly** : completely(완전하게), securely(안전하게), promptly(정각에)

- **의문부사** : when, where, how, why 등의 의문사가 부사로 쓰인다.
- **관계부사** : when, where, why, how 등으로 접속사와 부사의 역할을 동시에 한다.
  - Unit 19

접속 부사
문법적으로 부사이고 해석상으로만 접속사이다.
therefore(그러므로), however(그러나), nevertheless(그럼에도 불구하고) 등으로 두 문장을 의미상으로 이어주는 역할을 하는 부사.

Tom felt sick. **Nevertheless**, he attended the important meeting.
Tom felt sick**; nevertheless,** he attended the important meeting.
Tom은 아팠다. 그럼에도 불구하고, 중요한 회의에 참석했다.

UNIT 06 전치사

◎ GRAMMAR POINT

① 전치사의 위치

전치사 뒤에는 명사 및 대명사, 동명사가 나온다. 특히 대명사가 올 경우, 형태는 목적격이어야 한다.

(1) 전치사 + 명사

Perhaps immortality has been an ambition for many humans **throughout history**.
아마 불멸이란 역사상 많은 사람들이 바래왔던 것일 것이다.

(2) 전치사 + 동명사 + 명사(구)

You should get active **by doing** some physical activities every day to stay healthy.
건강을 위해 매일 신체활동을 하면서 활발하게 생활해야만 한다.

(3) 전치사 + 명사구

Both parties disagreed **on how to solve the problem**.
두 정당은 이 문제를 어떻게 풀 것인지 그 방법에 대해서는 동의하지 않았다.

② 시간을 나타내는 전치사 at / on / in

at + 시각, 시점	on + 요일, 날짜, 특정일	in + 주, 달, 계절, 년도, 세기
at five o'clock 5시에 **at** midnight 한밤중에 **at** night 밤에 **at** the beginning/end of the month 그 달 초/말에 **at** times 때때로 **at** the moment 그 순간	**on** Sunday 월요일에 **on** October 20th 10월 25일에 **on** Monday morning 일요일 아침에 **on** time 정시에 **on** Christmas Day 크리스마스 날에	**in** January 1월에 **in** winter 겨울에 **in** 21st century 21세기에 **in** 2027 2027년에 **in** the morning/afternoon/evening 아침/오후/저녁에

③ 장소를 나타내는 전치사 at / on / in

at + 좁은 장소, 한 지점, 번지	on + 표면 위, 일직선상의 지점	in + 넓은 장소[공간] 안
at the station 역에 **at** the intersection 교차로에 **at** work 직장에 **at** Washington street Washington 가에서	**on** the table 테이블 위에 **on** the grass 잔디 위에서 **on** the second floor 2층에 **on** the board 게시판에 **on** the ceiling 천장에	**in** the building 건물 안에 **in** the yard 뜰에서 **in** China 중국에서 **in** the world 세상에서 **in** the river 강에서

④ 분사형 전치사

| regarding ~에 대하여 | concerning ~에 대하여 | barring ~이 일어나지 않는다면 |
| following ~후에 | considering ~을 고려하면 | including ~을 포함하여 |

GRAMMAR PRACTICE

A in, on, at 중에서 알맞은 것을 넣으세요.

1. All the students are _____ school _____ the morning.
2. The students were born _____ 2015, and they are _____ the classroom.
3. Their classroom is _____ the fifth floor.
4. Some students will run _____ the playground _____ the afternoon.
5. The bus stops _____ the bus stop every 20 minutes.

B 괄호 안에서 알맞은 것을 고르세요.

1. (Regard, Regarding) this matter, both parties has concurred.
2. The pictures are hanging (on, in) the wall.
3. (Including, Considering) his age, William is strong and looks young.
4. (On, In) Sunday morning, we will do volunteer work.
5. All reports must be submitted (at, in) the end of the month.

C 보기와 같이 다음 주어진 단어를 이용하여 문장을 완성하세요.

보기   for / us / contact : Thank you <u>for contacting us.</u>

1. without / study / hard :

   He passed the test _____.

2. after / my homework / finish :

   I will play soccer with my friends _____.

3. before / go to bed :

   She gave me some medicine _____.

4. about / another city / move to :

   My family is thinking _____.

5. without / a washing machine / use :

   They do laundry _____.

VOCA   concur 동의하다   do laundry 세탁하다

◎ GRAMMAR POINT

⑤ 시간을 나타내는 전치사

(1) by vs. until

전치사	의미	특징	예시
by	까지	동작의 완료	All the guests are expected to leave **by** noon. 모든 손님들은 정오까지 떠날 것으로 예측된다.
until	까지	상태의 계속	She stayed there **until** 11:00 a.m. 그녀는 11시까지 그곳에 머물렀다.

(2) for vs. during

전치사	의미	특징	예시
for	동안	불특정 기간 (주로 시간 표현의 숫자)	**for** two months 두달 동안
during	동안	특정 기간 (행사, 사건의 명사)	**during** summer vacation 여름방학 동안

(3) throughout vs. over

전치사	의미	특징	예시
throughout	~동안 내내	장소 시간 모두 사용	**throughout** the city 도시 전역에 **throughout** the day 하루 종일
over	~동안에	주로 현재완료와 사용	**over** the last five years 지난 5년동안

(4) within vs. in

전치사	의미	특징	예시
within	~이내에	경계선 안쪽을 의미	**within** ten days 10일 이내에
in	~동안, 이후에	주로 현재 완료와 사용 주로 미래 시제와 사용	**in** the past two years 지난 2년동안 **in** ten minutes 10분 후에

(5) between vs. among

전치사	의미	특징	예시
between	~사이에	둘 사이	**between** you and me 너와 나 사이에
among	~ 사이에	셋 이상 사이	**among** the students 그 학생들 사이에

⑥ 이유, 양보를 나타내는 전치사

전치사	의미	예시
because of due to owing to on account of	~때문에	**because of** her experience 그녀의 경력 때문에 **due to** the bad weather 나쁜 날씨 때문에 **owing to** the rain 비 때문에 **on account of** his absence 그의 결석 때문에
in spite of despite	~에도 불구하고	**in spite of** numerous problems 여러 문제들에도 불구하고 **despite** being late 늦었지만

GRAMMAR PRACTICE

A 괄호 안에서 알맞은 것을 고르세요.

1. (Despite, Due to) system failures, all transactions were canceled all day long.

2. Our team will have finished the project (by, until) tomorrow.

3. We will discuss the issue (for, during) the meeting.

4. They sell their products to markets (throughout, over) the country.

5. Camels can live without water (for, during) almost 10 days.

6. (For, During) the flight, smoking is absolutely forbidden.

7. The contract has caused a lot of argument (among, between) the two companies.

8. This new policy will cause a lot of argument (over, among) members.

9. The plane was delayed (because of, in spite of) the weather.

10. (Because of, In spite of) the bad economy, luxury goods have been selling well.

B 어법상 틀린 문장은 바르게 고치고, 틀린 부분이 없으면 O로 표시하세요.

1. He has worked as an assistant manager during 30 years now.

2. Drinks will be provided with the recess.

3. Please send me the information until Monday.

4. He has to work overtime by 9:00 p.m. tonight.

5. Please hold all attendance until further notice.

VOCA system failure 시스템 오류   transaction 거래   camel 낙타   be forbidden 금지되어 있다   recess 휴식, 휴회
until further notice 추후통보가 있을 때까지

◎ GRAMMAR POINT

⑦ 위치와 방향을 나타내는 전치사

전치사	예문
by(= beside) ~옆에 near(= next to = close to) ~가까이에	stand **by** me 내 옆에 서다 the building **near** the post office 우체국 근처 건물
above 기준 위 **below** 기준 아래	the bridge **above** the river 강 위의 다리 the river **below** the bridge 다리 아래의 강
over 공간 위 **under** 공간 아래 **beneath** ~아래	the rainbow **over** the cloud 구름 위의 무지개 **under** the table 테이블 밑에 **beneath** the lake 호수 아래
in front of ~앞에 **behind** ~뒤에	the station **in front of** the building 건물 앞 역 the building **behind** the station 역 뒤의 건물
across 가로질러 **along** ~를 따라 **through** 관통하여 **past** ~를 지나서	**across** the street 길 건너 **along** the street 길을 따라 **through** the forest 숲을 통해 walk **past** the building 건물을 지나 걷다
opposite 반대편에	**opposite** the store 가게 반대편
to ~쪽으로 **toward** ~쪽으로 **for** + 목적지 ~를 향해	go **to** New York 뉴욕에 가다 walk **toward** the river 강을 향해 걷다 leave **for** New York 뉴욕으로 떠나다
into ~안으로 **out of** ~밖으로	**into** the room 방 안으로 **out of** my purse 지갑에서

⑧ 부가, 제외를 나타내는 전치사

의미	전치사	예문
besides in addition to apart from	~에 더해서 (게다가)	He speaks Chinese **besides** English. 그는 영어 이외에 중국어도 말한다.
instead of	~대신에	I'll take coffee **instead of** green tea this morning. 오늘 아침에는 녹차 대신 커피를 마시겠다.
except aside from apart from	~을 제외하고	**Apart from** its cost, the plan was a good one. 비용 문제만 뺀다면 그 계획은 훌륭한 것이었다.
regardless of	~에 상관없이	The trial took place **regardless of** gender or sexuality. 성별에 관계없이 재판이 일어났다.
except for but for without barring	~이 없다면	We'll arrive in half an hour **barring** traffic congestion. 교통 정체가 없다면, 우리는 30분 이내에 도착할 것이다. She would have failed **but for** his help. 그의 도움이 없었더라면 그녀는 실패했을 것이다.

GRAMMAR PRACTICE

A 괄호 안에서 알맞은 것을 고르세요.

1. This year's rainfall has been (above, beneath) normal.

2. Tourists are walking (under, along) the seashore.

3. (Regardless of, In addition to) signing a lease for the apartment, we also require a deposit.

4. I usually borrow books from the library (near, over) my house.

5. The woman keeps talking to herself (in front of, under) the mirror.

6. I put soy milk in my coffee (apart from, instead of) milk.

7. We have a lot in common (besides, regardless) food.

8. We'll have everything done by tomorrow (barring, except) an accident.

9. Many police officers have stood guard all (along, besides) the street.

10. (In addition, Aside from) the minor corrections Christina is working on, the booklet is almost ready for the event.

B 빈칸에 알맞은 전치사를 넣으세요.

| up   down   along   into   through |

1. A man and a dog are jogging _____ the river.

2. Many vehicles are passing _____ the tunnel.

3. Hikers climbed _____ to the top of the hill.

4. The host asked the guests to sit _____.

5. A woman walked _____ the restaurant.

VOCA seashore 해안가 lease 임대차 stand guard 경비를 서다 protest rally 항의 집회 minor 사소한, 대수롭지 않은 correction 수정, 교정 booklet 책자

GRAMMAR POINT

⑨ 전치사 + 명사(구)

at the owner's expense 사용자의 비용 부담으로

upon request 요청이 있을 때	**upon** receipt 수령하자마자
under construction 공사 중 **under** contract 계약상으로 **under** supervision 감독 하에	**under** consideration 고려중인 **under** the insurance policy 보험 정책 하에서 **under** the direction 지시 하에
in detail 자세히 **in** bulk 대량으로 **in** demand 수요가 있는 **in** advance 미리	**in** error 실수로 **in** duplicate 두 통으로 **in** writing 서면으로
beyond one's ability ~의 능력 이상의 **beyond** repair 수리할 수 없는	**beyond** one's limits ~의 한계를 넘어서 **beyond** description 말로 표현할 수 없을 정도의
out of date 구식의 **out of** order 고장 난 **out of** town 이 지역에 없는 **out of** room 공간이 부족한	**out of** reach 손이 닿지 않는 **out of** stock 재고가 떨어진 **out of** print 절판된
without a doubt 의심할 여지없이	

⑩ 전치사 + 명사 + 전치사

at the rate **of** ~의 비율로 **at** the expense[cost] **of** ~의 비용으로 **at** the pace **of** ~의 속도로 **at** the beginning/end **of** this month 이달 초/말쯤	**at** the price **of** ~의 가격으로 **at** the speed **of** ~의 속력으로 **at** the age **of** ~의 나이로
in defiance **of** ~를 무릅쓰고 **in** observance **of** ~를 준수하여	**in** honor **of** ~를 기념하여 **in** charge **of** ~에 책임이 있는
in comparison **with** ~와 비교하여 **in** compliance **with** ~를 따라서	**in** accordance **with** ~와 일치하여 **in** addition **to** ~에 더하여
on behalf **of** ~를 대신하여	**on** the first/last day **of** this month 이달 첫/마지막 날에
by means **of** ~에 의하여	
with the exception **of** ~를 제외하고	

GRAMMAR PRACTICE

A 괄호 안에서 알맞은 것을 고르세요.

1. You should book tickets in (advancement, advance).

2. The incident is reported in (a detail, detail) in today's newspaper.

3. The beautiful scene of the sunrise is (beyond, above) description.

4. They bought fruits and vegetables (with, in) bulk.

5. I was going to buy a novel, but it was (out, out of) print.

6. In order to meet the deadline, we should proceed (in, at) a fast pace.

7. The national bank will be closed in (observance, observation) of a public holiday.

8. All phases are conducted (under, with) the supervision of instructors.

9. Each year, most people set new goals (at, on) the beginning of the year.

10. The Sales Department holds monthly meetings (at, on) the first day of each month.

B 어법상 틀린 문장은 바르게 고치고, 틀린 부분이 없으면 **O**로 표시하세요.

1. Today, sugar is used on bulk in a lot of food products.

2. The bridges are currently under construction.

3. The agreement will automatically be terminated at the death of the resident.

4. This medicine is dangerous. Keep in out of the reach of children.

5. If you're not happy with your books, return them within 10 days of our expense.

VOCA incident 사건 proceed 나아가다 public holiday 공휴일 phase 단계 conduct 행하다 supervision 감독
agreement 계약 terminate 종결시키다 resident 거주자

GRAMMAR IN SENTENCE

▶ 의미 단위로 문장을 끊어 읽고, 해석하세요.
단, 경우에 따라 명사구 또는 명사절은 { }, 형용사구 또는 형용사절은 [ ], 부사 부사구 부사절은 ( )로 표시하세요.

1. Some students will run on the playground in the afternoon.

2. The bus stops at the bus stop every 20 minutes.

3. Regarding this matter, both parties have concurred.

4. Considering his age, William is strong and looks young.

5. The agreement will automatically be terminated upon the death of the resident.

6. If you're not happy with your books, return them within 10 days at our expense.

7. In order to meet the deadline, we should proceed at a fast pace.

8. The national bank will be closed in observance of a public holiday.

9. Many police officers stood guard all along the street.

10. Aside from the minor corrections Christina is working on, the booklet is almost ready for the event.

전치사

전치사

전치사는 명사나 대명사의 목적격 앞에 놓여 시간, 장소, 이유, 양보, 방법 등을 나타낸다.

The book is **on** the desk. 그 책은 책상 위에 있다.
　　　　　　명사

I bought a book **for** her. 나는 그녀를 위하여 책 한 권을 샀다.
　　　　　　　대명사(목적격)

Tom is accustomed **to** studying English every day.
　　　　　　　　　　동명사 + 명사
Tom은 매일 영어 공부하는 것이 습관이다.

전치사 vs 접속사

	전치사 + 명사(구)	접속사 + 절(주어 + 동사)
~이기 때문에	because of, owing to, due to	because, as, since, now that
~에도 불구하고	despite, in spite of	although, though, even though
~일 경우에	in case of, in the event of	in case that, in the event that
~를 제외하고	except, except for	except that
~에 따르면	according to	according as
~하는 동안	during, over	while
만약 ~ 않다면	without	if ~ not, unless

ACTUAL TEST 2

A 보기 중 맞는 것을 고르세요.

1 All of the participants will be asked to complete a ------- survey about the effectiveness of the session.
(A) briefed
(B) briefest
(C) briefly
(D) brief

2 Flight attendants must ensure that ------- of the passengers is properly seated prior to takeoff.
(A) every
(B) all
(C) each
(D) much

3 According to a recent survey, the abundance of college graduates makes the job market very ----------.
(A) competition
(B) compete
(C) competing
(D) competitive

4 It is absolutely necessary that all researchers wear -------- glasses and gloves while in the laboratory.
(A) protect
(B) protective
(C) protecting
(D) protected

5 The two laundry detergents showed in the study were found to be ------- effective.
(A) equal
(B) equally
(C) equality
(D) equaled

6 Charles Raven has had ------- 15 years of experience in marketing and he is a marketing manager for a medium-sized company in South Carolina.
(A) nearly
(B) currently
(C) completely
(D) closely

7 Dick Martins is ------------ interested in returning to Atlanta, which is his hometown, and he would like to move to a larger city.
(A) especial
(B) especially
(C) exceptional
(D) exceptionally

8 After interviewing the candidates, heads of each department will ---------- make a decision tomorrow.
(A) finally
(B) final
(C) finance
(D) financial

9 A dinner reception will be held at Hall's Guesthouse and Restaurant starting at 6:00 p.m. ------- Saturday, June 20th.
(A) from
(B) on
(C) in
(D) to

10 Our company will deliver items ------- three days of the date the order is placed.
(A) within
(B) sometime
(C) nearby
(D) during

B 보기 중 맞는 것을 고르세요.

Questions 11-16 refer to the following notice.

Attention! Movie Lovers!

When a movie becomes very **11** -------, we often sell out all our tickets for a show.

12 -------, we recommend that in order to get a ticket, you use our ticket reservation system. This system is **13** ------- by phone, through the Internet or by stopping **14** ------- our box office location. To reserve your ticket, select the movie, the time, and how **15** ------- tickets you will purchase. For very large groups, we recommend you talk to a service agent by phone. This way, you will be sure to receive all your tickets **16** ------- the same area.

11 (A) popular
(B) popularity
(C) popularly
(D) populate

12 (A) However
(B) Nevertheless
(C) Therefore
(D) For example

13 (A) avail
(B) available
(C) availability
(D) availably

14 (A) in
(B) on
(C) of
(D) at

15 (A) much
(B) lots
(C) many
(D) every

16 (A) in
(B) through
(C) to
(D) from

MINI TEST 1

A 보기 중 맞는 것을 고르세요.

1. The recent increase in sales taxes will result in a ---------- in employee benefits.
   (A) reduced
   (B) reducing
   (C) reduces
   (D) reduction

2. Professional and cultural organizations can be -------------- of information about scholarships.
   (A) source
   (B) sources
   (C) sourcing
   (D) sourced

3. Heather stated that her deep love of nature has been -------- main motivation for producing such brilliant works of art.
   (A) her
   (B) hers
   (C) she
   (D) herself

4. Because his secretary was out of the office yesterday, Mr. Shannon had to take his calls by -------.
   (A) he
   (B) his
   (C) him
   (D) himself

5. We have already received -------- membership packet in the mail since last year.
   (A) few
   (B) whole
   (C) many
   (D) every

6. The Health Care Institute prepares graduates to make ------- contributions to society.
   (A) valuably
   (B) values
   (C) valuable
   (D) value

7. It is extremely important to enter your personal information -------------- to be eligible for this sweepstakes.
   (A) correct
   (B) correctly
   (C) corrected
   (D) correction

8. In spite of several attempts, Ms. Gilbert has not ---------- been able to talk to any customers service representatives over the phone.
   (A) still
   (B) ahead
   (C) yet
   (D) already

9. Please -------- us for more information about special Saturday classes and other options.
   (A) comply
   (B) look
   (C) respond
   (D) contact

10. Employees enrolled in Applied Research in Business can fully ------- in group activities.
    (A) participating
    (B) participate
    (C) had participated
    (D) participant

B 보기 중 틀린 것을 고르세요.

1 Parents of young (A)[child] have to (B)[deal with] the commercial (C)[influence] of television every time they take them (D)[to] a supermarket or toy store.

2 (A)[An] e-mail will be sent (B)[to you] to confirm the (C)[cancel] of your registration (D)[for] the international business course.

3 Each regional manager (A)[handle] all health and social care complaints (B)[for] their respective districts (C)[so that] they (D)[become] familiar with local issues and services.

4 Jennifer (A)[plans] to apply (B)[hers] experience in the field of environmental science (C)[as] an undergraduate (D)[toward] an advanced degree in environmental law.

5 The new restaurant will (A)[be open] (B)[for business] (C)[near] the N&H Department Store (D)[on] the beginning of next month.

6 The new product design (A)[has not] generated (B)[many] interest (C)[from] consumers (D)[judging by] the survey results.

7 I (A)[ran into] (B)[an] acquaintance of (C)[me] from my former company (D)[on] the street.

8 Ms. Cruise will (A)[play] the (B)[title role] in the film, (C)[which] is an (D)[adapting] of the play, *The Merchant of Venice*.

9 The law firm (A)[met] yesterday and (B)[discussed about] the (C)[implications] of the (D)[recent] high court decision regarding a paint manufacturer.

10 (A)[To join] the member's club, (B)[completely] one of the forms (C)[by] the cash register and submit it (D)[to] the customer service desk.

MINI TEST 1

C 보기 중 맞는 것을 고르세요.

Questions 1-6 refer to the following e-mail.

Date: April 15

Subject: Revised Office Policies: Meeting

As of May 1, we will **1**. ------- some new office policies on safety and evacuation procedures. We will be holding a meeting **2**. ------- April 20th at 3:00 p.m. **3**. ------- the main auditorium. It is necessary that all employees **4**. ------- the meeting as we will be going over a number of important policy changes.

If you have any questions or concerns, please **5**. ------- them to Amy Jermons by e-mail at amyj@mail.org or by telephone at 654-1230. Thank you for your **6**. ------- .

---

1 (A) implement
    (B) implementing
    (C) implemented
    (D) implementation

2 (A) from
    (B) in
    (C) on
    (D) of

3 (A) in
    (B) on
    (C) above
    (D) below

4 (A) participate
    (B) attend
    (C) take part
    (D) go

5 (A) reply
    (B) deal
    (C) respond
    (D) direct

6 (A) cooperate
    (B) cooperative
    (C) cooperation
    (D) cooperatively

Questions 7-12 refer to the following flyer.

David Lucas will be performing live!

Finally, David Lucas **7** ------- that he can give a truly great performance.

☐ Venue: World Music Store	☐ Dates: Friday, December 20 to Sunday, December 22
☐ Time: 7:00 P.M.	☐ Cost: $50 adults / $20 children under fifteen

To purchase tickets in **8** -------, send a personal check or money order to the World Music Store **9** ------- Wednesday, December 4. You can **10** ------- by credit card by calling 1-800-123-1234. Any remaining tickets will be sold on a first-come, first-served basis **11** ------- the evening of each performance.

Cash will be the only **12** ------- form of payment on these evenings.

---

7 (A) will demonstrate
 (B) demonstrated
 (C) has demonstrated
 (D) demonstrates

8 (A) advancement
 (B) advance
 (C) advanced
 (D) advancing

9 (A) for
 (B) in
 (C) by
 (D) at

10 (A) pay
 (B) be paid
 (C) paying
 (D) have paid

11 (A) at
 (B) on
 (C) for
 (D) in

12 (A) accept
 (B) accepted
 (C) accepting
 (D) acceptable

잉글리쉬앤 그래머 MASTER

실전편

Unit 7 수일치
Unit 8 시제
Unit 9 태

UNIT 07 수일치

GRAMMAR POINT

문장에서 주어와 동사는 수를 일치시켜야 한다. 기본적으로 주어가 단수이면 동사도 단수, 주어가 복수이면 동사도 복수가 와야 한다.

① 단수 주어 + 단수 동사 / 복수 주어 + 복수 동사

단수 동사에는 is/was, has 등이 있고, 일반 동사는 현재 시제일 경우에 동사 뒤에 -(e)s를 붙인다.
복수 동사에는 are/were, have 등이 있고, 일반 동사일 경우에는 동사원형을 쓴다.

Many **experts explain** that playing music helps plants grow.
많은 전문가들은 음악을 들려주면 식물이 잘 자란다고 설명한다.

② 주어 and 주어 + 복수 동사

접속사 and로 연결되는 주어는 두 개이므로 복수 주어가 되며, 복수 동사가 나와야 한다.

Coffee and tea **have** long and historic pasts. 커피와 차는 오랜 역사적인 과거를 가지고 있다.
　A and B　　복수 동사

③ 등위 상관접속사로 연결된 주어

등위 상관접속사는 반드시 짝을 맞추어 같이 쓰여야 하며, A와 B는 같은 문법 구조를 가져야 한다.

다음은 동사의 수를 B에 일치시킨다.

Either A or B A 또는 B	Neither A nor B A도 아니고 B도 아니고
Not A but B A가 아니라 B	Not only A but also B A뿐만 아니라 B도
B as well as A A뿐만 아니라 B도	

Not only my friends but also **my sister hasn't** been to Paris.
= **My sister** as well as my friends **hasn't** been to Paris.
내 친구뿐만 아니라 내 여동생도 파리에 가본 적이 없다.

④ 주어 + (수식어구) + 동사

주어와 동사 사이에 in addition to ~, along with ~, together with ~ 등의 수식어구가 있으면, 맨 앞에 나온 명사가 주어가 된다. 수식어구는 괄호로 묶는 연습을 평상시에 해두면 도움이 된다.

The reduction in salaries and benefits **has** depressed all of the employees.
봉급과 복지 혜택의 감소로 직원들은 모두 우울해했다.

⑤ 관계대명사절의 수일치

주격 관계대명사의 선행사와 관계대명사절의 동사는 일치한다.

I know **the man** who **is** walking on the street. 나는 길을 걷고 있는 그 남자를 안다.

GRAMMAR PRACTICE

A 괄호 안에서 알맞은 것을 고르세요.

1. Either you or your boyfriend (washes, wash) the dishes.

2. Neither my father nor I (is, am) a smoker.

3. Thomas as well as his friends (are, is) going to visit you.

4. Ms. Johnson, together with her family, (goes, go) to church every Sunday.

5. The (applicant, applicants) who meet the requirements for the position will be contracted.

6. The next item on today's meeting agenda (is, are) our company's expansion into Asia.

7. Residents adjacent to the airport (has, have) filed a lawsuit because of the noise.

8. Not only exam results but also class participation (is, are) included in the score.

9. Both furniture and clothes (is, are) on display.

10. Anyone with an interest in classical music (is, are) welcome to attend this event.

B 어법상 틀린 문장은 바르게 고치고, 틀린 부분이 없으면 O로 표시하세요.

1. Either a bus or a taxi are available at the airport.

2. Neither my parents nor my sister like pork.

3. I met a woman who work at a department store.

4. Our top priority for the remainder of the year are revenue growth.

5. Not only the students but also their teacher is attending the event.

VOCA meet the requirements for ~에 대한 요건을 충족시키다　agenda 안건　expansion 확장　adjacent to ~에 인접한
file a lawsuit 소송을 제기하다　priority 우선　revenue 수익　growth 성장

◎ GRAMMAR POINT

⑥ 동명사나 명사절은 단수 취급한다.

Taking advantage of advancements in technology **has** made our manufacturing process more streamlined. 진보된 기술을 이용하니 우리의 생산 공정이 더욱 합리화되었다.

⑦ The number of vs. A number of

> **The number of** + 복수 명사 → 단수 동사: ~의 수
>   주어
> **A number of** + 복수 명사 → 복수 동사: 많은 ~
>   주어

The number of complaints **has** increased this month. 이번 달에 불만사항의 수가 증가하고 있다.
    주어   단수 동사

A number of people were interested in the movie. 많은 사람들이 그 영화에 관심이 있었다.
           주어   복수 동사

⑧ There + 자동사 + 주어

유도부사 There ~ 구문에서는 <There + 자동사 + 주어>의 어순으로 주어와 동사가 도치된 형태로 쓰인다.

There	자동사	주어
	be동사	(형용사) **명사** (전치사구)
	remain	(부사)
	exist	(형용사구: 분사 구문, to부정사)
	live	(형용사절: 관계대명사절)
	완전 자동사	

There **are** so many **countries** to visit in the world. 세상에는 방문할 나라들이 아주 많다.
    be동사   주어

There **remains** great **advice** for the readers to discover.
       자동사   주어(불가산 명사, 단수 취급)

독자들이 알아낼 수 있는 좋은 조언이 여전히 남아 있다.

⑨ 그 외에 주어를 단수 취급하는 경우

(1) 복수지만 하나의 덩어리로 파악되는 무게, 거리, 가격, 시간 등의 개념

또한 and로 연결됐지만 개별적으로 이해하면 안 되는 것들도 단수 취급한다.

Ten years **is** a long time. 십 년은 긴 시간이다.

Gin and tonic **is** my favorite drink. 나는 진토닉을 좋아한다.

(2) -s로 끝나는 학문명, 국가명, 병명

mathematics (수학)	economics (경제학)	physics (물리학)
the Philippines (필리핀)	the United States (미국)	diabetes (당뇨병)

GRAMMAR PRACTICE

A 괄호 안에서 알맞은 것을 고르세요.

1. There (was, were) a few paintings and a clock on the walls.
2. There (is, are) a broad consensus in the country on this issue.
3. During late summer, swimming in this river (is, are) very dangerous.
4. What we want to know (are, is) if Ann will come to the party tomorrow.
5. Half of the students (was, were) getting less than 50% on tests.
6. Why Tom left Jenny (is, are) still unknown.
7. Physics (is, are) not easy to study.
8. The number of tourists in this area (has, have) increased recently.
9. A number of students (is, are) studying hard in the library.
10. Playing games for too long (is, are) not good for children's health.

B 어법상 틀린 문장은 바르게 고치고, 틀린 부분이 없으면 O로 표시하세요.

1. There was a demonstration, a discussion and a presentation yesterday.
2. The clerks in this store works overtime every Monday.
3. What the president said were true.
4. Eating breakfast everyday are good for your health.
5. Since it was a holiday, the number of cars on the road was noticeably reduced.

VOCA broad 광범위한 consensus 합의 issue 쟁점 demonstration 실연 discussion 토론 presentation 발표
clerk 점원 noticeably 확연히 reduce 줄다

GRAMMAR IN SENTENCE

▶ 의미 단위로 문장을 끊어 읽고, 해석하세요.
단, 경우에 따라 명사구 또는 명사절은 { }, 형용사구 또는 형용사절은 [ ], 부사 부사구 부사절은 ( )로 표시하세요.

1. There were a demonstration, a discussion and a presentation yesterday.

2. What we want to know is if Ann will come to the party tomorrow.

3. Half of the students were getting less than 50% on tests.

4. The clerks in this store work overtime every Monday.

5. Eating breakfast everyday is good for your health.

6. Since it was a holiday, the number of cars on the road was noticeably reduced.

7. The next item on today's meeting agenda is our company's expansion into Asia.

8. Residents adjacent to the airport have filed a lawsuit because of the noise.

9. Not only exam results but also class participation is included in the score.

10. Anyone with an interest in classical music is welcome to attend this event.

 **Outro**

수일치

수일치

주어가 단수이면 동사도 단수, 주어가 복수이면 동사도 복수가 와야 한다.

단수 주어 + 단수 동사	**A scientist is explaining** that playing music helps plants grow. 어떤 과학자는 음악을 들려주면 식물이 잘 자란다고 설명한다.
복수 주어 + 복수 동사	**Some scientists are explaining** that playing music helps plants grow. 과학자들은 음악을 들려주면 식물이 잘 자란다고 설명한다.

-s를 꼭 붙여서 써야 하는 명사들

headquarters 본사	belongings 소지품	sales 판매
customs 세관	measures 수단, 대책	savings 저축
earnings 소득	human resources 인력 자원	

단수와 복수가 동일한 명사

| sheep 양 | barracks 병영 | species 종 | means 수단 |
| series 연속 | crossroads 십자로 | headquarters 본사 | |

Unit 07 | 수일치 89

UNIT 08 시제

◎ GRAMMAR POINT

① 단순 시제

영어 문장에서 가장 기본적인 시제는 현재, 과거, 미래를 나타내는 단순 시제이다. 각각 어떨 때 어떤 형태로 쓰이는지를 알아두어야 한다.

(1) 현재 시제
현재 시제는 불변의 진리, (일정 기간) 변함없는 사실, 습관, 반복을 나타내는 경우에 쓴다.
주로 every day, each month, often, frequently, regularly, usually 등과 함께 쓴다.
주어가 3인칭 단수인 경우에는 동사 뒤에 -(e)s를 붙여 써야 한다.

The sun **rises** in the east. (불변의 진리) 태양은 동쪽에서 뜬다.
The train **starts** at 6:00 p.m. (일정 기간 변함없는 사실) 그 기차는 오후 6시에 출발한다.
He **attends** the workshop every month. (현재의 습관, 반복) 그는 강습회에 매달 참석한다.

(2) 과거 시제
과거 시제는 이미 끝난 과거의 동작이나 상태를 나타낸다. 주로 last year, two years ago 등과 함께 쓴다.

He **attended** the workshop last year. 그는 작년에 강습회에 참석했었다.

(3) 미래 시제: will + 동사원형
미래 시제는 <will + 동사원형>이 기본적인 형태이며, 미래의 상황에 대한 추측이나 의지를 나타낸다.
<be going to + 동사원형> 또는 <be + -ing> 형태도 미래를 나타낸다. tomorrow, next year 등과 함께 쓴다.

He **will attend** the workshop tomorrow. 그는 내일 강습회에 참석할 것이다.

② 진행 시제

현재, 과거, 미래의 각 시점에서 진행 중인 동작이나 상황을 나타낼 때 쓰이는 시제가 바로 진행 시제이다. 즉, 진행 시제에는 현재 진행, 과거 진행, 미래 진행이 있다.

(1) 현재 진행: am/is/are + -ing
현재 시점에 진행되고 있는 일을 표현할 때 쓰며, **now, currently** 등과 함께 쓴다.

What **are** you **doing** now? 당신은 지금은 무엇을 하는 중입니까?
He **is** currently **attending** the workshop. 그는 현재 강습회에 참석 중이다.

(2) 과거 진행: was/were + -ing
특정한 과거 시점에 진행되고 있었던 일을 표현할 때 쓴다.

He **was attending** the workshop at 5:00 p.m. yesterday.
그는 어제 오후 5시에 강습회에 참석하고 있었다.

(3) 미래 진행: will be + -ing
특정한 미래 시점에 진행되고 있을 일을 표현할 때 쓴다.

He **will be attending** the workshop after work tomorrow.
그는 내일 일을 마친 후에 강습회에 참석하고 있을 것이다.

GRAMMAR PRACTICE

A 주어진 동사를 알맞은 형태로 고쳐 쓰세요.

1. go : Ann _____ to the grocery store every weekend.

2. walk : Andrew was _____ the dog in the park when I called him.

3. take : He is currently _____ a class on safety regulations.

4. break : The American Civil War _____ out in April 1861.

5. travel : Next month, Tom _____ _____ with his family to Switzerland.

B 괄호 안에서 알맞은 것을 고르세요.

1. I (will have, have) a meeting with a client at 3:00 p.m. tomorrow.

2. The Korea-Japan World Cup (is, was) held in 2002.

3. Water (is, was) made up of an oxygen atom and two hydrogen atoms.

4. Tomorrow, he (goes, will go) on a business trip to San Francisco.

5. I (drive, was driving) a car when you contacted me yesterday.

C 어법상 틀린 문장은 바르게 고치고, 틀린 부분이 없으면 O로 표시하세요.

1. I check in at the airport next Sunday morning.

2. Early retirement packages are usually available for long-term working employees.

3. Our company has introduced the new system last month.

4. I was now studying hard to study abroad.

5. Next month, the Marketing Department implements a strategy to increase the company's revenue.

VOCA grocery 식료품류 safety regulations 안전 규정 oxygen 산소 atom 원자 hydrogen 수소 retirement 은퇴
implement 이행하다

GRAMMAR POINT

③ 완료 시제

이전에 시작됐던 일이 말하고 있는 그 시점까지 계속해서 영향을 미치고 있음을 나타내는 시제가 완료 시제이다. 기본적인 형태는 <have동사 + p.p.>로, 크게 현재 완료, 과거 완료, 미래 완료가 있다.
완료 시제를 진행형으로 표현하고 싶으면 <have동사 + been + -ing>의 형태로 나타내면 된다.

(1) 현재 완료: have + p.p.
<have + p.p.> 형태인 현재 완료는 과거부터 현재까지 이어지는 내용이므로 현재의 의미로 간주하면 된다. <since + 과거 시점>, <for + 기간>, in the past ~ years 등과 함께 쓴다.

He **has attended** the workshop since last year. 그는 작년부터 그 강습회에 참석해 오고 있다.

(2) 현재 완료 진행: have been + -ing
과거에 시작된 일이 현재까지 진행 중임을 나타낼 때 쓴다.

He **has been attending** the workshop for an hour.
(한 시간 전부터 시작한 일이 지금 말하는 순간에도 진행되고 있음을 나타냄)
그는 한 시간 동안 강습회에 참석하고 있는 중이다.

(3) 과거 완료: had + p.p.
과거를 기준으로 그 과거 이전에 일어난 일을 표현할 때 쓴다.

He **had** already **attended** the workshop when I arrived at his office yesterday.
　　　　　과거 완료　　　　　　　　　　　　　　과거
(내가 그의 사무실로 갔던 과거 시점을 기준으로 해서 이전에 이루어진 일이 그가 강습회에 간 일이라는 것을 알 수 있음)
내가 어제 그의 사무실에 도착했을 때 그는 이미 강습회에 가 있었다.

(4) 과거 완료 진행: had been + -ing
과거를 기준으로 그 과거 이전에 일어난 일이 과거의 그 순간에도 진행 중이었음을 나타내는 표현이다.

He **had been attending** the workshop for an hour when she left.
　　　　　과거 완료 진행　　　　　　　　　　　　　　　과거
(그녀가 떠난 과거 시점을 기준으로 강습회는 이미 시작했고 그녀가 떠나는 순간에도 강습회는 하고 있었다는 것을 알 수 있음)
그녀가 강습회장을 떠났을 때 그는 한 시간째 강습회에 참석 중이었다.

(5) 미래 완료: will have + p.p.
미래 완료(will + have + p.p.)는 과거의 어떤 사건이나 동작이 미래의 특정한 시점까지 완료될 것임을 말할 때 쓴다. 주로 <by + 미래 시간의 부사구>와 함께 쓰이거나, 또는 <By the time S2 + V2(현재시제), S1 + V1(will + have + p.p.)>의 형태로 많이 쓰인다.

He **will have attended** the workshop 5 times by next month.
(이전부터 참석하기 시작했던 강습회가 다음 달이 되면 5번이 됨을 나타냄)
그는 다음 달까지면 강습회에 5번 참석했을 것이다.

GRAMMAR PRACTICE

A 주어진 동사를 알맞은 형태로 고쳐 쓰세요.

1. introduce : Our company _____ the new system since last month.
2. rise : Recently, oil prices _____ due to strong global demand.
3. play : Jane _____ the piano for two hours.
4. live : Austin _____ in Atlanta before he moved to Seattle.
5. repair : By the time I get to the auto repair shop, my car _____ _____.

B 괄호 안에서 알맞은 것을 고르세요.

1. The opera had already started by the time we (arrived, will have arrived) at the theater.
2. Since last year, we (have been working, will have worked) in the same department.
3. I've been busy this week, so I (haven't finished, hadn't finished) the report yet.
4. By the time he travels to Canada next year, he (has been, will have been) there three times so far.
5. When we got home last night, we found that somebody (will have broken, had broken) in to the flat.

C 어법상 틀린 문장은 바르게 고치고, 틀린 부분이 없으면 O로 표시하세요.

1. I have called the technician about fixing this machine yesterday.
2. The detective looked into the accident thoroughly since last month.
3. He will have met his girlfriend for two years by the end of this month.
4. The technician has been fixing the computer since this morning.
5. By the time we got to the theater, the film had started.

VOCA auto repair shop 자동차 정비소   so far 지금까지   break into 침입하다   flat 아파트   thoroughly 철저히

GRAMMAR POINT

④ 특정 시제와 함께 쓰이는 부사(구)

현재	과거	현재완료	미래, 미래완료
every day each month often frequently usually generally	yesterday recently two years ago last month (year) in 과거 (in 2010) once (한번은)	for 기간 since 과거시점 recently in the last(past)~ over the year(month)	tomorrow next month (year) as of 미래 by/until + 미래 in the near future * 단, until은 미래완료와 함께 쓰지 않는다.

⑤ 시간, 조건의 부사절

시간이나 조건을 나타내는 부사절에서는 현재시제가 미래를 나타낸다.
이 때 주절은 미래 시제 또는 명령문을 쓴다.

| 시간 | before, after, when, until, as soon as, while | 조건 | if, unless, as long as, once (일단~하면) |

When you **get** home, please **call** me again. 집에 도착하면, 내게 다시 전화 하세요. (시간을 나타내는 부사절)

If you **need** money, he **will lend** you some. 당신이 돈이 필요하면 그가 조금 빌려줄 겁니다.
(조건을 나타내는 부사절)

⑥ 현재완료 vs. 과거

현재완료는 계속, 경험, 결과, 완료의 의미를 나타낸다.

He **has** just **finished** his homework. 그는 숙제를 막 마쳤다. (완료)

I **have been to** Rome. 나는 Rome에 가본 적이 있다. (경험)

She **has gone to** Rome. 그녀는 Rome으로 떠나 버렸다. (결과)

have been to ~ 해 본 적이 있다 vs. have gone to~ 가버리고 이곳에 없다.

	현재 완료 (과거- 현재) 현재에 초점을 맞춤	과거 : 과거 일만 얘기함
계속	He has worked for CNN since last year. 그는 작년이래로 줄 곳 CNN에서 일하고 있다. 그는 작년부터 지금까지 CNN에서 일하고 있다.	He worked for CNN last year. 그는 작년에 CNN에서 일했다. 작년의 과거 사실만을 알 수 있다.
경험	A: Do you know the novel? 그 소설을 아세요? B: Yes, I have read the book before. 네, 전에 읽은 적이 있어요. 소설을 읽었다는 경험을 강조한다.	A: When did you read the novel? 언제 그 소설을 읽으셨어요? B: I read the novel last month. 지난달에 읽었어요. 소설을 읽은 과거 시점 자체를 강조한다.
결과	I have lost my purse. 나는 내 지갑을 잃어버렸다. 과거에 잃어버린 결과 현재에도 계속 잃어버린 상태임을 나타낸다.	I lost my purse yesterday. 나는 나의 지갑을 어제 잃어버렸다. 과거에 잃어버렸고, 지금은 어떻게 되었는지 알 수 없다. (찾았을 수도 아직 못 찾은 상태일 수도 있다)

GRAMMAR PRACTICE

A 두 문장이 같은 의미가 되도록, 주어진 표현을 이용하여 빈칸을 채우세요.

1. Anna is currently traveling in Paris. This is the first time there.

   = Anna _____ to Paris. (be, never)

2. Linda was on a business trip in Paris last month.

   = Linda _____ in Paris last month. (go)

3. Tim noticed that his wallet was missing last night, but he found it at his desk this morning.

   = Tim _____ his wallet last night. (lose)

4. Tim noticed that his wallet was missing last night and he still can't find it.

   = Tim _____ his wallet. (lose)

5. The room was dark an hour ago, but now the lights are on.

   = Someone _____ on the lights. (turn)

B 괄호 안에서 알맞은 것을 고르세요.

1. Our company (have introduced, will have introduced) the new system by next month.
2. Denver University (will have attracted, has attracted) young professionals recently.
3. If all of the team members (will work, work) cooperatively, we can meet the deadline.
4. The Sales Department (spent, has spent) a lot of money on courier services in the past two months.
5. As soon as you (wire, will wire) the advance payment early next month, we will prepare for the October shipment.

C 어법상 틀린 문장은 바르게 고치고, 틀린 부분이 없으면 O로 표시하세요.

1. I've gone to the museum when I was a child.
2. The interview schedules will be set shortly after we will review the applications.
3. I'm looking for David. I haven't been able to contact him all day.
4. They haven't visited him for a long time.
5. I have forgot the appointment with the doctor yesterday.

VOCA wallet 지갑   attract 유치하다   meet the deadline 마감일을 맞추다   wire 송금하다   advance shipment 선금

◎ GRAMMAR POINT

⑦ 과거 vs 과거완료

(1) 과거: 동작이 과거에 한 번 발생한 것이다. 현재와 관련이 없으며 과거에 어느 정도 지속됐는지 알 수 없다.

He **met** his girlfriend. 그는 어제 여자 친구를 만났다. (어제 만난 동작으로 끝이 났다. 얼마나 만났는지 알 수 없다.)

(2) 과거 완료: 먼 과거에 시작해서 과거에 완료된 동작이다. 현재와는 상관이 없지만 과거에 어느 정도 지속해서 발생한 것이다.

He **had met** his girlfriend <u>for about two years</u>. 그는 여자친구와 2년 정도 만났다.
(분명한 기간이 들어가 있다. 물론 과거 완료이므로 지금은 더 이상 안 만난다는 것을 알 수 있다.)

⑧ 미래 vs 미래완료

(1) 미래: 행위가 현재가 아닌 미래에 발생할 것이다.

He **will meet** his girlfriend <u>tomorrow</u>. 그는 여자 친구를 내일 만날 것이다.
(지금도 만나는 행위가 진행 중인지는 알 수 없다. 내일 만난다는 것만 알 수 있다.)

(2) 미래 완료: 과거에 시작된 동작이 현재를 지나 미래의 특정한 시점에 완료될 때 사용하기 때문에 상당한 기간을 의미한다.

He **will have met** his girlfriend for two years <u>by the end of this month</u>.
이번 달 말이 되면 그는 자신의 여자 친구를 만난 지 2년이 된다.
(과거부터 남자친구를 만나왔고 현재도 만나고 있지만 아직 2년은 되지 않았다. 이번 달 말이 되면 2년이란 기간이 되는 셈이다.)

⑨ 동사원형을 쓰는 특수 구문

요구, 주장, 제안, 명령을 나타내는 동사	
요구하다: require, request, demand, ask	주장하다: insist
제안하다: suggest, propose, recommend, advise	명령하다: order

이성적 판단에 근거를 둔 형용사			
necessary 필요한	important 중요한	imperative 필수적인	
essential 필수적인	vital 중요한	advisable 권고할 만한	urgent 위급한

요구, 주장, 제안, 명령을 나타내는 동사와 이성적인 판단에 근거를 둔 형용사가 쓰이면, 종속절의 동사 앞에는 should를 쓰거나 생략한다. 문장에서는 주로 should를 생략하는데, 이 경우 동사원형만 남게 된다.

The supervisor **has demanded** that all the reports **(should) <u>be submitted</u>** by tomorrow.
상관이 내일까지는 모든 보고서가 제출되어야 한다고 요청했다.

📝 시제 일치하는 경우

One of the onlookers **insisted that** the suspect **hadn't started** the scuffle.
한 목격자가 용의자는 싸움을 시작하지 않았다고 주장했다.

▶ insist가 that절에서 단순히 지난 일을 얘기하고 있는 경우는 that절 안에서 동사원형이 사용되지 않는 것에 유의한다. 가정 동사나 가정 형용사라 하더라도 that절에서 동사원형이 쓰이기 위해서는 반드시 that절의 내용이 '**실현되어야 함**'이 요지여야 한다.

GRAMMAR PRACTICE

A 괄호 안에서 알맞은 것을 고르세요.

1. These safety regulations (will come, will have come) into effect on the 1st of next month.

2. By the time I get to the airport, he (has, will have) already left.

3. Tom (has been, had been) abroad three times before he graduated from college.

4. When I (get, got) to the bus stop, the bus had just left.

5. We asked that our customers (filled, fill) out the form completely.

B 주어진 동사를 알맞은 형태로 고쳐 쓰세요.

1. work : The manager suggested we _____ together.

2. finish : It is imperative that our team _____ the project by next week.

3. wear : It is essential that employees _____ protective clothing in this area.

4. be : The doctor insisted that the patient ____ operated on immediately.

5. take : It is recommended that the sales manager _____ a vacation for his health.

C 어법상 틀린 문장은 바르게 고치고, 틀린 부분이 없으면 O로 표시하세요.

1. The teacher asked that all students submitted their reports by noon.

2. By next month, I will have been to the museum 5 times.

3. When I arrive at the airport, the plane had already departed.

4. Before he joined our company, he has already worked at an advertising agency for 5 years.

5. Regulations require that all passenger trains maintain low speeds as they pass through towns.

VOCA safety regulations 안전 규정   come into effect 효력을 발생하다   protective 보호하는

GRAMMAR IN SENTENCE

▶ 의미 단위로 문장을 끊어 읽고, 해석하세요.
단, 경우에 따라 명사구 또는 명사절은 { }, 형용사구 또는 형용사절은 [ ], 부사 부사구 부사절은 ( )로 표시하세요.

1. Early retirement packages are usually available for long-term working employees.

2. Before he joined our company, he had already worked at an advertising agency for 5 years.

3. Regulations require that all passenger trains maintain low speeds as they pass through towns.

4. The interview schedules will be set shortly after we review the applications.

5. I called the technician about fixing this machine yesterday.

6. The detective has looked into the accident thoroughly since last month.

7. He will have met his girlfriend for two years by the end of this month.

8. The technician has been fixing the computer since this morning.

9. By the time we get to the theater, the film will have started.

10. Next month, the Marketing Department will implement a strategy to increase the company's revenue.

 **Outro**

시제

단순시제	현재 -s	(일정기간) 변함없는 사실, 습관, 반복 또는 불변의 진리 David attends the seminar **every month**. David 는 매달 세미나에 참석한다.	
	과거 -ed/ 불규칙변화	과거 특정 시점의 동작, 행동, 과거의 사실 David **attended** the seminar **last month**. David는 지난달에 세미나에 참석했다.	
	미래 will + 동사원형	미래의 특정 시점의 동작, 행동, 미래의 사실 David **will attend** the seminar **tomorrow**. David는 내일 세미나에 참석할 것이다.	
진행시제	현재진행 am/is/ are +-ing	현재 진행 중인 일이나 사건, 또는 단순한 미래 David **is attending** the seminar **now**. David는 세미나에 참석중이다.	
	과거진행 was/ were +-ing	과거의 어느 시점에 진행 중이었던 일 David **was attending** the seminar **at 2:00 p.m. yesterday**. David는 내일 오후 2시에 세미나에 참석 중일 것이다.	
	미래진행 will be-ing	미래의 어느 시점에 진행 될 일 David **will be attending** the seminar tomorrow afternoon. David는 내일 오후에는 한참 세미나에 참석 중일 것이다.	
완료시제	현재완료 have + p.p.	과거에 사실이 현재에 영향을 미치거나 지속될 때 David **has attended** the seminar **since last year**. David는 작년부터 계속 세미나에 참석해 오고 있다.	
	과거완료 had + p.p.	언급된 과거보다 더 과거에 있었던 일 David **realized** that he **had lost** his key trying to open the door. David는 문을 열려고 했을 때 열쇠를 잃어버렸다는 것을 깨달았다.	
	미래완료 will have p.p.	과거부터 진행되어 미래의 특정 시점에 어떤 일이 완료될 때 David **will have attended** the seminar 10 times **by next month.** David 는 다음 달 까지면 10번 세미나에 참석하는 것이 된다.	

UNIT 09 태

GRAMMAR POINT

일반적으로 주어가 동작을 하는 주체이면 능동태, 주어가 동작의 대상이 되면 수동태를 쓴다.

① 수동태, 능동태 구분하기

자동사의 경우 보편적으로 능동형으로 표현을 한다.
타동사의 경우 능동태 동사 뒤에는 목적어가, 수동태 동사 뒤에는 전치사나 부사가 온다.

📒 **타동사의 경우**

능동태	주어 + **타동사** + **목적어**
	a/the/소유격 + (형용사) + 명사
	this/that + (형용사) + 명사
	명사s
	형용사 + 명사
수동태	주어 + **be동사 + p.p.** + 전치사/부사

능동태 They <u>accepted</u> <u>the proposal</u>. 그들은 그 제안을 받아들였다.
　　　　　　타동사　　목적어(the + 명사)

수동태 The proposal <u>was accepted</u> <u>by them</u>. 그 제안은 그들에 의해 받아들여졌다.
　　　　　　　　　be + p.p.　　전치사

② 수동태 뒤에 명사가 올 수 있는 경우

(1) 4형식 동사

4형식 동사 give, send, show, lend, offer, award, grant 등은 수동태 뒤에 능동태의 직접 목적어였던 명사가 올 수 있다.

능동 I **gave** my sister a book. = I **gave** a book to my sister. 나는 여동생에게 책 한 권을 주었다.

수동 My sister **was given** <u>a book</u>. = A book **was given** to my sister.
　　　내 여동생은 책을 한 권 받았다.

(2) 5형식 동사

① 상태와 판단을 나타내는 5형식 동사인 consider, think, make, find, elect, call, name, appoint 등은 수동태 뒤에 목적 보어인 명사가 올 수 있다.

능동 All the employees **considered** the new vice president a great leader.
　　　모든 직원들은 그 신임 부사장이 훌륭한 지도자라고 여겼다.

수동 The new vice president **was considered** <u>a great leader</u> (by all the employees).

A 괄호 안에 알맞은 것을 고르세요.

1. We (was held, held) the party last night.
2. The meeting (was held, held) at 1 o'clock yesterday.
3. A report (was given, gave) to the manager this morning.
4. Breakfast (will serve, will be served) at 6:00.
5. Ted (wounded, was wounded) in the factory.

B 어법상 틀린 문장은 바르게 고치고, 옳은 문장에는 표시 (O) 하세요.

1. The president respected by all the employees.
2. Your sister has seen at the party before.
3. Quarterly earnings are regularly reported to board members.
4. All my friends will invite to my housewarming party.
5. All the proceeds will use to acquire more properties.

C 다음 능동태 문장을 수동태 문장으로 바꾸세요.

1. She gave me a novel I wanted to read yesterday.

2. He must send the loan payments to the national bank by the fifteenth of this month.

3. People consider Mr. Wilson one of the best public speakers because his speech is powerful and impressive.

4. They held an exhibition of Erica's paintings and sculptures at the BACO Gallery in New York.

5. They should lock maintenance equipment that is not in use in the warehouse.

VOCA wound 다치다 property 재산, 자산, 소유물 loan payments 대출 상환금 due 만기가 된 public speaker 대중연설가 exhibition 전시회 painting 그림 sculpture 조각 maintenance 수리, 장비 유지 be in use 사용 중이다 warehouse 창고 lock 챙겨

GRAMMAR POINT

② to부정사를 목적 보어로 취하는 동사들

능동태에서 **to** 부정사를 목적보어로 취하는 **5형식** 동사들은 수동형태가 **S + be p.p + to** 부정사의 형태로 전환된다.

능동태 The president **encouraged** the employees **to work** hard.
= **수동태** The employees **were encouraged to** work hard (by the president).
사장님은 직원들이 열심히 일하도록 격려했다.

be enabled to do 가능하도록 되다	**be encouraged to** do ~하라고 권장 받다
be expected to do ~할 예정이다	**be persuaded to** do ~하라고 설득되다
be instructed to do ~하라고 지시[설명]하다	**be asked to** do ~해달라고 요청받다
be allowed to do ~할 수 있게 허락받다	**be advised to** do ~하라고 조언을 받다
be required to do ~하라고 요구되다	**be requested to** do ~하라고 요청받다
be reminded to do ~하라고 상기되다	**be forced to** do ~하라고 강요받다

③ 목적격 보어가 바뀌는 동사들

사역동사는 **make**만 수동태로 바뀔 수 있으며, 이때 목적격보어로 쓰인 동사원형은 **to** 부정사로 바뀐다. 지각동사는 목적격 동사로 쓰인 동사원형이 수동태에서 현재분사나 **to** 부정사로 바뀐다.

I **saw** Laura **cry** → Laura **was seen crying (to cry)** by me.
나는 Laura가 우는 것을 보았다.

They **made** her **cry**. → She **was made to cry** by them.
그들은 그녀를 울렸다.

③ 감정동사의 능동태, 수동태 구별

감정을 나타내는 타동사는 주어가 감정을 느끼는 주체가 되면 수동태를, 주어가 감정의 원인이면 능동태를 쓴다.

People **were disappointed** at the results. (주어가 감정을 느끼는 주체)
사람들은 결과에 실망했다.
▶ disappointed 실망한

The results **were disappointing**. (주어가 감정의 원인)
결과는 실망스러웠다.

감정동사의 수동태 관용표현

be interested in ~에 관심이[흥미가] 있다	be pleased with ~에 기쁘다
be tired of ~에 싫증나다	be surprised at ~에 놀라다
be amazed at ~에 놀라다	be frightened at ~에 두려움을 느끼다, 깜짝 놀라다
be disappointed at ~에 실망하다	be satisfied with ~에 만족하다

GRAMMAR PRACTICE

A 다음 능동태 문장을 수동태 문장으로 바꾸세요.

1. They require all employees to wear protective equipment in the workplace.

2. The company requires all visitors to present identification.

3. They expect heavy rains to continue throughout the day.

4. They ask guests dining at this restaurant on weekends to make reservation.

5. Someone heard him shout, "Watch out!"

B 다음 수동태 문장을 능동태 문장으로 바꾸세요.

1. I was allowed to throw a party by my parents.

2. He was encouraged to write poems by me.

3. The boy was made to read a book by a teacher.

4. Tony was advised to study a foreign language by the professor.

5. Children were heard laughing(to laugh) loudly in the classroom by them.

C 괄호 안에 알맞은 것을 고르세요.

1. His fans are very interested (by, in) his new song.
2. They were surprised (at, with) the news.
3. The candidate was disappointed (at, to) the outcome of the election.
4. My boss is satisfied (at, with) their manner of doing business.
5. All my family members were pleased (at, with) my passing the exam.

VOCA watch out 조심하다   poem 시

◎ GRAMMAR POINT

④ 자동사의 수동태

자동사 뒤에는 목적어가 없기 때문에 수동태로 바꿀 때 주어 자리로 나가는 명사가 없으므로 수동태로 바꿔 쓸 수 없다. 단, 자동사라 하더라도 전치사와 함께 쓰여 타동사 역할을 할 수 있는 표현들은 자동사와 전치사 가 한꺼번에 수동태로 쓰일 수 있다.

능동 The police **looked at** every document. 경찰이 모든 문서를 보았다.

수동 Every document **was looked at** by the police.

① 수동태가 될 수 있는 자동사

look at 보다	look after 돌보다	refer to 참고하다
deal with 다루다	dispose of 처분하다	pay for 지불하다

② 수동태가 될 수 없는 자동사

rise 오르다	arrive 도착하다	happen = take place (~일이) 일어나다
occur 발생하다	appear 나타나다	disappear 사라지다
remain 남아있다	exist 남다	expire 만기가 되다
function 기능을 하다	proceed 나아가다, 진행하다	decline 감소하다, 하락하다
deteriorate 쇠퇴하다	walk 걷다	work(labor) 일하다
come 오다	go 가다	live 살다
participate in ~에 참여하다	specialize in ~을 전문으로 하다	

The book was disappeared. (X) 책이 사라졌다.
The book has disappeared. (O)   The book disappeared. (O)

⑤ 수동태 관용표현: by 이외의 전치사를 쓰는 수동태

be covered with ~으로 덮여 있다	be dressed in ~을 입고 있다
be involved in ~에 연관이 있다	be absorbed in ~에 빠져 있다
be exposed to ~에 노출되다	be based on ~에 근거를 두다
be worried about ~을 걱정하다	be convinced of ~을 확신하다
be known as ~으로 알려지다	be known for ~으로 유명하다 (이유)
be known to ~에게 알려지다 (대상)	be noted for ~으로 유명하다 (이유)
be tired of ~으로 피곤하다	be made up of ~으로 구성되다
be related to ~과 관련되다	be associated with ~ ~과 연관되다
be blamed for ~으로 비난받다	be concerned with ~와 관계가 있다
be confused at ~에 혼란스럽다	be attached to ~ ~에 첨부되다
be equipped with ~의 장비를 갖추다	be limited to ~에 제한되다
be enclosed with ~과 함께 동봉되다	be skilled at(in) ~에 숙련되다
be opposed to ~에 반대하다	be committed to~ ~에 전념하다
be dedicated to ~에 헌신하다	be devoted to ~에 헌신하다

⑥ made by / of / from / out of

be made by: 물건을 만든 사람, 회사 등 출처를 표시할 때	**be made out of:** 재활용으로 만들어진 경우
be made of: 물리적으로 화학적으로 바뀌지 않은 경우	**be made from:** 물리적으로 화학적으로 바뀌는 경우

GRAMMAR PRACTICE

A 괄호 안에 알맞은 것을 고르세요.

1. One of my credit cards (expired, was expired) last month.
2. A variety of areas (dealt with, were dealt with) in the seminar.
3. The roads were very dangerous because they were covered (with, on) ice.
4. In Japan, everyone is dressed (by, in) new clothes on New Year's Day.
5. It is rock music that I was absorbed (in, of) when I was young.

B 다음 중 알맞은 전치사를 빈칸에 넣으세요.

for   as   to   of   from

1. Mr. Mandela is known _____ one of the world's greatest leaders.
2. It is known _____ the shortest subway lines in the world.
3. Iraq used to be known _____ the West by the Greek name Mesopotamia.
4. This chair is made _____ wood.
5. This cake is made _____ milk and eggs.

C 어법상 틀린 문장은 바르게 고치고, 옳은 문장에는 표시 **(O)** 하세요.

1. Attention, all employees.
2. The annual Christmas dinner will be taken place on Friday, December 20th at 6:00 p.m.
3. Every attendee asked to drop their name in the Secret Santa Box in your office.
4. Names will draw by Lisa Ring on December 10th and your partner's name will be placed in your mailbox.
5. The gift should cost under $20.00.

VOCA expire 만기가 되다　leader 지도자　draw 추첨하다

GRAMMAR POINT

⑦ 수동태의 시제

현재	능동	She washes the car everyday.
	수동	The car **is washed** everyday (by her).
미래	능동	She will wash the car tomorrow.
	수동	The car **will be washed** tomorrow (by her).
과거	능동	She washed the car yesterday.
	수동	The car **was washed** yesterday (by her).
현재완료	능동	She has washed the car for two hours.
	수동	The car **has been washed** for two hours (by her).
미래완료	능동	She will have washed the car by 2:00 in the afternoon.
	수동	The car **will have been washed** by 2:00 in the afternoon (by her).
과거완료	능동	She had washed the car when I arrived at home.
	수동	The car **had been washed** when I arrived at home (by her).
현재진행	능동	She is washing the car now.
	수동	The car **is being washed** now (by her).
과거진행	능동	She was washing the car when I called her yesterday.
	수동	The car **was being washed** when I called her yesterday (by her).

⑧ 의문문의 수동태

의문문을 수동태로 전환할 때는 능동태를 평서문으로 만들어서 바꾸면 된다.

(1) 일반의문문

Did you submit the report yesterday? 보고서를 제출했어요?
→ 의문문 수동태 Was the report submitted yesterday?

(2) 의문사가 있는 의문문 수동태

Where did you buy the shirt? 어디서 셔츠를 구매했어요?
→ (Where) You bought the shirt.
→ (Where) The shirt was bought by you.
→ Where was the shirt bought by you?

(3) 의문대명사가 주어로 쓰인 수동태

Who cleans the room every day? 누가 매일 방을 청소하나요?
→ The room is cleaned every day by whom?
→ By whom is the room cleaned every day?

(4) 의문대명사가 목적어로 쓰인 수동태

What did they do last week? 지난주에 그들은 무엇을 했어요?
→ What was done by them last week?

⑨ 명령문의 수동태

Close the door. 문을 닫아라. → Let the door be closed

GRAMMAR PRACTICE

A 빈칸을 채워 다음 문장을 수동태로 바꾸어 쓰시오.

1. 현재   능동   They discuss the matter every day.
              수동   The matter _____

2. 미래   능동   They will discuss the matter tomorrow.
              수동   The matter _____

3. 과거   능동   They discussed the matter yesterday.
              수동   The matter _____

4. 현재완료   능동   They have discussed the matter since yesterday.
              수동   The matter _____

5. 미래완료   능동   They will have discussed the matter by tomorrow.
              수동   The matter _____

6. 과거완료   능동   They has discussed the matter when I arrived there.
              수동   The matter _____

7. 현재진행   능동   They are discussing the matter now.
              수동   The matter _____

8. 과거진행   능동   They were discussing the matter when I arrived there.
              수동   The matter _____

B 다음 문장을 수동형으로 바꾸세요.

1. Did you do your homework last night?

   → 평서문 _____

   → 평서문 수동태 _____

   → 의문문 수동태 _____

2. When did you take these pictures?

   → _____

3. Who washed the dishes?

   → _____

   → _____

4. Open the window.

   → _____

5. Do your homework.

   → _____

GRAMMAR IN SENTENCE

▶ 의미 단위로 문장을 끊어 읽고, 해석하세요.
단, 경우에 따라 명사구 또는 명사절은 { }, 형용사구 또는 형용사절은 [ ], 부사 부사구 부사절은 ( )로 표시하세요.

1. All my friends will be invited to my housewarming party.

2. All of the proceeds will be used to acquire more properties.

3. The roads were very dangerous because they were covered with ice.

4. In Japan, everyone is dressed in new clothes on New Year's Day.

5. It is rock music that I was absorbed in when I was young.

6. Mr. Mandela is known as one of the world's greatest leaders.

7. Iraq used to be known to the West by the Greek name Mesopotamia.

8. Mr. Wilson is considered one of the best public speakers because his speech is powerful as well as impressive.

9. An exhibition of Erica's paintings and sculptures has been held at the BACO Gallery in New York.

10. Maintenance equipment that is not in use should be locked in the warehouse.

Outro

태

be + p.p

시제	능동태	수동태
현재	현재동사	is/are + p.p
과거	과거동사	was/were + p.p
미래	will + 동사원형	will be p.p
진행	be+~ing	be being p.p
완료	have + p.p	have been p.p

수동태의 기본 형태

시제	태	예문
현재	능동	She write a letter every day.
	수동	A letter **is written** every day.
미래	능동	She will write a letter tomorrow.
	수동	A letter **will be written** tomorrow.
과거	능동	She wrote a letter yesterday.
	수동	A letter **was written** yesterday.
현재완료	능동	She has written a letter since last month.
	수동	A letter **has been written** since last month.
미래완료	능동	She will have written a letter by 8:00 in the evening.
	수동	A letter **will have been written** by 8:00 in the evening.
과거완료	능동	She had written a letter when I arrived at home.
	수동	A letter **had been written** when I arrived at home.
현재진행	능동	She is writing a letter now.
	수동	A letter **is being written** now.
과거진행	능동	She was writing a letter when I called her yesterday.
	수동	A letter **was being written** when I called her yesterday.

ACTUAL TEST 3

A 보기 중 맞는 것을 고르세요.

1 Building a factory ------- a good way to offer local residents more job opportunities efficiently.
(A) is
(B) are
(C) has
(D) have

2 Our customer service representatives ---------- you with a registration number and coupons for free drinks.
(A) provision
(B) providing
(C) provides
(D) provide

3 A number of middle school students in the city --------- in the special event held by Dell this weekend.
(A) participates
(B) are participated
(C) is participating
(D) are participating

4 The board of directors ------- sometime next week to discuss the renovation of the Dows Building.
(A) to convene
(B) will convene
(C) convening
(D) convened

5 Best Buys -------- a mutually amicable purchasing agreement with Happy Electronics Trade for over 3 years.
(A) has
(B) had
(C) has had
(D) will have

6 Researchers at the University of Chicago ------- that tea has the potential to cure diabetes.
(A) believe
(B) believes
(C) is believing
(D) are believed

7 After the committee -------- discussing the contract, they moved onto the next item.
(A) finishes
(B) had finished
(C) has finished
(D) will have finished

8 Mr. Taylor --------- a short speech after dinner to express his appreciation for the retirement gift yesterday.
(A) delivers
(B) delivered
(C) is delivered
(D) has delivered

9 The client's request to revise the contracts -------- considerable problems for the Legal Department since last week.
(A) is caused
(B) has caused
(C) will cause
(D) is causing

10 Because of the heavy traffic jam, the film ------- by the time we got to the cinema.
(A) has been started
(B) started
(C) is starting
(D) had started

B 보기 중 맞는 것을 고르세요.

Questions 11-16 refer to the following article.

The Mentor Language Study School **11** ------- a problem with student work levels. From the middle of the term this year, the average student **12** ------- at least one homework assignment every week. Half of the students **13** ------- less than 50% on tests. The teachers decided that something had to **14** ------- to help the students want to study.

The manager suggested that the teachers **15** ------- a class award system. Every class of students who completed their homework assignments and received over 85% on tests would **16** ------- a pizza party at the end of the term. Within 3 weeks, student work levels improved by 70%.

11 (A) have had
(B) has had
(C) have
(D) had had

12 (A) was missing
(B) were missing
(C) was missed
(D) were missed

13 (A) receive
(B) receives
(C) was receiving
(D) were receiving

14 (A) do
(B) did
(C) be done
(D) done

15 (A) begin
(B) began
(C) begun
(D) was beginning

16 (A) received
(B) receives
(C) receive
(D) receiving

잉글리쉬앤 그래머 MASTER

실전편

 코스

Unit 10 부정사
Unit 11 동명사
Unit 12 분사

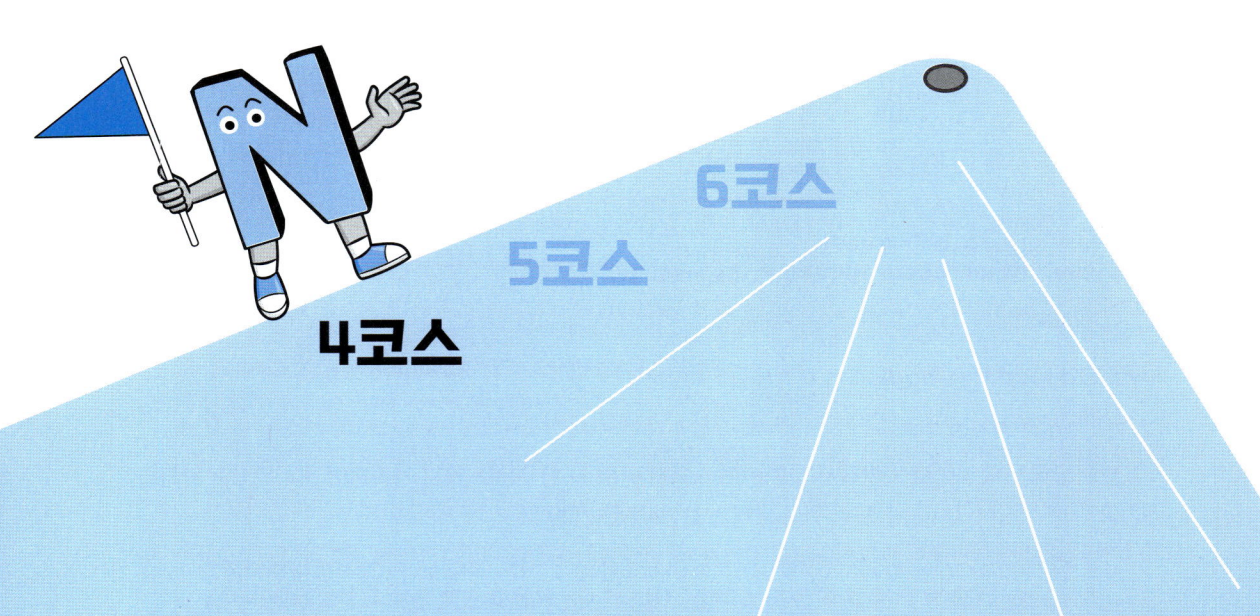

UNIT 10 부정사

◎ GRAMMAR POINT

① to부정사의 개념과 역할

to부정사, 분사, 동명사는 동사에서 만들어졌지만 본동사의 역할은 할 수 없으므로 준동사라고 한다. to부정사는 문장 안에서 절대 본동사로 쓰일 수 없다.

(1) 명사 역할: 주어, 목적어, 보어 자리

'~하는 것, ~하기'로 해석되며, 문장 안에서 명사가 할 수 있는 역할(주어, 목적어, 보어)로 쓰일 경우에 해당된다. 주어로서 부정사구가 문두에 오는 일은 드물며, 그 대신 문두에는 형식 주어 It를 쓰고 to부정사는 문미로 돌리는 게 보통이다(가주어-진주어 구문).

① 주어

To get up early is easy for me. 나는 아침에 일찍 일어나는 것이 쉽다.
= **It** is easy for me **to get up early**. (가주어 - 진주어 구문)

📝 가주어-진주어 구문

주어가 to부정사나 that절이 와서 너무 길어지면 가주어 It이 주어 자리를 지키고, to부정사나 that절은 문장 뒤로 돌리는 것을 가주어-진주어 구문이라고 한다.

> **It** is/was + 형용사/분사 + **to부정사/ that절**
> 　　가주어　　　　　　　　　　진주어
>
> **It** is easy for me **to get up early**.
> **It** is possible **that nobody will attend the meeting**.

② 목적어

I want **to read this book**. 나는 이 책을 읽기를 원한다.

📝 가목적어-진목적어 구문

5형식 문장에서 목적어로 to부정사나 that절이 와서 너무 긴 경우에도 역시 가목적어 it이 목적어 자리를 지키고, to부정사나 that절은 문장 뒤로 돌려 쓰는 것이 일반적이다.

> 주어 + make/find/deem/consider/think/keep/ leave + **it** + 목적 보어 + **to부정사/that절**
> 　　　　　　　　　　　　　　　　　　　　　　　　　가목적어　　　　　　　진목적어

I found English difficult. 난 영어가 어렵다는 걸 알았다.
I found to study English alone difficult.
→ I found **it** difficult **to study English alone**. 난 혼자서 영어 공부를 하는 게 힘들다는 걸 알았다.

③ 주격 보어

The objective of the conference is **to discuss the issue**. 회의의 목적은 그 사안을 논의하는 것이다.

④ 목적격 보어

His wealth enables him **to do what he likes**. 그의 재산은 그가 원하는 것을 할 수 있도록 해준다.

GRAMMAR PRACTICE

A 다음을 같은 의미의 문장으로 바꾸세요.

1. To exercise every day is good for our health.
   → It is _____.

2. To be polite to others is important.
   → It is _____.

3. To answer this question is very difficult.
   → It is _____.

4. To finish the project on time is imperative.
   → It is _____.

5. To be kind to our guests is important.
   → It is _____.

6. To wear protective clothing is essential.
   → It is _____.

7. I made to use the machine possible.
   → I made it _____.

8. I found to finish the project on time impossible.
   → I found it _____.

9. You'll find to stay up all night difficult.
   → You'll find it _____.

10. I made to complete the assignment possible.
    → I made it _____.

B 어법상 틀린 문장은 바르게 고치고, 틀린 부분이 없으면 O로 표시하세요.

1. Jenny decided to study Spanish because she wanted to traveling to Mexico.

2. My plan is to travel around Italy in the near future and visit historical sites.

3. The purpose of this study is investigate the correlation between age and learning ability.

4. The doctor advised his patients taking vitamin C daily.

5. My grandparents made it possible for me to rest comfortably.

VOCA exercise 운동하다   polite 예의 바른   imperative 강제적인   essential 필수의

GRAMMAR POINT

(2) 형용사 역할: 명사 수식

① 한정적 용법: 명사 뒤에서 수식
'~하는, ~할'로 해석되며, 명사, 대명사의 뒤에서 앞에 있는 명사나 대명사를 수식하는 역할을 한다.

I don't have time **to go on a picnic**. (to부정사가 앞의 time을 수식) 나는 소풍을 갈 시간이 없다.

> **to부정사의 수식을 받는 명사들**
>
> | | |
> |---|---|
> | **ability to** do ~할 수 있는 능력 | **authority to** do ~할 수 있는 권한 |
> | **opportunity to** do ~할 기회 | **capacity to** do ~할 수 있는 수용력 |
> | **chance to** do ~할 기회 | **claim to** do ~할 권리 |
> | **decision to** do ~하기로 한 결정 | **effort to** do ~하려는 노력 |
> | **need to** do ~해야 할 필요성 | **right to** do ~할 권리 |
> | **time to** do ~할 시간 | **way to** do ~하는 방법[길] |

② 서술적 용법: be to do 용법
be to do가 문장 안에서 주격 보어(형용사 보어)로 쓰여서 예정, 의무, 가능, 운명(~할 운명이다), 의도(~하려면: intend to) 등을 나타낸다. 특히 미래의 예정된 일을 의미할 때 사용하는 be to do의 용법은 주로 '공식적인 일정'을 표현하는데 사용된다.

We **are to meet** at the post office. (예정) 우리는 우체국에서 만날 예정이다.

(3) 부사 역할: 목적이나 원인을 나타내는 경우
to부정사가 문장 안에서 부사적 기능을 하며 목적, 결과 등을 나타낸다. 특히 '목적'을 나타내는 '~하기 위하여, ~하러'의 의미로 가장 많이 쓰이고, 이때 to부정사는 <in order to + 동사원형 = so as to + 동사원형>으로 바꿔쓸 수 있다. 목적을 표현하는 to부정사는 긍정문에서는 in order나 so as를 생략해도 무방하지만 부정문에서는 in order not to, so as not to가 사용된다.

I got up early **to catch the train**. 나는 기차를 타기 위해서 일찍 일어났다.
We came here **to study English**. 우리는 영어를 공부하기 위하여 이곳에 왔다
He tried **not to smile**. (to smile을 부정) 그는 웃지 않으려 애썼다.

> **too ~ to do와 enough to do**
>
> **too** + 부사/ 형용사 + **to** + 동사원형 너무 ~해서 …할 수 없다
> = so + 부사/형용사 + that 주어 + cannot ~
>
> 부사/ 형용사 + **enough to** + 동사원형 너무 ~해서 …할 수 있다
> = so + 부사/형용사 + that 주어 + can ~

This stone is **too** heavy for me **to** lift. 이 돌은 너무 무거워서 내가 들 수 없다.
= This stone is **so** heavy **that** I **cannot** lift it.

This book is easy **enough** for me **to** read. 이 책은 너무 쉬워서 나도 읽을 수 있다.
= This book is **so** easy **that** I **can** read it.

GRAMMAR PRACTICE

A 다음 밑줄 친 부분의 의미를 찾아 번호를 쓰고, 한글로 해석하세요.

> ① 가능 ② 예정 ③ 의무 ④ 의도 ⑤ 운명

1. The president **is to visit** our new factory next week.
2. You **are to finish** it by six.
3. No one **was to be seen** on the street.
4. If you **are to succeed,** you must work hard.
5. He **was never to return** to his hometown.

B 빈칸을 채워서 같은 의미의 문장으로 만드세요.

1. Angela wants to win the contest, so she has been playing the violin for five hours a day.

   = _____, Angela has been playing the violin for five hours a day.

2. Our team wanted to participate in the seminar, so we left the office early.

   = Our team left the office early _____.

3. If you want to get 20% off your airfare, book now.

   = Book now _____.

4. The boy is so smart that he can solve the math problem.

   = The boy is _____ the math problem.

5. It was so cold that we couldn't sleep in tents.

   = It was _____ in tents.

C 어법상 틀린 문장은 바르게 고치고, 옳은 문장에는 표시 (O) 하세요.

1. It's time get ready to go back to school now!
2. I had the opportunity to learning many things through them.
3. The workshop will be a chance to familiar oneself with some new trends.
4. In an effort to satisfy his customers, Mr. Johnson conducted several surveys.
5. An employee has the right receive at least one month's notice of dismissal or intention to leave.

VOCA factory 공장   hometown 고향   participate in 참석하다   book 예약하다   conduct a survey 설문 조사를 실시하다

◎ GRAMMAR POINT

② to부정사를 목적어나 목적격 보어로 취하는 동사들

(1) to부정사를 목적어로 취하는 동사: 대개 미래 지향적인 성향

- **원하다**: want to, hope to, wish to, expect to, desire to
- **(앞날을) 계획하고 제안하고 약속하다**: plan to, promise to, decide to, offer to, propose to, agree to, demand to
- **부정적인 의미**: refuse to, fail to, pretend to, struggle to
- **기타**: afford to, manage to, choose to, deserve to

I **decided to study** Spanish. 나는 스페인어를 공부하기로 결심했다.
I **managed to arrive** there by six. 나는 6시까지 그곳에 도착할 수 있었다.

(2) to부정사를 목적 보어로 취하는 동사들

<동사 + 목적어 + to부정사> 형태와 같이 부정사를 목적격 보어 자리에 취하는 동사들을 살펴보면, 목적격 보어가 '목적어의 동작'을 나타내는 경우가 많다. 이러한 동사들은 '목적어로 하여금 ~하게 하다' 라는 의미를 갖고 있다.

enable A to do A가 ~할 수 있게 하다	**encourage** A to do A에게 ~하라고 권장하다, 격려하다
persuade A to do A에게 ~하라고 설득하다	**instruct** A to do A에게 ~하라고 지시[설명]하다
allow A to do A에게 ~할 수 있게 허락하다	**advise** A to do A에게 ~하라고 조언하다
invite A to do A에게 ~하도록 초대하다	**require** A to do A에게 ~하라고 요구하다
request A to do A에게 ~하라고 요청하다	**cause** A to do A가 ~하도록 야기시키다

The doctor **advised** the patient **to lose** weight. 의사는 환자에게 몸무게를 줄이라고 권유했다.

(3) to 부정사의 의미상의 주어

문장 전체의 주어와 to부정사의 주어가 다를 때는 to부정사 앞에 의미상 주어를 명시해주어야 한다. 위와 같이 to부정사를 목적 보어로 취하는 5형식 문장에서 목적어는 to부정사의 의미상 주어이다. 하지만 의미상 주어가 문장의 목적어 역할을 하지 못하는 경우에는 <for + 의미상 주어> 또는 <of + 의미상 주어>의 형태로 to부정사 앞에 명시해준다.

① for + 의미상 주어

I think it is difficult **for him to solve** the problem. 그 남자는 그 문제를 풀기 어려울 것 같아요.

② of + 의미상 주어

<It is+사람의 성질이나 특징을 나타내는 형용사> 뒤에 to부정사가 올 경우에는 의미상 주어 앞에 of를 붙인다.

> **사람의 성질이나 특징을 나타내는 형용사**
> good, fine, bad, nice, honest, kind, unkind, wise, clever, stupid, foolish, silly, polite, sweet, wrong, right, thoughtful, considerate, cruel, rude, careful, careless, generous ...

It is very kind **of you to say** that. 그렇게 말씀하시다니 당신은 정말 친절하시군요.
= You are very kind to say that.

GRAMMAR PRACTICE

A 다음 주어진 단어와 **to** 부정사를 이용하여 빈칸을 완성하세요.

1. promise / to keep in touch / with me

    → Richard _____ last week.

2. plan / for a month / stay here

    → Jane _____.

3. struggle / make ends meet.

    → He has _____.

4. afford / a sports car / buy

    → I can't _____.

5. manage / the deadline / meet

    → They were able _____.

B 괄호 안에서 알맞은 것을 고르세요.

1. The parents (allowed, are allowed) their children to have a party.
2. A professor persuaded him (go, to go) to graduate school.
3. The United Nations has failed (reach, to reach) a consensus on the issue of economic expansion.
4. The editor asked all of the writers to (submission, submit) their articles by the tenth of the month.
5. It is so generous (of, for) you to forgive my mistakes.

C 어법상 틀린 문장은 바르게 고치고, 틀린 부분이 없으면 **O**로 표시하세요.

1. Alex persuaded his son change his mind.
2. My parents allowed me to participating in the festival.
3. My professor encouraged me to write novels.
4. This book is too difficult of you to read.
5. It was very foolish for you to do that.

VOCA keep in touch 연락하다　make ends meet 수입과 지출의 균형을 맞추다, 수입에 알맞은 생활을 하다　dispute 논쟁
expertise 전문지식　inception 시초, 발단　generous 관대한　forgive 용서하다

◎ GRAMMAR POINT

③ 형용사와 함께 쓰이는 to부정사 표현

📝 **be + 형용사(과거 분사) + to부정사**

be (un)able to ~할 수 있다(없다)	be ready to ~할 준비가 되다
be likely to ~할 것 같다	be expected to ~할 예정이다
be supposed to ~하기로 되어 있다	be willing to 기꺼이 ~하겠다
be eager to ~하고 싶다	be reluctant to ~하는 게 내키지 않다
be liable to 걸핏하면 ~한다	

Jack **is likely to** pass the exam. 잭은 시험에 합격할 것 같다.

④ 원형부정사

어떤 동사들은 to부정사가 들어갈 자리에 동사원형만 쓰는 경우가 있다. 이를 바로 원형부정사라고 한다.

(1) let, have, make + 목적어 + 목적 보어

문장의 동사가 사역동사일 때 목적어와 목적격 보어의 관계가 능동인지 수동인지 구분해야 한다.
즉, 목적어와 목적 보어가 능동 관계이면 목적 보어 자리에 동사원형을, 수동 관계이면 과거 분사를 쓴다.

- **사역동사 + 목적어 + 동사원형 (능동)**: 누구에게 ~하도록 시키다
- **사역동사 + 목적어 + p.p. (수동)**: (목적어가) ~ 되도록 시키다

Parents don't **let** their children **drink** alcohol. (the children과 drink가 능동 관계)
부모는 자녀가 술 마시는 것을 허락하지 않는다.

The boss **made** his employees **follow** his order. (his employees와 follow가 능동 관계)
상사는 직원들이 자신의 명령을 따르도록 했다.

I **had** the roof **painted.** (the roof와 painted가 수동 관계)
나는 지붕에 페인트칠을 하도록 시켰다.

(2) 준사역동사 help

동사 help의 목적어나 목적 보어 자리에 to부정사가 올 경우, to를 생략하고 동사원형만 써도 상관없다.

- **help + 목적어 + (to) 동사원형**: ~가 …하는 것을 돕다
- **help + (to) 동사원형**: ~하는 것을 돕다

I **helped** my sister (to) do her homework. 나는 나의 여동생이 숙제하는 것을 도와주었다.
I **helped (to) do** her homework. 나는 그녀가 숙제하는 것을 도와주었다.

GRAMMAR PRACTICE

A 괄호 안에서 알맞은 것을 고르세요.

1. You will be (able, capable) to find more information on our products.

2. Angela is (like, likely) to pass the exam.

3. How much are you (will, willing) to pay?

4. John is (liable, eager) to get angry.

5. The airport construction project will help the company (diversify, diversity).

6. The competition is (suppose, supposed) to be held in Tokyo, Japan, next year.

7. Climate change is likely (hit, to hit) some nations more than others.

8. This year, over 1,000 people are (expecting, expected) to visit the ski festival.

9. People are aware of the risks and are (ability, willing) to take them.

10. Our company is (willing, reluctant) to launch the new product due to the market uncertainty.

B 어법상 틀린 문장은 바르게 고치고, 틀린 부분이 없으면 O로 표시하세요.

1. The manager is suppose to hold the meeting this afternoon.

2. Jack is likeness to pass the exam this time.

3. I am liable to catch a cold when the season changes.

4. A lot of people were eagerly to give their help to the organization.

5. The teacher let the students to look around the museum.

VOCA airport construction project 항공 공사 프로젝트   competition 대회   market uncertainty 시장의 불확실성
look around 둘러보다

GRAMMAR IN SENTENCE

▶ 의미 단위로 문장을 끊어 읽고, 해석하세요.
단, 경우에 따라 명사구 또는 명사절은 { }, 형용사구 또는 형용사절은 [ ], 부사 부사구 부사절은 ( )로 표시하세요.

1. Jenny decided to study Spanish because she wanted to travel to Mexico.

2. My plan is to travel around Italy in the near future and to visit historical sites.

3. The purpose of this study is to investigate the correlation between age and learning ability.

4. The doctor advised his patients to take vitamin C daily.

5. My grandparents made it possible for me to rest comfortably.

6. The airport construction project will help the company diversify.

7. Climate change is likely to hit some nations more than others.

8. This year, over 1,000 people are expected to visit the ski festival.

9. I had the opportunity to learn many things through them.

10. An employee has the right to receive at least one month's notice of dismissal or intention to leave.

부정사

준동사

동사에서 비롯되었으나, 본동사 역할은 못한다.

- 문장에서 명사, 형용사, 부사의 역할을 하여 주어, 보어, 목적어, 수식어구 자리에 와서 동사의 성질을 가진다.
- to 부정사, 동명사, 분사가 있다.

부정사

to 동사원형

- **명사 역할** : <~하는 것, ~하기>

  문장에서 주어 목적어 보어로 쓰인다.

  To teach is **to learn**. 가르치는 것이 배우는 것이다.
  　주어　　　보어

  Craig wants **to work** at a law firm. Craig는 법률회사에서 일하기를 원한다.
  　　　　　목적어

- **형용사 역할** : <~할, ~하는>

  　뒤에서 앞의 명사 수식

  Everyone in this area has **the right to vote**. 이 지역에 있는 모든 사람들은 투표할 권리가 있다.

- **부사 역할** : <~하기 위하여, ~하기 위해>

  　문장의 맨 앞이나 뒤에서 부가적으로 의미 보충
  　목적이나 원인을 나타냄

  All the equipment needs to be replaced **to avoid any unnecessary accidents.**
  모든 장비들은 불필요한 사고를 피하기 위해서 교체되어야 한다.

UNIT 11 동명사

◎ GRAMMAR POINT

① 동명사의 개념과 역할

> 동명사 = 동사적 의미 + 명사적 역할

동명사란 동사에 -ing가 붙은 형태의 준동사이다. 동명사는 문장에서 본동사로 쓰일 수 없고, 명사로서 주어, 목적어, 보어 자리에 쓰인다. 하지만, 동사의 성격은 여전히 가지고 있어서 목적어나 보어를 취하고 부사의 수식도 받을 수 있다.

(1) 주어 자리

Swimming is a good sport. 수영은 좋은 스포츠이다.

(2) 명사 보어 자리(주어 = 명사 보어)

His hobby is **collecting** stamps. 그의 취미는 우표를 수집하는 것이다.

(3) 타동사의 목적어

He stopped **reading** and began **strolling** along the beach.
그는 독서를 멈추고, 바닷가를 산책하기 시작했다.

(4) 전치사의 목적어

He is above **telling** me a lie. 그는 나에게 거짓말 할 사람이 아니다.

Thank you for **answering** so promptly. 즉시 답변을 해 주셔서 감사합니다.
동명사 answering은 전치사 for의 목적어(명사적 성질)이면서 so promptly의 수식(동사적 성질)을 받고 있다.

(5) 동명사의 의미상의 주어

동명사의 의미상의 주어는 소유격으로 쓴다.

Everybody was upset **about Mark's getting** a raise.
Mark의 급여가 인상된 것에 대해 사람들이 모두 화를 냈다.

② 동명사를 목적어로 취하는 동사

(1) 동명사를 목적어로 취하는 동사

- ~하다 멈추다: stop, quit, finish, give up, discontinue
- ~을 연기하다: delay, put off, postpone
- ~을 심사숙고하다, 고려하다, 추천하다: consider, recommend, suggest
- ~을 싫어하다, 부인하다, 꺼려하다: mind, deny, avoid, escape, resist
- ~을 즐기다: enjoy
- ~을 학수고대하다: anticipate

Jenny will **consider working** for a new company. Jenny는 새로운 회사에서 일하는 것을 고려중이다.

GRAMMAR PRACTICE

A 다음의 단어를 이용하여 빈칸에 알맞은 동명사를 넣으세요.

> go achieve listen speak walk swim write invest exercise help

<동명사의 주어 역할>

1. _____ in stocks is inherently risky.

2. _____ other people makes me happy.

3. _____ in the sea is dangerous, so you should be careful.

4. _____ every day is good for our health.

<동명사의 보어 역할>

5. Angela's hobby is _____ to music.

6. His plan is _____ English fluently.

<동명사의 타동사 목적어 역할>

7. Alex has finished _____ a letter to his friend.

8. I'm considering _____ to London.

<동명사의 전치사 목적어 역할>

9. Before _____ in the park, drink plenty of water.

10. All the students are capable of _____ their goals.

B 어법상 틀린 문장은 바르게 고치고, 틀린 부분이 없으면 **O**로 표시하세요.

1. Please quit worry about me.

2. Both riding a bicycle and take a walk every day are good for your health.

3. He discontinued taking piano lessons.

4. On hot summer days, people often feel like to eating ice cream.

5. The teacher summarized a long report by given its main ideas.

VOCA inherently 본질적으로 risky 위험한 plenty of 많은 be capable of~ ~할 능력이 있다 achieve 달성하다

(2) 의미 변화 없이 to부정사와 동명사를 모두 목적어로 취하는 동사

| like 좋아하다 | hate 싫어하다 | prefer 선호하다 | begin 시작하다 |
| start 시작하다 | love 사랑하다 | continue 계속하다 | |

I **like** swimming. = I **like** to swim. 나는 수영하는 것을 좋아한다.

(3) stop

	to부정사	동명사
stop	~하기 위해 멈추다 I stopped (in order) **to smoke.** 나는 담배를 피우려고 멈췄다.	~하는 것을 멈추다 I stopped **smoking.** 나는 담배를 피우던 것을 멈췄다.

(4) to부정사와 동명사를 목적어로 취할 때 의미가 바뀌는 동사들

	to부정사	동명사
remember	앞으로 할 일을 기억하다 I remembered **to turn** off the light. 나는 불을 꺼야 한다는 것을 기억해냈다.	했던 일을 기억하다 I remembered **turning** off the light. 나는 불을 껐다는 것을 기억했다.
forget	앞으로 할 일을 잊다 I forgot **to buy** some books. 나는 책을 몇 권 살 것을 잊었다.	했던 일을 잊다 I forgot **buying** some books. 나는 책을 몇 권 샀던 것을 잊었다.
regret	~하게 되어 유감이다 I regret **to go** there. 나는 그곳에 가게 되어 유감이다.	~했던 일을 후회하다 I regret **going** there. 나는 그곳에 갔던 것을 후회한다.
try	애써 ~하다 I tried **to do** my best for the test. 나는 시험을 위하여 최선을 다했다.	시험 삼아 해보다 I tried **opening** the door. 나는 그 문을 열려고 했다.
mean	의도하다 I meant **to call** you last night. 어젯밤에 네게 전화하려고 했어.	의미하다 Getting there by 7:00 means **waking** up before 5:00. 거기 7시 까지 가는 것은 5시 전에 일어나야 한다는 의미야.
go on	하던 일을 마치고 ~하다 After the break, the chairman went on **to talk** about the project. 휴식 후에 의장은 프로젝트에 대해 얘기를 시작했다.	계속 하던 일을 하다 She went on **tapping** her pencil on the table. 그녀는 탁자에 계속 연필을 탁탁 쳤다.

GRAMMAR PRACTICE

A 다음 중 알맞은 것을 고르세요. 단, 둘 다 답인 경우는 모두 고르세요.

1. I like (to cook, cooking) for other people.

2. I enjoy (to play, playing) computer games.

3. They have given up (to smoke, smoking) recently.

4. The police officer seemed to (avoid, refuse) looking into the case.

5. The teacher continued (to tell, telling) the story to the students.

B 다음 한글 해석에 맞게 알맞은 동사의 형태를 넣으세요.

1. lock : Don't forget _____ the door at night.

2. see : I remember _____ him somewhere.

3. study : I regret not _____ hard when I was young.

4. sell : Do you remember _____ the ticket by tomorrow?

5. fight : They suddenly stopped _____.

C 어법상 틀린 문장은 바르게 고치고, 틀린 부분이 없으면 O로 표시하세요.

1. Mr. Johnson decided to discontinue to smoke yesterday.

2. Although she is busy, Ms. Lee will continue to studying English.

3. Jane suddenly started to eating the leftovers.

4. I never meant to make her cry.

5. No matter how difficult it may seem, keep trying to do your best.

VOCA   somewhere 어디선가   suddenly 갑자기

◎ GRAMMAR POINT

③ 동명사 vs. 명사

동명사와 명사는 문장에서 하는 역할이 주어, 목적어, 보어로 동일합니다.
동사에 -ing가 붙은 형태인 동명사는 동사의 의미에 명사의 기능이 합쳐진 것이기 때문에 동사의 특성도 가지고 있다.

(1) 동명사는 목적어나 보어를 취할 수 있다. 그러나 명사는 취할 수 없다.

I will have lunch after **discussing** the issue. 나는 그 문제를 의논한 후에 점심 식사를 하겠다.
I will have lunch after the discussion. 나는 의논 후에 식사를 하겠다.

(2) 동명사 앞에는 관사가 올 수 없다. 그러나 명사 앞에는 관사가 위치한다.

The researchers are dedicated to **developing** new products.
그 연구원들은 신제품 개발하는 일에 전념하고 있다.

The researchers are dedicated to **the development** of new products.
그 연구원들은 신제품 개발에 전념하고 있다.

(3) 동명사는 부사의 수식을 받는다. 그러나 명사는 형용사의 수식을 받는다.

After **having dinner** deliciously, they took a walk. 저녁식사를 맛있게 한 후에, 그들은 산책을 갔다.
After a delicious **dinner**, they took a walk. 맛있는 저녁식사 후에, 그들은 산책을 갔다.

(4) 명사 vs 명사화 된 동명사

advertisement 광고	advertising 광고업	means 수단, 방법	meaning 의미
coverage (보험)보상범위	covering 덮개	plan 계획	planning 기획
fund 기금	funding 자금지원	process 과정, 공정	processing 처리. 절차
heat 열	heating 난방	seat 좌석	seating 좌석배치
house 집	housing 주택(공급)	spend 지출액, 비용	spending 지출, 소비
mail 우편물	mailing 우송	staff 직원	staffing 직원배치
market 시장	marketing 마케팅	ticket 표	ticketing 발권

GRAMMAR PRACTICE

A 주어진 단어를 변형해서 빈칸을 완성하세요.

1. develop : He is interested in _____ natural resources.

2. develop : He is interested in the _____ of natural resources.

3. ship : I'd like to check on the products before _____ your order.

4. organize : Without different _____ of the jobs, introducing computers is of no use.

5. organize : Without _____ jobs differently, introducing computers is of no use.

6. introduce : Before the _____ of the product, I will show you the sample.

7. introduce : Before _____ the product, I will show you the sample.

8. expand : The next item on today's meeting agenda is our company's _____ into Asia.

9. expand : The next item on today's meeting agenda is about _____ into Asia.

10. have : After _____ lunch together, they went shopping.

B 어법상 틀린 문장은 바르게 고치고, 틀린 부분이 없으면 **O**로 표시하세요.

1. We cannot be too careful in the choosing books.

2. Smart home appliances will be a success in the market.

3. I've been working for five years in the market division at Intel.

4. The head of the Planning Department will attend the meeting.

5. When a celebrity appears in an advertising, people want to buy that product.

VOCA natural resources 천연자원   ship 배송하다   order 주문   of no use 소용없는   agenda 안건   home appliance 가전제품   celebrity 유명인   appear 나오다

◎ GRAMMAR POINT

④ 동명사 관용어구

(1) 전치사 + -ing

to + -ing형	
be accustomed to -ing ~에 익숙하다	be used to -ing ~에 익숙하다
be devoted to -ing ~에 몰두하다	be committed to -ing ~에 헌신하다
be dedicated to -ing ~에 전념하다	look forward to -ing ~을 기대하다
when it comes to -ing ~에 관해서는	as opposed to -ing ~에 반해서, ~이 아니라
object to -ing ~에 반대하다	be subject to -ing ~하기 쉽다

in + (동)명사 vs. with + 명사	
problems in -ing ~에 대한 문제	problem with + 명사 ~에 대한 문제
assist in -ing ~하는 것을 돕다	assist with + 명사 ~하는 것을 돕다
be finished (in) -ing ~을 끝내다	be finished with + 명사 ~을 끝내다
be busy (in) -ing ~하느라 바쁘다	be busy with + 명사 ~로 바쁘다

(in) + -ing
have difficulty (trouble, a hard time) (in) -ing ~하는 데 어려움을 겪다
spend + 시간/돈 + (in) -ing ~하는 데 시간/돈을 쓰다

on + -ing	
keep (on) -ing 계속 ~하다, 자꾸 ~하다	insist on -ing ~하기를 주장하다

at + -ing	
be skilled at -ing ~하는 데 능숙하다	be aimed at -ing ~을 겨냥하다

of + -ing	
instead of -ing ~대신에	be aware of -ing ~을 알고 있다
be capable of -ing ~할 수 있다	

He **is accustomed to working** in dangerous environments.
그는 위험한 환경에서 일하는 것에 익숙하다.

(2) 여러 가지 관용어구와 용법

> cannot help -ing ~할 수밖에 없다 = cannot but + **동사원형** = have no choice but to + **동사원형**

I **can't help falling** in love with you. = I **cannot but fall** in love with you.
= **I have no choice but to fall** in love with.
나는 당신과 사랑에 빠지지 않을 수가 없다.

> be worth -ing = be worthwhile + **동명사, 부정사** ~할 만한 가치가 있다 = be worthy of + **동명사, 명사**

It **is worth reading** this book. = It **is worthwhile to read** this book.
= **It is worthy of reading** this book.
이 책은 읽을 가치가 있다.

> It is no use -ing = It is no good -ing ~해도 소용없다

It is no use[good] crying over spiled milk. 엎지른 우유를 놓고 울어봐야 소용없다.

GRAMMAR PRACTICE

A 다음 중 알맞은 것을 고르세요.

1. They are dedicated (to preserve, to preserving) natural resources.
2. She was busy (tidy, tidying) up her room.
3. I am accustomed (to jog, to jogging) every morning.
4. This course is aimed (at, of) enabling employees to become mature contributors to their customers.
5. I look forward (to speak, to speaking) with you soon.
6. They are committed (to preserve, to preventing) the accident.
7. Dr. Phillips is seeking (to broaden, to broadening) his research by conducting a genetic study.
8. Most of the residents objected (to build, to building) the factory in this area.
9. The purpose of the program is (to enhance, to enhancing) the effectiveness of the organization.
10. This training program will enable employees (to perform, to performing) better.

B 어법상 틀린 문장은 바르게 고치고, 틀린 부분이 없으면 O로 표시하세요.

1. Ms. Ruppert recommends that we seek legal advice before sign any agreement.
2. David spends most of his time prepare for the entrance exam.
3. I am busy with my task these days.
4. Your suggestion is worthy considering.
5. Most workers are used to work in dangerous environments.

VOCA preserve 보호하다, 지키다, 보존하다   tidy 정돈하다, 치우다   mature 성숙한   contributor 기부자, 공헌자   resident 주민   legal advice 법률자문

GRAMMAR IN SENTENCE

▶ 의미 단위로 문장을 끊어 읽고, 해석하세요.
단, 경우에 따라 명사구 또는 명사절은 { }, 형용사구 또는 형용사절은 [ ], 부사 부사구 부사절은 ( )로 표시하세요.

1. Both riding a bicycle and taking a walk every day are good for your health.

2. The teacher summarized the long report by giving its main ideas.

3. No matter how difficult it may seem, keep trying to do your best.

4. David spends most of his time preparing for the entrance exam.

5. Ms. Ruppert recommends that we seek legal advice before signing any agreement.

6. When a celebrity appears in an advertisement, people want to buy that product.

7. Dr. Phillips is seeking to broaden his research by conducting a genetic study.

8. Most of the residents objected to building the factory in this area.

9. The purpose of the program is to enhance the effectiveness of the organization.

10. This training program will enable employees to perform better.

 **Outro**

동명사

동명사

동사원형 + -ing

- 명사 역할 : ~하는 것, ~하기

주어역할	**Teaching** is **learning** 주어 보어
보어역할	**Seeing** is **believing**. 주어 보어
목적어 역할	Ann finished **typing** a letter. Ann은 편지를 타이핑하는 것을 끝냈다. 목적어

동명사의 특징

- 동명사는 목적어나 보어를 취할 수 있다. 그러나 명사는 **No!**

  Please send your supervisor a letter **accepting** his offer.
  그의 제안을 받아드리는 편지를 당신의 상관에게 보내세요.

- 동명사 앞에는 관사가 올 수 없다.

  They are devoted to **developing** natural resources.
  그들은 천연자원을 개발하는 것에 전념하고 있다.

- 동명사는 부사의 수식을 받는다.

  They went shopping after **having** a lunch deliciously.
  점심식사를 맛있게 한 후에, 그들은 쇼핑을 갔다.

UNIT 12 분사

GRAMMAR POINT

분사는 동사에서 만들어졌지만, 문장에서 단독으로는 본동사로 쓰일 수 없다. 분사는 형용사 역할을 하기 때문에 명사의 앞이나 뒤에서 명사를 수식하고, 주격 보어나 목적격 보어 자리에도 쓰일 수 있다. 자동사 및 능동, 진행의 의미를 가진 타동사는 -ing 형태를, 타동사이면서 수동이자 완료의 의미를 지니고 있으면 p.p. 형태를 쓴다.

① 명사를 수식하는 분사

(1) 명사의 앞에서 수식하는 분사 : 분사 + 명사

분사에는 동사에 -ing가 붙은 현재분사와, -ed가 붙은 과거분사(p.p.)가 있다. 일반적으로 현재분사는 '능동과 진행'의 의미를 갖고 과거분사는 '수동과 완료'의 의미를 갖는다.

현재분사	과거분사
surprising news 놀라운 소식	damaged luggage 파손된 수화물
a boring book 지겨운 책	bored people 지겨워하는 사람들

This is an **interesting** book. 이 책은 흥미로운 책이다.
  → interest는 '~에게 흥미를 갖게 하다'라는 타동사이다. 책 자신이 흥미를 느낀(interested) 것이 아니라 흥미를 준다는 능동이 어울리므로 현재분사(interesting)가 쓰이고 있다.

(2) 명사의 뒤에서 수식하는 분사 : 명사 + 분사

분사가 보어나 목적어, 부사(구) 등을 동반할 때는 통상 명사의 뒤에 놓인다. 분사 앞에 <주격 관계대명사 + be동사>가 생략된 형태라고 보면 된다. 이때 수식을 받는 명사를 주어라고 생각하고 분사를 동사로 보았을 때 그 관계가 능동이면 현재 분사(-ing)를, 수동이면 과거 분사(p.p.)를 써야 한다.

명사 + 현재분사 + (명사)	명사 + 과거분사 + 전치사구
people working for small companies 작은 회사에서 일하는 사람들	customers interested in our products 우리 제품에 관심 있는 고객들
members using the exercise facility 운동 시설을 이용하는 회원들	cars provided by our hotel 저희 호텔에서 제공하는 자동차
e-mail containing detailed information 상세한 정보가 들어 있는 이메일	examples listed in the document 서류에 나열되어 있는 예들
employees seeking reimbursement for travel expenses 출장비 변제 요청하는 직원들	survey conducted by the health department 건강 관리국에 의해서 시행된 조사

With all the people **coming and going**, this place looks busy.
모든 사람들이 오고 가는 것으로 이 장소는 분주해 보인다.
  → coming and going이 all the people 수식하고 있으며, 사람들이 오고 가는 능동의 의미이므로 현재분사가 쓰여야 한다.

GRAMMAR PRACTICE

A 다음 중 알맞은 것을 고르세요.

1. We live in a large house (building, built) of stone and brick.
2. A man (naming, named) Aesop wrote this famous storybook.
3. I know the girl (wearing, worn) the big straw hat.
4. Of those (inviting, invited), only a few came to the party.
5. Anyone (inviting, invited) to the party can enjoy dancing and singing.
6. The man (wearing, worn) glasses is my boyfriend.
7. The workshop (holding, held) last month was to increase productivity.
8. They expressed significant interest for the newly (proposing, proposed) production schedule.
9. There is a fee (charging, charged) for each transaction.
10. We will be happy to refund or replace any (damaging, damaged) goods if they are returned within 15 days of purchase.

B 보기 중 알맞은 것을 고르세요.

1. _____ harvesting techniques and various machines have helped farmers make more earnings.
    (A) improving   (B) improved   (C) improvement   (D) improves

2. A person _____ in the building after 10:00 p.m. is requested to lock the door when he leaves.
    (A) remained   (B) remain   (C) remaining   (D) who remaining

3. Anyone _____ to apply for the accounting position advertised must submit their resumes and cover letters by the end of the month.
    (A) wants   (B) to want   (C) wanted   (D) wanting

4. She could figure out the amount of time _____ for the job since she had had a similar experience.
    (A) requiring   (B) required   (C) requires   (D) to require

5. There are a wide range of conservation organizations _____ to protect endangered animals and habitats.
    (A) working   (B) worked   (C) works   (D) which working

VOCA be built of~ ~으로 지어진   transaction 거래   refund 환불하다   replace 교체하다   revise 교정하다, 개정하다   return 반품하다   harvesting 수확하는, 거두어들이는   earning 소득   a wide range of 광범위한   endangered 멸종 위기에 처해 있는   habitat 서식지

GRAMMAR POINT

② 명사를 서술하는 분사

2형식 문장의 주격 보어 자리에는 주어와의 의미 관계를 따지고, 5형식 문장의 목적격 보어 자리는 목적어와의 의미 관계를 따져서 능동이면 현재 분사를 수동이면 과거분사를 넣는다.

(1) 주격 보어로 쓰일 때 : 주어 + 자동사 + 주격보어(분사)

S	V	C
	be / become / get feel / smell / sound / taste look / seem / appear remain / stay / prove / turn out	형용사 (주격보어: 분사)

She **remained standing** for some time. 그녀는 한동안 서 있었다.
→ stand는 자동사이므로 현재 분사를 써야 한다.

(2) 주어 + 타동사 + 목적어 + 목적보어

S	V	O	OC
	make / find think / deem / consider keep / leave		형용사 (목적보어 : 분사)

특히, 목적 보어가 excite, bore, tire, impress, satisfy 등과 같은 감정동사에서 파생된 경우에는 목적어와의 능동, 수동 관계에 주의한다.

Laura **makes** me **annoyed** because she called me late last night.
Laura가 어젯밤 늦게 전화를 해서 나를 귀찮게 했다.

③ 명사를 수식하는 현재 분사와 과거 분사

현재 분사 관용표현	과거 분사 관용표현
demanding job 까다로운 일	**attached** files 첨부 파일
existing equipment 현재의 장비	**complicated** matter 복잡한 문제
incoming calls 걸려오는 전화	**dedicated** employees 헌신적인 직원들
fascinating painting 매혹적인 그림	**designated** parking area 지정된 주차 장소
growing reputation 오르고 있는 명성	**detailed** information 상세한 정보
lasting impression 지속되는 인상	**discounted** price 할인된 가격에
misleading information 잘못된 정보	**enclosed** document 동봉된 서류
missing baggage[luggage] 분실물	**finished** products 완제품
opening remarks 개회사	**guided** tour 가이드가 동반하는 여행
opposing point of view 반대의 관점	**limited** capacity 제한된 용량
overwhelming support 압도적인 지지	**preferred** means 선호되는 수단
rewarding careers 보람 있는 직업들	**projected** budget 추정 예산
rising costs 오르는 비용	**restricted** area 제한 구역
leading company 선두 기업	**qualified** candidate 자격을 갖춘 후보자
surrounding cities 주변 도시들	**skilled** programmer 숙련된 프로그래머
promising workers 전도유망한 직원들	**unlimited** access 무제한 접근

GRAMMAR PRACTICE

A 다음 주어진 감정 동사를 이용하여, 빈칸에 알맞은 분사형태나 형용사를 넣으세요.

1. excite: I found the movie _____ and the movie made people _____.
2. impress: I found the opera _____ and the opera made audience _____.
3. satisfy: The boss found the report _____, and the report made the boss _____.
4. disappoint: Parents deemed results _____, and results made parents _____.
5. surprise: The girl thought the news _____, and the news made the girl _____.

B 다음 중 알맞은 것을 고르세요.

1. He remained (satisfying, satisfied) with his salary.
2. The company is seeking (skillfully, skilled) workers.
3. We will choose the next manager from among the (qualified, qualifies) applicants.
4. For a (limiting, limited) time only, we offer free shipping on orders over $50.00.
5. Through books and websites, we aim to enable young people to make (informing, informed) decisions about their future careers.

C 보기 중 알맞은 것을 고르세요.

1. United Delivery Service remains _____ to reviewing and modifying security measures on a regular basis to ensure the safety of our truck drivers.
   (A) committment   (B) commit   (C) committing   (D) committed

2. Building contractors have founded the city's building codes too _____ to accommodate their needs.
   (A) to frustrate   (B) frustrating   (C) frustrated   (D) frustrate

3. The pamphlets were redesigned to include photographs of the hotel's _____ interior design.
   (A) updating   (B) update   (C) updates   (D) updated

4. The new president must take the _____ role in planning the company's success in the future.
   (A) leading   (B) leaded   (C) leader   (D) lead

5. This year, we intend to conduct a _____ survey to gather more data in order to address specific graduate student complaints.
   (A) detail   (B) detailing   (C) details   (D) detailed

VOCA free shipping 무료 배송   committed to ~에 헌신하다   modify 수정하다   security measures 안전규정
building code 건축규정   frustrate 실망시키다   accommodate 수용하다, 충족시키다   pursue 추구하다, 종사하다
detailed 상세한, 정밀한   address 역점을 두어 다루다   specific 구체적인, 상세한   graduate student 대학원 학생

◎ GRAMMAR POINT

④ 분사 구문

분사를 이용하여 부사절을 간단히 부사구로 고친 것으로, 그 구가 주절을 부사적으로 수식할 때 이를 분사 구문이라고 하며, 때(시간), 이유·원인, 조건, 양보, 부대 상황(동시 동작, 연속 동작)을 의미하는 접속사의 뜻이 내포되어 있다.

(1) 주절과 시제가 일치할 때

능동이면 -ing로, 수동이면 p.p. 형태로 시작된다.

① 시제 일치, 능동

While he was taking a walk in the park yesterday, Tom **met** a colleague of his.

→ ***Taking*** *a walk in the park yesterday*, Tom **met** a colleague of his.
　　　분사 구문
Tom은 어제 공원을 산책하다가 동료를 만났다.

② 시제 일치, 수동

When she was left alone, she **began** to cry.

→ ***Left*** *alone*, she **began** to cry.
　　분사 구문
그녀는 혼자 있게 되자 울기 시작했다.

(2) 주절과 시제가 일치하지 않을 때(완료 분사 구문)

<having + p.p.>의 형태를 취하는 완료 분사 구문은 주절의 시제보다 앞선 시제를 나타내게 된다.

① 한 시제 앞설 때, 능동

After he had taken a shower, Bob **went** to school.

→ ***Having taken*** *a shower*, Bob **went** to school.
　　완료 분사 구문(샤워를 한 게 학교에 간 것보다 앞선 일임을 나타냄)
Bob은 샤워를 한 후에 학교에 갔다.

② 한 시제 앞설 때, 수동

After he had been warned to be punctual by his boss, Tom **began** to get up early.

→ ***Having been warned*** *to be punctual by his boss*, Tom **began** to get up early.
　　완료 분사 구문(상관에게 경고를 들은 게 일찍 일어나기 시작한 것보다 앞선 일임을 나타냄)
Tom은 그의 상사로부터 시간을 지키라는 경고를 받고 난 후에 일찍 일어나기 시작했다.

(3) 분사 구문의 부정

분사 구문의 부정은 분사 앞에 not이나 never를 붙인다.

Having money, I can buy the car. (긍정) 나는 돈이 있기 때문에 차를 살 수가 있다.

→ **Not having any money**, I can't buy the car. (부정) 나는 돈이 없기 때문에 차를 살 수가 없다.

= As I don't have any money, I can't buy the car.

GRAMMAR PRACTICE

A 밑줄 친 부사절을 분사 구문으로 바꾸세요.

1. When she was happy, Jenny used to sing loudly.
    → _____, Jenny used to sing loudly.
2. Because he was born in April, Tony likes spring very much.
    → _____, Tony likes spring very much.
3. After he had been advised to lose weight by his doctor, he began to diet.
    → _____, he began to diet.
4. The chair left the conference room abruptly, as he disappointed everybody.
    → The chair left the conference room abruptly, _____.
5. After they had discussed possible measures, they moved on to the next item.
    → _____, they moved on to the next item.
6. As I didn't know the man at all, I couldn't say a word.
    → _____, I couldn't say a word.

B 밑줄 친 분사 구문을 부사절로 바꾸세요.

1. Living next door to her, I hardly ever talk to the old lady.
    → _____, I hardly ever talk to the old lady.
2. Having traveled abroad many times, Linda knows a lot about other countries.
    → _____, Linda knows a lot about other countries.
3. Arriving at the bus station, I found that the last bus had left.
    → _____, I found that the last bus had left.
4. Applying for the position, you are asked to include your salary history.
    → _____, you are asked to include your salary history.
5. Built in 1990, the library has offered residents various kinds of books and events.
    → _____, the library has offered the residents various kinds of books and events.
6. Not knowing what to say, I sat quietly.
    → _____, I sat quietly.

VOCA detective 탐정의　excursion 여행　for a change 기분전환을 위해　reject 거절하다

GRAMMAR POINT

⑤ with + 목적어 + 분사

<with + 목적어 + 분사> 형태의 분사 구문을 쓰면 생생한 묘사적 효과를 나타낼 수 있다.

(1) with + 목적어 + 현재 분사(목적어의 능동적 행동)

It was a misty morning **with little wind blowing**. 바람이 거의 불지 않는 안개 낀 아침이었다.
= It was a misty morning and little wind was blowing.

(2) with + 목적어 + 과거 분사(목적어의 수동적 행동)

With an eye bandaged, I could not write properly.
한 눈에 붕대를 감고 있었으므로 나는 글을 제대로 쓸 수 없었다.

⑥ 독립 분사 구문 : 문장 전체를 꾸미는 부사구

부사절의 주어가 you, they, we, people등과 같이 일반인이거나 주절과 같을 때, 주어를 생략하고 분사 구문으로 시작하며, 관용적인 표현들은 기억해 두도록 하자.

Generally speaking 일반적으로 말해	**Judging from** ~으로 판단하건대
Speaking of ~에 대해 이야기하자면	**Granting that** ~을 인정한다면
Compared with ~을 비교하면	**Frankly speaking** 솔직히 말해서
Strictly speaking 엄격히 말해서	**Seeing that** ~을 보면, ~이므로

If we speak generally, English is not easy to speak. 일반적으로 말해 영어는 말하기 쉽지 않다.
= **Generally speaking**, English is not easy to speak.

⑦ 준동사의 시제, 태, 부정

	to 부정사	동명사	분사	
			현재분사	과거분사
수동태	to be p.p	being p.p	X	(being) p.p
진행형	to be -ing	X	V-ing	X
완료형	to have p.p	having p.p	having p.p (능동)	having been p.p (수동)
부정	not to V	not V~ing	not V-ing	not p.p.
의미상의 주어	for 명사 to V	소유격 + -ing 또는 명사 + -ing		

① to 부정사

Sara seems **to be reading** a newspaper. Sara는 신문을 읽고 있는 중인 것 같았다.
Sara seems **to have been** sick. Sara는 아팠던 것 같다.

② 동명사

He regretted **not having spoken** to me. 그는 나에게 그렇게 말하지 않았던 것을 후회한다.
I know the fact of **his having** done it. 나는 그가 그것을 했다는 사실을 알고 있다.

③ 분사 구문

Not knowing how to cook, Linda asked me some questions.
Linda는 요리하는 방법을 몰라서, 나에게 몇 가지 질문을 했다.

GRAMMAR PRACTICE

A 다음 주어진 문장과 독립 분사 구문 함께 사용하여 문장을 완성하세요.

| Compared with last year | Frankly speaking | Judging from his accent |
| Strictly speaking | Speaking of bears | |

1. _____, he seems to be an American.
2. _____, here is a story for you.
3. _____, I didn't do my homework yet.
4. _____, prices have risen by 20 percent.
5. _____, she is not so good at math.

B 어법상 틀린 문장은 바르게 고치고, 틀린 부분이 없으면 O로 표시하세요.

1. Grant that you were drunk, you are responsible for your conduct.
2. The event was initially scheduled to hold in Tokyo in March.
3. We decided against it in order not to borrow more money.
4. You should be careful to not get involved in that complication.
5. Make sure not to eat too many cookies.

C 보기 중 알맞은 것을 고르세요.

1. With winds _____ from the southwest, atmospheric conditions will stay unstable and cause sporadic rain or snow in certain areas.
   (A) blow   (B) blowing   (C) blew   (D) blown

2. Generally, casinos can create new jobs and allow money _____ on infrastructure.
   (A) spending   (B) to spend   (C) to be spent   (D) having spent

3. The chemical EGCG in green tea can prevent nerve cells from _____.
   (A) being damaged   (B) to damage   (C) damaging   (D) damages

4. Since the money that the developers offered was not enough for him _____ another residence, he refused to leave his home.
   (A) buy   (B) to buy   (C) buying   (D) bought

5. His English is not bad, _____ he has learned it for six months.
   (A) considers   (B) to be considered   (C) considered that   (D) considering that

VOCA get involved in ~에 관련되다, 연루되다 unstable 불안정한 sporadic 산발적인 create 만들다 infrastructure 기반시설 residence 주택, 거주지

GRAMMAR IN SENTENCE

▶ 의미 단위로 문장을 끊어 읽고, 해석하세요.
단, 경우에 따라 명사구 또는 명사절은 { }, 형용사구 또는 형용사절은 [ ], 부사구 부사절은 ( )로 표시하세요.

1. We live in a large house built of stone and brick.

2. A man named Aesop wrote this famous storybook.

3. I know the girl wearing the big straw hat.

4. The workshop held last month was to increase productivity.

5. They expressed significant interest for the newly proposed production schedule.

6. There is a fee charged for each transaction.

7. We will be happy to refund or replace any damaged goods if they are returened within 15 days of purchase.

8. Anyone remaining in the building after 10:00 p.m. is requested to lock the door when he leaves.

9. Anyone wanting to apply for the accounting position must submit a résumé and a cover letter by the end of the month.

10. She could figure out the amount of time required for the job since she had had a similar experience.

 **Outro**

분사

분사
동사의 의미와 함께 문장 안에서는 명사를 수식하는 형용사로 쓰이는 것

- **과거분사** : p.p 형태. 수동과 완료의 의미

    Report **damaged** luggage immediately to the airport baggage center.
    파손된 수화물을 공항 수화물 센터로 즉시 보고하세요.

- **현재분사** : V-+ing 형태. 능동과 진행의 의미

    The boy **sleeping** in the bed is my son.
    침대에서 자고 있는 소년은 내 아들이다.

분사 구문

'접속사 + 주어 + 동사'로 시작하는 부사절에서, 주절과 주어가 일치하는 경우, 부사절의 접속사와 주어를 생략하고 현재분사와 과거분사를 이용해 축약해서 표현하는 구문

- **기본형태** : 시제 일치, 능동

    Having money, I can buy the car.
    나는 돈이 있기 때문에 차를 살 수가 있다.

- **수동형태** : 시제 일치, 수동

    Left alone, she **began** to cry.
    그녀는 혼자 있게 되자 울기 시작했다.

- **완료 형태** : 주절의 시제보다 부사절 시제가 앞설 때

    Having taken a shower, Bob **went** to school.
    완료 분사 구문(샤워를 한 게 학교에 간 것보다 앞선 일임을 나타냄)
    Bob은 샤워를 한 후에 학교에 갔다.

ACTUAL TEST 4

A 보기 중 맞는 것을 고르세요.

1 In an effort to ------- many travelers, the travel agency has made the cheapest package tour of Europe.
(A) attracting
(B) attractively
(C) attraction
(D) attract

2 The new system will encourage students ------- their behavior instead of simply punishing them.
(A) modifying
(B) to modify
(C) modify
(D) modified

3 Friendly Messenger lets you instantly -------- with your coworkers over long distances all around the world.
(A) communicate
(B) to communicate
(C) communicating
(D) communicated

4 Trainers who have completed their daily tasks should spend time ------- manuals on company policies.
(A) read
(B) to read
(C) reading
(D) with reading

5 Terry is used to -------- on the left side of the road because he has lived in Tokyo for a long time.
(A) drive
(B) drove
(C) driven
(D) driving

6 Every employee should remember that all items -------- directly from the local manufacturer will take an additional two days.
(A) shipped
(B) shipping
(C) ships
(D) was shipping

7 ------- requests for a better work environment, the company decided to renovate the building.
(A) Received
(B) Having received
(C) Having been received
(D) Being received

8 Before visitors could enter the --------- parking area, they had to have security passes.
(A) designate
(B) designating
(C) designation
(D) designated

9 Emergency rescue teams will conduct an active search of the area for the -------- children.
(A) miss
(B) missing
(C) missed
(D) misses

10 ------- customer satisfaction, the fast-growing company established a new Customer Service Department last year.
(A) To improve
(B) Improving
(C) Improves
(D) Improved

B 보기 중 맞는 것을 고르세요.

Questions 11-16 refer to the following leaflet.

Attention All Pet Owners!

Do your pets have all their vaccine and immunization shots? Have these records been filed with The Federal Bureau for Animal Control or your local Animal Control Office?

11 ------- your pet safe and healthy is both your and our goal. It is important **12** ------- records of your pet's immunization for international travel purposes, in the event that your pet gets lost, goes missing or becomes ill.

To check on the status of your pet's immunization and vaccine record, or **13** ------- your pet's file, please bring **14** ------- documents of your pet's medical history from a licensed veterinarian to your local Animal Control Office. Mandatory vaccinations and immunizations can also **15** ------- by the Animal Control Office. Please call ahead **16** ------- an appointment for these services.

---

11 (A) Keep
(B) Kept
(C) Keeping
(D) Being kept

12 (A) to maintain
(B) to be maintained
(C) to maintaining
(D) maintains

13 (A) updating
(B) updated
(C) updates
(D) to update

14 (A) certify
(B) certified
(C) certifying
(D) certificate

15 (A) provide
(B) have provided
(C) provides
(D) be provided

16 (A) book
(B) to book
(C) booking
(D) booked

MINI TEST 2

A 보기 중 맞는 것을 고르세요.

1. Together they began a -------- study of the funeral industry, and Bob suggested that they publish their findings.
   (A) detailing
   (B) detailed
   (C) details
   (D) detail

2. Despite the recent economic recession, high-technology venture firms keep growing in size, ------- numerous college graduates with degrees in engineering and technology.
   (A) hire
   (B) hires
   (C) hiring
   (D) hired

3. ------- the chief executive officer, Ms. Lucas has access to confidential information and statistics regarding the company's performance.
   (A) To be
   (B) Be
   (C) Being
   (D) Has been

4. The number of freelance writers ------- remarkably in recent years at a significantly faster rate than that of dependent writers.
   (A) will increase
   (B) are increased
   (C) have increased
   (D) has increased

5. The recent issue of the journal *Science*, written by famous scientists, --------- by a courier service next week.
   (A) will deliver
   (B) is delivering
   (C) will be delivered
   (D) delivers

6. Our supervisor requested that some equipment --------- from the basement to the newly built warehouse.
   (A) be moved
   (B) move
   (C) is moved
   (D) moves

7. Our flight attendants -------- complimentary beverages once we are airborne.
   (A) provides
   (B) are provided
   (C) will be providing
   (D) have provided

8. It is recommended that a driver -------- a minimum of 8 hours of sleep prior to driving on long trips.
   (A) obtain
   (B) is obtained
   (C) obtained
   (D) obtaining

9. The company's advisor suggested -------- the releasess of the new products due to unfavorable conditions in the market.
   (A) postpone
   (B) to postpone
   (C) postponing
   (D) postponed

10. Failing -------- with the new regulations can lead to serious consequences, including fines and imprisonment.
    (A) to comply
    (B) complying
    (C) complied
    (D) to be complied

B 보기 중 틀린 것을 고르세요.

1 This year's (A)[annual] Multimedia Art Asia Pacific media arts festival will be (B)[holding] in Brisbane, Australia, (C)[from] October 23 (D)[to] November 10.

2 (A)[After] hearing and considering the (B)[views of] the members of the union, the executive committee drew up a (C)[report on] the issue that will be (D)[sent it] to the Ministry of Industry and Energy.

3 Before (A)[clean] the copy machine, the user (B)[should] make sure (C)[that] he (D)[removes] the cord from the outlet.

4 Mr. Thompson (A)[resigned as] the administrative head (B)[in order pursue] other (C)[activities] (D)[for] the local community.

5 It is predicted (A)[that] the (B)[representatives] of different (C)[company] all over the world will also (D)[copy] this kind of device.

6 Questions (A)[involve] product (B)[warranties], repair, and pricing (C)[should be] (D)[directed to] Mr. Harrison in Sales.

7 Graduate students (A)[interested] in (B)[pursue] careers (C)[in] agriculture are recommended (D)[to] attend the farmer's conference in Maine.

8 The sales representative (A)[informed] us (B)[that] Mr. Green was (C)[satisfaction] with our (D)[after sales service] and will continue to do business with our company.

9 (A)[Applicants] are (B)[reminded obtain] all the necessary personal (C)[documents] to (D)[apply for] any jobs at this company.

10 The NK Newspaper (A)[allow] readers (B)[to] check for (C)[updated] news at any time (D)[on] their cell phones as a bonus for subscribing.

MINI TEST 2

C 보기 중 맞는 것을 고르세요.

Questions 1-6 refer to the following letter.

September 10

Karl Leman
Taylor Bay Apartments
335 Waterfront Ave.
San Francisco, CA 10009

To Karl Leman:

I **1.** ------- a tenant in your building on Waterfront Avenue for the past 5years. I have always paid my rent on time and have never had any issues arise with respect to the level of service offered. However, last month, my bathroom sink began **2.** -------, and I immediately called the building manager, who told me she would contact a maintenance person. It took 2 days for a maintenance person to arrive, by which time a significant amount of water **3.** ------- onto the dining room carpet. While I did my best to dry up the water, it has left a permanent stain.

I **4.** ------- the building manager of the stain, and she sent a cleaner to steam-clean the carpet. The stain **5.** -------, but I arrived home today to find a bill for $75.00 for the cleaning services.

I paid the bill but request that I **6.** ------- the full amount (or have it deducted from next month's rent of $450.00).

Thank you,
Julie Andrews, Apartment 1208

---

1 (A) am
　　 (B) was
　　 (C) have been
　　 (D) had been

2 (A) leaking
　　 (B) to leaking
　　 (C) leaks
　　 (D) leaked

3 (A) has leaked
　　 (B) leaks
　　 (C) will have leaked
　　 (D) had leaked

4 (A) informed
　　 (B) announced
　　 (C) said
　　 (D) mentioned

5 (A) removes
　　 (B) removed
　　 (C) is removed
　　 (D) was removed

6 (A) refund
　　 (B) be refunded
　　 (C) refunds
　　 (D) refunded

Questions 7-9 refer to the following advertisement.

BRIGHT CLEANETTES: HOME DRY-CLEANING KIT

Owning wool clothing **7** ------- a luxury many of us enjoy. However, **8** ------- it to the dry cleaner's every time can be a money-consuming problem! Now, you don't have to spend much money **9** ------- your wool clothing. With the new Bright Cleanette Home Dry-Clean Kit, you can **10** ------- clean wool clothing in your own home. Don't miss out on the quality of wool clothing. Bright Cleanette **11** ------- you with quality cleaning for less! You can also save up to thirty percent by **12** ------- Bright Cleanette through the catalogue before the end of the month.

---

7 (A) is
    (B) are
    (C) has
    (D) have

8 (A) taking
    (B) take
    (C) taken
    (D) took

9 (A) clean
    (B) to clean
    (C) cleaning
    (D) cleaned

10 (A) ease
     (B) easy
     (C) easily
     (D) easier

11 (A) gives
     (B) sends
     (C) offers
     (D) provides

12 (A) ordered
     (B) orders
     (C) order
     (D) ordering

잉글리쉬앤 그래머 MASTER

실전편

 코스

Unit 13 접속사 I
Unit 14 접속사 II
Unit 15 관계사

4코스　5코스　6코스

UNIT 13 접속사 I

GRAMMAR POINT

① 등위접속사와 상관접속사

등위접속사와 상관접속사는 접속사를 중심으로 앞뒤에 문법적으로 같은 구조가 와야 한다는 특징이 있다.

(1) 등위접속사: and, but, or, so, for

등위접속사 and, but, or는 앞뒤를 대등하게 연결한다. 즉, 앞뒤가 형용사-형용사, 구-구, 절-절 등과 같이 문법적으로 같은 구조를 취해야 한다.
단, so와 for는 오직 절과 절을 연결할 수 있으며, 단어나 구는 연결하지 못한다.

단어 / 구 / 절	and but (= yet) or	단어 / 구 / 절
절	so for	절

Do you like beef **or** pork? (명사 or 명사) 소고기를 좋아하세요, 돼지고기를 좋아하세요?

He enjoys dancing, swimming **and** hiking every weekend. (동명사 and 동명사)
그는 주말마다 춤추기, 수영하기 그리고 하이킹하는 것을 즐긴다.

He should stay home, **for** he is sick. (절 for 절) 그는 집에 있어야만 한다, 왜냐면 아프기 때문이다.

He can speak Spanish very well **but** (he) cannot speak English. (절 but 절)
등위접속사로 연결된 경우 중복된 단어들은 생략될 수 있다.
그는 스페인어는 잘하지만 영어는 하지 못한다.

(2) 등위 상관접속사

등위 상관접속사는 반드시 짝을 맞춰 같이 쓰며, A와 B는 같은 문법 구조를 가진다.

상관 접속사의 수일치	
either A or B A 또는 B neither A nor B A도 B도 아닌 not only A but also B = B as well as A A뿐만 아니라 B도 not A but B = B but not A A가 아니라 B	B에 동사 일치
both A and B A와 B 둘 다	항상 복수 동사

Either a bus **or** a taxi <u>is</u> available at the airport. 버스나 택시를 공항에서 이용할 수 있다.
Both coffee **and** tea <u>have</u> long and historic pasts. 커피와 차는 오랜 역사를 가지고 있다.

GRAMMAR PRACTICE

A 괄호 안에서 알맞은 것을 고르세요.

1. Neither my parents (or, nor) my sister likes pork.
2. We need signatures from both you (but, and) your spouse.
3. I had no choice but to listen to him, (for, so) he was my boss.
4. Not only my friends (as well, but also) my sister hasn't been to Paris.
5. She likes to go on a picnic, (but, so) doesn't like to watch soccer at the stadium.

B 어법상 틀린 문장은 바르게 고치고, 틀린 부분이 없으면 O로 표시하세요.

1. The movie was interesting so exciting.
2. Either visiting us or to call us is up to you.
3. Which do you prefer, apples or pears?
4. I like to read books and listening to music.
5. The teacher as well as the students have never read the novel.

C 보기 중 알맞은 것을 고르세요.

1. He was rather disappointed, _____ his loved one had left him for no good reason.
   (A) so   (B) for   (C) but   (D) or

2. Severe illness will create a crisis not only for the individual concerned _____ for his family.
   (A) as well   (B) or   (C) nor   (D) but also

3. Three of the job candidates had worked with this software, _____ only one was familiar with data management.
   (A) not   (B) for   (C) but   (D) or

4. Neither the reduction of parking fees _____ the expansion of the parking area will increase the number of the customers at that shopping mall.
   (A) and   (B) nor   (C) so   (D) but

5. If you arrive at Vancouver International Airport, you can travel to Whistler either by bus _____ by train.
   (A) and   (B) or   (C) nor   (D) but

VOCA signature 서명   spouse 배우자   have no choice but to~ ~할 수 밖에 없다   candidate 지원자, 후보자
be familiar with ~에 익숙한   data management 자료관리   reduction 감소   expansion 확장   travel 다니다
by bus/train 버스/기차로

◎ GRAMMAR POINT

② 명사절 접속사

'절'이란 주어와 동사를 갖춘 것이다. 명사절이란 '절'이 문장 안에서 명사의 역할, 즉, 주어, 목적어, 보어의 역할을 한다. 명사절은 '명사절 접속사 + 주어 + 동사'의 형태로 이루어진다.

(1) 명사절을 이끄는 접속사 that

접속사 that은 문장에서 명사절을 만들어 주어, 목적어, 보어의 역할을 하는 문장을 이끈다. 접속사 that이 이끄는 명사절은 **완전한 문장 구조**를 갖는다.

That the Earth is round is an absolute truth. (주어) 지구가 둥글다는 것은 명백한 진리이다.
People believe **that Michael is innocent**. (목적어) 사람들은 Michael이 결백하다고 믿는다.
His problem is **that he is too lazy.** (보어) 그의 문제점은 그가 너무 게으르다는 것이다.

(2) 명사절을 이끄는 접속사 if나 whether

① if나 whether는 명사절을 이끌어 '~인지 아닌지'의 의미를 나타낸다. 명사절 이하는 불확실한 의문 (~인지 아닌지)을 나타내며 주어, 보어, 목적어로 쓰인다.

I am not sure **if** he will attend the seminar. 그가 세미나에 참석할지 아닐지 확실하지 않다.

② if/whether가 이끄는 명사절 중 if로 구성된 명사절은 주어로 사용될 때와 be동사의 보어로 사용할 때는 사용되지 않는다.

The problem is **whether** our competitor will launch the product this month.
= **Whether** our competitor will launch the product this month is the problem.
문제는 경쟁사가 그 제품을 이번 달에 출시하느냐는 것이다.

③ **whether**는 whether A or B나 whether or not으로도 쓰이고 주어자리나 전치사 다음에도 쓰일 수 있지만 if는 이런 경우 쓸 수 없다.

I don't know **whether he will come or not**. (목적어) 나는 그가 올지 안 올지 모른다.

④ 조건(만약에 ~면)의 부사절에서는 whether를 쓰지 않는다.

We can see you **if** you arrive on time. (O) 당신이 정각에 도착하면, 우리는 당신을 볼 수 있다.
We can see you whether you arrive on time. (X)

⑤ whether가 부사절로 쓰이면, '~에 상관없이'를 의미하게 된다.

Whether you like it or not, I'm going to see you.
네가 좋아하건 싫어하건 상관없이, 나는 너를 보러 갈 것이다.

GRAMMAR PRACTICE

A 주어진 표현들을 적절히 배열하여 문장을 완성하세요.

1. in the east / rises / the sun / that

   Everyone knows _____.

2. too critical / you / are / that

   Your problem is _____.

3. was / doing / worth / the work / that

   I encouraged him _____.

4. the meeting / will attend / you / if

   I wonder _____.

5. sign the contract / they will / whether

   We don't know _____.

B 어법상 틀린 문장은 바르게 고치고, 틀린 부분이 없으면 O로 표시하세요.

1. If or not he will serve as the chairman is an important issue.
2. The problem is that you were not at the meeting yesterday.
3. It is a great relief to know if the report is not due until Monday.
4. Please let me know if or not you can help in this matter.
5. Whether Mr. Murphy is elected as the new chairman is quite surprising.

C 다음 중 알맞은 것을 고르세요.

1. The law states (if, that) children under seventeen must be accompanied by their parent or guardian to view an R-rated movie.
2. John Black, the regional manager in Asia, wonders (whether, that) he can sign a long-term agency contract with Mr. Lay.
3. It is true (that, if) water is made up of a combination of oxygen and hydrogen.
4. We would like to know (what, if) you could offer us full coverage against fire, accident and industrial injuries.
5. We wonder (that, whether) we can sign a long-term agency contract with you.

VOCA state 명시하다 be accompanied by~ ~를 동반하다 guardian 보호자 view 시청하다 fire 화재
industrial injury 산업재해

GRAMMAR POINT

(3) 동격절을 이끄는 that : 동격절 that을 이끄는 명사들

that 바로 앞에 fact, news, suggestion 등의 명사가 오고 that절 뒤에는 주로 완전한 절이 사용되어 어떤 사실인지, 어떤 소식인지, 어떤 제안인지를 구체적으로 알려주는 경우가 있는데, 이런 절을 동격절 that이라고 한다.

the fact that, the truth that ~라는 사실	the report that ~라는 보도
the rumor that ~라는 소문	the news that ~라는 소식
the advice that ~라는 충고[조언]	the suggestion that, the idea that ~라는 제안

His success is attributed to **the fact that** he is a very industrious person.
그의 성공은 그가 근면한 사람이라는 사실 때문이다.

(4) 형용사와 함께 쓰이는 that 절

be afraid that ~여서 유감이다	be aware that ~을 알고 있다
be happy that ~여서 기쁘다	be sure that ~을 확신하다
be glad that ~여서 반갑다	be sorry that ~여서 유감이다

I'm glad that you are interested in this film. 저는 당신이 이 영화에 관심이 있어서 기쁘다.

(5) 명사절을 이끄는 접속사 what

what은 명사절을 만들어 주어, 목적어, 보어의 역할을 하는 문장을 이끈다. 관계대명사로 분류되는 what이 이끄는 명사절은 <동사 + 보어> 또는 <주어 + 타동사> 등 주어, 목적어, 보어 중 한 가지 필수성분이 없는 불완전한 문장 구조를 갖는다.

What he wants is unclear. 그가 원하는 것이 불분명하다.
(주어로 쓰임. 타동사 want 뒤에 목적어가 없음)

I want to know **what** makes you so depressed. 나는 무엇이 너를 우울하게 만드는지를 알고 싶다.
(타동사 know에 대한 목적어로 쓰임. what 뒤에 주어가 없음)

That is **what** he checked at the conference. 그것은 그가 회의에서 확인한 것이다.
(is의 보어로 쓰임. checked 뒤에 목적어가 없음)

(6) 명사절 that, if, whether, what 구별하기

that, if, whether가 이끄는 명사절에서는 완전한 절이 오고, what이 이끄는 명사절에서는 주어나 목적어가 빠진 불완전한 절이 온다. 명사절 that절 뒤에는 확실한 사실이, if나 whether절 뒤에는 불확실한 사실을 나타내는 문장이 온다.

I believe **that you are telling me the truth**. 나는 네가 나에게 진실을 말한다고 믿는다.
I believe **what you said yesterday.** 나는 어제 네가 나에게 말한 것을 믿는다.
I wonder **if your company will develop the new software.**
나는 귀사가 그 새로운 소프트웨어를 개발할 것인지가 궁금하다.

GRAMMAR PRACTICE

A 빈칸에 **that** 또는 **what**을 넣어 완성하세요.

1. Tom knows _____ is good for him.
2. _____ makes the desert beautiful is _____ it hides a well somewhere.
3. I didn't know _____ she was an actress.
4. He's not _____ he used to be.
5. _____ I need right now is your report.
6. _____ the Earth is round is true.
7. My idea is _____ we should have a promotional campaign.
8. I know _____ the convention is very important.
9. _____ I want to know now is if my team can meet the deadline.
10. _____ we are experiencing now is unprecedented in world history.

B 어법상 틀린 문장은 바르게 고치고, 틀린 부분이 없으면 **O**로 표시하세요.

1. The fact that you've worked as a secretary will help you find a job.
2. If he will go on a business trip next week or not will be decided tomorrow.
3. This is not what we are used to seeing this time of the year.
4. The problem is what the same mistake has been made many times before.
5. He is afraid that the company is losing clients.

VOCA   well 우물   promotion campaign 판매촉진 캠페인   unprecedented 전례가 없는

◎ GRAMMAR POINT

③ 명사절을 이끄는 접속사 what, who, which

의문대명사인 what, who, which가 명사절을 이끄는 경우, <동사 + 보어> 또는 <주어 + 타동사> 등 주어, 목적어, 보어 중 한 가지 필수성분이 없는 **불완전한 문장 구조**를 갖는다.

What I need right now is your report. (주어) 내가 지금 필요한 것은 당신의 보고서이다.

I can't tell **what** she wants. (목적어) 그녀가 무엇을 원하는지를 모르겠다.

He didn't know **who** needed the file. (보어) 그는 누가 그 파일을 필요로 하는지를 몰랐다.

Do you know **which** department Anna works in? (which 가 department를 수식하는 의문형용사로 쓰였다.)
어느 부서에서 Anna 가 일하는 지 아세요?

④ 명사절을 이끄는 접속사 when, where, why, how

의문부사인 when, where, why, how가 이끄는 명사절은 **완전한 문장 구조**를 갖는다.

We wondered **where** the file had been found. 그 파일이 어디에서 발견되었는지 궁금했습니다.

Nobody knows **how(why)** he got married to Linda.
아무도 그가 어떻게(왜) 그의 Linda와 결혼했는지 모른다.

⑤ 의문사 / whether + to 부정사 = 의문사+주어+should+동사

Tell me **when to** call you. = Tell me **when I should** call you.
언제 전화해야 할지 말해줘.

Please decide **whether to** join us as soon as possible.
= Please decide **whether you should** join us as soon as possible.
참여 여부를 가능한 빨리 결정해주세요.

→ 의문사 why는 이 구조로 사용하지 않는 것에 유의한다.

⑥ 간접의문문

(1) 의문사가 있는 경우 : 의문사 + 주어 +동사

Do you know? + Where is the gas station?
= Do you know where the gas station is?
주유소가 어디 있는지 아세요?

(2) 의문사가 없는 경우 : if(whether) + 주어 +동사

Can you tell me? + Will she like this cake?
= Can you tell me if she will like this cake?
그녀가 이 케이크를 좋아 할지 말 해 줄 수 있어요?

GRAMMAR PRACTICE

A 두 문장의 의미가 같도록 빈칸을 채우세요.

1. I'd like to know how to get to the building.
   = I'd like to know _____ get to the building.

2. I can't decide whether I will go to the concert or not.
   = I can't decide _____ or not.

3. I'd just like to ask when I am supposed to give a speech.
   = I'd just like to ask _____ a speech.

4. I can't decide what I should eat tomorrow.
   = I can't decide _____ tomorrow.

5. He wants to know what he should wear and how he should behave.
   = He wants to know _____ and _____.

B 빈칸에 알맞은 명사절 접속사를 넣어서 문장을 완성하세요.

who　　how　　when　　where　　why

1. The chart illustrates _____ the body works.
2. That sign indicates _____ the restroom is.
3. It is impossible to predict _____ an earthquake will happen.
4. I don't know _____ the man is.
5. May I ask _____ you are canceling the meeting?

C 어법상 틀린 문장은 바르게 고치고, 틀린 부분이 없으면 O로 표시하세요.

1. It has not yet been decided that department he will be transferred to.
2. Do you happen to know why Mr. Johnson was late this morning?
3. That the boss is worried about right now is whether he can pay his employees a salary.
4. Can you show me when the concert hall is?
5. They know how to use their time wisely and effectively.

GRAMMAR IN SENTENCE

▶ 의미 단위로 문장을 끊어 읽고, 해석하세요.
단, 경우에 따라 명사구 또는 명사절은 { }, 형용사구 또는 형용사절은 [ ], 부사구 부사절은 ( )로 표시하세요.

1. The fact that you've worked as a secretary will help you find a job.

2. Whether he will go on a business trip next week or not will be decided tomorrow.

3. This is not what we are used to seeing this time of the year.

4. The problem is that the same mistake has been made many times before.

5. He is afraid that the company is losing clients.

6. It has not yet been decided which department he will be transferred to.

7. Do you happen to know why Mr. Johnson was late this morning?

8. What the boss is worried about right now is whether he can pay his employees their salaries.

9. Can you show me where the concert hall is?

10. They know how to use their time wisely and effectively.

 **Outro**

접속사 I

접속사
단어와 단어 구와 구, 또는 절과 절을 연결해 주는 말

등위접속사
and, but, or, for, so 등으로 문법상 대등하게 단어, 구, 절을 연결한다.

<u>He is a teacher</u> **and** <u>I am a student</u>. 그는 교사이고 나는 학생이다.
    등위절   등위절

종속접속사
주절과 종속절을 연결한다.

- **명사절을 이끄는 접속사**

    관계대명사 what, 접속사 that과 if[whether], 간접 의문문의 의문사 등으로 유도되어 주어, 목적어, 보어로 쓰이므로 명사절은 생략할 수 없다.

    I bought some milk this morning, **but** I didn't drink it.
    나는 오늘 아침에 우유를 샀지만, 나는 그것을 마시지 않았다.

- **부사절을 이끄는 접속사**

    when, while, although, because, if 등으로 유도되는 절로서, '시간, 장소, 조건, 이유, 양보' 등을 나타낸다. 주절을 보충해주는 역할을 하므로 부사절은 생략 가능하다.

    <u>Please answer the phone</u> **when** <u>it rings</u>. 전화벨이 울리면 받아주세요.
         주절   종속절

    Because <u>he felt sick</u>, <u>Tom was absent</u>. Tom 아파서 결근했다.
            종속절   주절

UNIT 14 접속사 II

◎ GRAMMAR POINT

① 부사절 접속사

부사절이란 하나의 절(주어와 동사를 갖춤)이 시간, 이유, 조건, 양보, 목적, 대조 등을 나타내는 부사로 쓰이는 것을 말한다. 부사절은 '부사절 접속사 + 주어 + 동사'로 이루어지며, 부사절 접속사가 이끄는 부사절은 주절의 앞이나 뒤에 위치한다.

(1) 시간을 나타내는 부사절 접속사

when ~할 때	while ~하는 동안	until ~할 때까지
before ~전에	after ~한 후에	by the time ~할 때까지는
as soon as ~하자마자	as ~할 때	since ~이래로

We will contact you **as soon as** we have a job opening.
우리에게 공석이 나자마자 당신께 연락드리겠습니다.

After the movie is over, we will hand out questionnaires to people.
영화가 끝나면, 우리는 사람들에게 질문서를 나눠줄 것이다.

📝 by the time vs until

by the time은 주절의 내용은 항상 어떤 사건의 결과를 표현해야 하고, until을 사용하면 주절은 항상 무슨 일이 벌어지고 있는가를 표현하는 진행의 의미를 담고 있어야 한다.
즉 by the time을 이용하여 하고 싶은 말은 결국 어떤 상태에 이르렀다는 것이고 until로 표현하고자 하는 내용은 어떤 일을 계속했다는 것이다. by the time은 주절이 어떻게든 결과만 표시하면 되므로 주절이 항상 완료시제와 쓰일 필요는 없다. until은 전치사로도 사용할 수 있고 by the time과 같은 의미의 전치사는 by이다.

By the time we got there, everybody **had left**. 우리가 거기 도착했을 때는 모두 떠나버렸다.
We kept on driving until the sun went down. 해가 떨어질 때까지 우리는 계속 운전했다.

(2) 이유를 나타내는 부사절 접속사

because ~때문에	since ~이므로	as ~이므로	now that 이제 ~이니까

He was absent **because** he was sick. 그는 아팠기 때문에 결석을 했다.
Now that he is poor, Richard cannot buy the house. Richard는 가난하기 때문에, 그 집을 살 수 없다.

GRAMMAR PRACTICE

A 다음 중 알맞은 것을 고르세요.

1. Make sure you turn off the radio (though, before) you go to bed.

2. (While, As long as) I buy my ticket, keep an eye on my suitcase.

3. It's been a long time (if, since) we have seen each other.

4. The weather is getting hotter (now that, by the time) the rainy season is over.

5. Let's wait (by the time, until) it stops raining.

6. I'm upset (so, because) it's not going as well as I expected.

7. (So that, Now that) our company has gone out of business, we are all in the same boat.

8. (By the time, Until) the snowstorm stops, the damage will have been tremendous.

9. (If, Since) several guests are invited to dinner this evening, my wife is busily preparing it for them.

10. It's always good to have a mop or a broom and clean the floor periodically (meanwhile, while) you're working.

B 내용상 어색하거나, 어법상 틀린 문장은 바르게 고치고, 틀린 부분이 없으면 O로 표시하세요.

1. Consumers have become suspicious of travel prices as they have found different rates for airlines on various websites.

2. Because of plastic is more durable than wood, it is ideal for window frames.

3. We hired Joe Smith though his portfolio was the most unique and innovative among the applicants.

4. By the time the classroom is poorly lit, students can't take notes.

5. Mobile professionals require access to important company resources so that they are away from the office.

VOCA be in the same boat 같은 처지다　snowstorm 눈보라　periodically 주기적으로　unclear 명확하지 않은, 불확실한
mobile 이동하는　professionals 전문직 종사자　impression 인상　be away from ~에서

(3) 조건을 나타내는 부사절 접속사

if 만약 ~하면	unless 만약 ~하지 않으면	as long as ~하는 한
once 일단 ~하면	in case ~한 일이 일어날 경우에	on condition that ~라는 조건으로

If all your work is done, you may go home. 일이 다 끝나면 당신은 집에 가도 좋다.

in case vs if

in case that은 주절이 in case ~보다 시간상으로 선행한다는 점에서 if와 다르다.

Keep an eye on the birds **in case** they fly away. 새들이 날아가 버릴지 모르니 잘 감시해라.
Contact the customer service first **if** the reception is bad.
수신이 안 좋으면 먼저 고객센터에 전화하세요.

(4) 양보를 나타내는 부사절 접속사

although, even though, even if, though, whereas 비록 ~이지만

Although she couldn't afford it, Ms. Tylor just bought a new house.
Tylor 씨는 경제적 여유가 없었지만 새 집을 구입했다.

(5) 목적을 나타내는 부사절 접속사

so[in order] that ~하기 위해서

I went early **in order that** I might find him at home. 나는 그가 집에 있을 때 만날 수 있도록 일찍 갔다.
We left early **so that** we could get there on time. 거기 제 시간에 도착하려고 일찍 출발했다.

② 시간, 조건의 부사절

시간이나 조건을 나타내는 부사절에서는 현재시제 또는 현재완료시제가 미래를 나타낸다. 이 때 주절은 will, can, may, should 등의 조동사와 함께 미래 시제 쓰거나 또는 명령문을 쓴다.

시간	before, after, when, until, as soon as, while, by the time, as soon as
조건	if, unless, as long as, once (일단~하면), In case

When you **finish/have finished** the report, send it over to Josh.
보고서를 마치면 Josh 에게 그것을 보내시오.

GRAMMAR PRACTICE

A 다음 중 알맞은 것을 고르세요.

1. Switch the light off (as long as, so that) we can sleep well.

2. Do not begin (unless, if) you intend to finish.

3. (In case, Although) you fail, you must have something to fall back on.

4. He just bought a new minivan (unless, even though) he couldn't afford it.

5. (Unless, If) the national budget doesn't increase, the problem will continue.

6. Mr. Johnson is reserved (if, whereas) his wife is very sociable.

7. (Once, Although) they are poor, they like to help other people.

8. Austin works hard (so that, in case) he can pass the examination.

9. (Once, Unless) you sign a contract, your rights and obligations are determined.

10. Please let us know (even though, if) you are interested in our proposal as soon as possible.

B 내용상 어색하거나, 어법상 틀린 문장은 바르게 고치고, 틀린 부분이 없으면 **O**로 표시하세요.

1. We are seriously thinking we may need to throw a party for Kennedy once he gets the chairmanship.

2. Unless your application has been approved, we will send you a written notification of your acceptance to the program.

3. Please refrain from utilizing our services in case you object to the terms and conditions of this agreement.

4. We need to increase our advertising budget if we hope to expand our customer base.

5. Please let me know this itinerary is to your satisfaction though I can reserve flights.

VOCA fall back on ~까지 후퇴하다   reserved 내성적인   sociable 사교적인   right 권리   obligation 의무   objective 목적, 목표   customer base 고객층

◎ GRAMMAR POINT

③ 접속사 vs 전치사 vs 접속부사

접속사 뒤에는 문장이 나오며, 전치사 뒤에는 명사나 동명사가 나온다. 같은 의미를 지닌 전치사와 접속사를 구분해서 외워두도록 한다. 또한 접속사와 접속 부사도 비교해서 인식해 두도록 한다. 접속부사는 부사이기 때문에 접속사의 의미를 가지고 있으면서도 문장과 문장을 연결하는 기능은 없다. 대신 세미콜론(;)으로 앞의 문장과 연결하거나, 문장의 맨 앞에 오는 경우에는 콤마(,)를 붙여 문장을 연결한다.

	접속사	전치사	접속 부사
~이기 때문에	because as since now that	because of owing to due to on account of	
~에도 불구하고	although though even though even if whereas	despite in spite of	however nevertheless nonetheless
~일 경우에	in case that in the event that	in case of in the event of	
~를 제외하고	except that	except except for	
~에 따르면	according as	according to	
~하는 동안	while	during over	meantime meanwhile
만약 ~ 않다면	if ~ not unless	without	otherwise

④ 접속사 + 분사(-ing 또는 p.p), S + V ~.

분사구문을 만들 때 접속사를 생략하는 것이 보편적이지만, 유의할 것은 누구나 쉽게 어떤 접속사가 생략되었는지 알 수 있을 때만 생략을 한다는 점이다. 혼란이 발생할 우려가 있는 경우 접속사를 그대로 둔다.

As p.p, S +V	~된 대로	As planned/scheduled/expected,
Once p.p, S +V	일단 ~되면	Once merged,
Unless p.p, S +V	만일 ~되지 않으면	Unless accompanied,
Before, After +-ing, S +V	~하기 전/후에	Before going to school,
When, While +-ing /p.p S +V	~할 때/ 동안에	While walking on the street,

Unless <u>they are accompanied</u> by their parents, children under 10 may not enter.
→ Unless **accompanied** by their parents, children under 10 may not enter.
부모에 의해 동반되지 않으면, 10세 이하 어린이들은 입장할 수 없다.

GRAMMAR PRACTICE

A 동일한 의미의 문장이 되도록 빈칸에 알맞은 전치사, 접속사 또는 접속부사를 넣으세요.

1. **While** I was flying back to Chicago, I met an old friend.

    = _____ the flight to Chicago, I met an old friend.

    = _____ flying back to Chicago, I met an old friend.

    = I was flying back to Chicago. _____, I met an old friend.

    = I was flying back to Chicago; _____, I met an old friend.

2. **Although** he was sick, he went to school.

    = _____ his sickness, he went to school.

    = He was sick. _____, he went to school.

    = He was sick; _____, he went to school.

B 다음 중 알맞은 것을 고르세요.

1. (In case, In case of) emergencies, simply press 4.
2. (If, Unless) there are emergencies, simply press 4.
3. You need to pay your taxes on time; (otherwise, unless) you will be punished.
4. Application forms will not be accepted (otherwise, unless) all the required information is included.
5. We Koreans have a strong attachment to our climate (nevertheless, though) we always complain that winter is too cold and summer is too hot.

C 내용상 어색하거나, 어법상 틀린 문장은 바르게 고치고, 틀린 부분이 없으면 **O**로 표시하세요.

1. While cleaning out the room, they found several umbrellas which had fallen behind the sofa.
2. In the event any problem or complaint, all calls and e-mails will be handled in a timely manner.
3. Visitors should be conscious of health precautions and should consult a tropical medical adviser before traveling to or in India.
4. Cars have a permit attached to the rear window during parked on company property.
5. Reservations are subject to cancelation otherwise confirmed at least 3 days in advance of your arrival.

VOCA punish 처벌하다 consistent 일관성 있는 precaution 예방 조치 reservation 예약 cancelation 취소 confirm (예약 등을) 확인하다 in advance 미리

GRAMMAR IN SENTENCE

▶ 의미 단위로 문장을 끊어 읽고, 해석하세요.
단, 경우에 따라 명사구 또는 명사절은 { }, 형용사구 또는 형용사절은 [ ], 부사구 부사절은 ( )로 표시하세요.

1. We are seriously thinking we may need to throw a party for Kennedy once he gets the chairmanship.

2. Once your application has been approved, we will send you written notification of your acceptance to the program.

3. Please refrain from utilizing our services if you object to the terms and conditions of this agreement.

4. We need to increase our advertising budget if we hope to expand our customer base.

5. Please let me know this itinerary is to your satisfaction so that I can reserve flights.

6. While cleaning the room, they found several umbrellas which had fallen behind the sofa.

7. In the event of any problems or compaints, all calls and e-mails will be handled in a timely manner.

8. Visitors should be conscious of health precautions and should consult a tropical medical adviser before traveling to or in India.

9. Cars must have a permit attached to the rear window while parked on company property.

10. Reservations are subject to cancelation unless confirmed at least 3 days in advance of your arrival.

접속사 II

부사절이란 하나의 절(주어와 동사를 갖춤)이 시간, 이유, 조건, 양보, 목적 등을 나타내는 부사로 쓰이는 것을 말한다. 부사절은 <부사절 접속사 + 주어 + 동사> 로 이루어진다.

의미	부사절 접속사
시간	**when** ~할 때　　**while** ~하는 동안　　**until** ~할 때까지 **before** ~전에　　**after** ~한 후에　　**by the time** ~할 때까지는 **since** ~이래로　　**as soon as** ~하자마자　　**as** ~할 때
조건	**if** 만약 ~하면　　**unless** 만약 ~하지 않으면　　**as long as** ~하는 한 **once** 일단 ~하면　　**in case** ~, **in the event (that)** ~한 일이 일어날 경우에
양보	**although, even though, even if, though, whereas** 비록 ~이지만
이유	**because** ~때문에　　**since** ~이므로 **as** ~이므로　　**now that** 이제 ~이니까
목적	**so that S + may(can) ~ , in order that ~** ~하기 위해서

As Mr. Kent was on vacation, I took on his job during his absence.
(Mr. Kent씨가 휴가를 갔기 때문에 그가 없는 동안 내가 그의 업무를 맡았다.)

As Dr. Karl is out for lunch, he will be able to see you after 2.
Karl 선생님께서 점심 드시러 나가셔서 2시가 지나서 만나보실 수 있습니다.

She left **as** I came in.
내가 들어오는 중에 그녀는 떠났다.

UNIT 15 관계사

◎ GRAMMAR POINT

관계사절은 다른 말로 형용사절이라고 한다. 즉, 절이 형용사로 쓰여 명사를 뒤에서 수식한다. 이때 관계사절 앞에서 수식을 받는 명사를 선행사라고 한다.

① 관계대명사의 격

관계대명사는 접속사와 대명사의 역할을 하기 때문에 관계절에 명사가 하나 빠진 불완전한 문장이 온다. 선행사가 사람이면 who나 whom(목적격인 경우)을, 사물이면 which를, 소유격인 경우 whose를 쓴다. 관계대명사 that은 선행사가 사람인 경우나 사물인 경우 모두 쓸 수 있으며, 주격, 목적격에도 사용할 수 있지만, 전치사와 콤마(계속적 용법) 뒤에는 쓸 수 없다.

(1) 주격 관계대명사

선행사(명사) +	관계대명사 +	동사 ~ (주어가 없는 절)
사람	who[that]	V ~
사물	which[that]	
X	what	

I met <u>a woman</u> **who** works for ABC Motors. 나는 ABC 자동차 회사에 근무하는 여성을 만났다.
　　　선행사(사람)　관계대명사　동사
(선행사와 주격 관계대명사절의 동사는 수일치가 되어야 한다.)

(2) 소유격 관계대명사

선행사(명사) + <u>whose</u> + 명사 + 동사 ~
　　　　　　　　(~의)

I bought <u>a car</u> **whose color** is red. 나는 빨간색인 차를 구입했다.
　　　선행사　관계대명사　명사　동사

= I bought <u>a car</u>, the color **of which** is red.
(선행사가 사물인 경우 of which로 나타낼 수도 있다. 소유격 관계대명사도 소유격이므로 바로 뒤에 반드시 명사가 있어야 한다.)

(3) 목적격 관계대명사

선행사(명사) +	관계대명사 +	주어 +	동사 (목적어가 없는 절)
사람	who[whom, that]	주어 +	타동사/자동사 + 전치사
사물	which[that]		
X	what		

The man **(who/whom/that)** Lisa is talking with is the president.
선행사(사람)　　관계대명사　　　주어　동사
Lisa가 함께 얘기를 하고 있는 사람이 회장님이다.

This is the book **which (that)** I have been reading since last week.
　　　선행사(사물)　관계대명사　주어 동사
이것이 내가 지난부터 읽고 있는 책이다.

GRAMMAR PRACTICE

A 주어진 표현들을 적절히 배열하여 문장을 완성하세요.

1. was teaching / I / who
   The man _____ is 70 years old.

2. to see / wanted / I / whom
   The man _____ was out of town.

3. the president of our company / is / father / whose
   That's the man _____.

4. respects / everyone / whom
   Rex, _____, donated $5,000 to charity recently.

5. describes / the performance / which
   I need a report _____.

B 다음 주어진 표현과 who / which / whose를 함께 사용하여 문장을 완성하세요.

| lands are seized | will disturb other people | lag behind schedule |
| provides the job to the right people | have maintained a perfect attendance record |

1. We are the reliable organization _____.
2. We must give adequate compensation to farmers _____.
3. Awards are given to students _____.
4. Residents should refrain from playing musical instruments _____.
5. Most of the people _____ have to pay a penalty.

C 보기 중 알맞은 것을 고르세요.

1. Most bosses prefer leaders _____ an emphasis on productivity.
   (A) which place   (B) who place   (C) who places   (D) whose place

2. The purpose of this investment is to develop a new spacecraft _____ our scientific advancement.
   (A) which reflect   (B) who reflects   (C) which reflects   (D) whose reflect

3. Teams should consist of the employees _____ representative of various organizational units.
   (A) which are   (B) who is   (C) which is   (D) who are

VOCA performance 업무성과 detail 상세히 기술하다 donate 기부하다 charity 자선 reliable 믿을 수 있는 organization 기관 adequate 충분한 compensation 보상 seize 빼앗다 refrain 삼가다 musical instrument 악기 disturb 방해하다 lag behind the schedule 일정에 뒤처지다 penalty 벌금 place an emphasis 강조하다

◎ GRAMMAR POINT

② 관계대명사 that vs what

(1) 관계대명사 that

① 관계대명사 that은 주격(who, which), 목적격 (who, whom, which) 을 대신할 수 있다.

A nurse is a person **who(that)** takes care of patients. 간호사는 환자들을 돌봐주는 사람이다.

② 소유격 whose 자리, 콤마(쉼표) 다음, 전치사 뒤에는 관계대명사 that이 올 수 없다.

Jack tried not to cry, **which** made me feel sad.
Jack은 울지 않으려고 애썼는데, 그것이 나를 슬프게 만들었다.

③ **all, every, some, any, no, none, only** 최상급이 선행사를 한정하고 있으면 관계대명사 that이 주로 쓰인다.

All (that) I want is attention. 내가 원하는 것은 관심뿐이다.

(2) 관계대명사 what: ~하는 것

반드시 선행사가 필요한 다른 관계대명사와는 달리 what은 선행사가 필요 없다. 선행사와 관계대명사가 함께 있기 때문이다. what = the thing which(that) 이기 때문에 주어 자리, 목적어 자리에 자유롭게 사용된다.

I don't know **what** you're talking about. 당신이 무슨 말을 하는지 알 수 없다.

(3) that과 what의 용법 구분

관계대명사 **that**	뒤에 주어나 목적어가 없는 불완전한 문장이 온다. that은 전치사와 같이 쓸 수 없고, 계속적 용법(,)으로도 쓰지 않는다.
접속사 **that**	뒤에는 <주어 + 동사 + 목적어>가 있는 완전한 문장이 온다.
관계대명사 **what**	앞에는 선행사가 없고, 뒤에는 주어나 목적어가 없는 불완전한 문장이 온다.

Here is the book **that** he was looking for. (관계대명사) 그가 찾던 책이 여기 있다.
We know **that** he is looking for a job. (접속사) 우리는 그가 직장을 구하고 있다는 것을 알고 있다.
We know **what** is good for us. (관계대명사) 우리는 무엇이 우리에게 좋은지 알고 있다.

③ 관계 대명사의 계속적 용법

관계대명사 앞에 콤마(,)를 찍어 순차적으로 해석하는 방식으로 문장을 표현하기도 하는데 이를 관계대명사의 계속적 용법이라고 한다. 특히, 관계대명사 which는 계속적 용법에서 앞 문장 전체를 가리키는 용도로도 사용한다.

Jack tried not to cry, **which** made me feel sad.
Jack이 울지 않으려고 했는데, 그것이 나를 더 슬프게 만들었다.

GRAMMAR PRACTICE

A 빈칸에 **that** 또는 **what**을 넣어 완성하세요.

1. Are you carrying anything _____ is dangerous with you?
2. _____ I need right now is your support.
3. His wealth enables him to do _____ he likes.
4. Here is the watch _____ you were looking for.
5. Can you believe _____ she is talking about?

B 보기 중 알맞은 것을 고르세요.

1. There's something _____ people don't know about her.
   (A) which (B) that (C) whose (D) whom

2. The woman _____ lives next door is a singer.
   (A) whom (B) that (C) whose (D) who

3. Big cities, _____ consume a lot of energy, cause most of the pollution.
   (A) which (B) that (C) where (D) what

4. I met a young man _____ can speak five languages.
   (A) which (B) that (C) whose (D) whom

5. You will be reimbursed on an hourly basis, _____ is the standard practice.
   (A) who (B) which (C) whose (D) that

C 어법상 틀린 문장은 바르게 고치고, 틀린 부분이 없으면 O로 표시하세요.

1. This request is for the position what needs to be filled due to the resignation of the present director.
2. Please find copies of all your outstanding accounts, that are past due over 30 days.
3. Thousands have taken these courses, what are available through private organizations across Canada.
4. We are the organization which is reliable in terms of offering jobs to people who would be appropriate for it.
5. The notice stated that only students that are members of the band will be allowed to use the practice room.

> **VOCA** support 지지, 응원 consume 소비하다 cause 원인이 되다 reimburse 이미 지급한 비용에 대해 돈을 받다 practice 관행 on a ~ basis ~기준/기반으로 fill 채워 넣다 resignation 사임 outstanding 미지불금의 in terms of ~한다는 면에서 appropriate 적합한 notice 공지 state 명시하다, 진술하다 be allowed to~ ~하도록 허락되다 practice room 연습실

◎ GRAMMAR POINT

④ 전치사 + 관계대명사

(1) 전치사 + 관계대명사
관계대명사가 전치사의 목적어로 쓰이는 경우로, 이때 전치사는 문장 맨 뒤로 보낼 수 있다.
목적격 관계대명사 whom과 which에 한하여 전치사를 수반할 수 있다.

This is **the office**. + I work in **the office.**
= This is **the office which** I work in.
= This is **the office in which** I work. (전치사를 관계대명사 앞으로 이동)
이곳이 내가 일하는 사무실이다.

(2) 전치사 + whom = who ~ 전치사
① 전치사와 함께 쓸 수 있는 관계대명사는 whom 과 which 이다.
② 관계대명사 that 앞에는 전치사가 올 수 없다는 점도 기억한다.
③ 현대 영어에서는 계속적 용법이 아닌 이상, 목적격 관계대명사 whom 대신 who를 많이 쓴다.
　단 이 경우에는 문장 끝의 전치사를 who 앞에 둘 수 없다는 점에 유의한다.

This is the student. + I gave a book to him.
= This is the student **whom** I gave a book **to**.
= This is the student **who** I gave a book **to**.
= This is the student **to whom** I gave a book. 이 학생이 내가 책을 준 학생이다.

(3) 장소를 나타내는 전치사 + 관계 대명사 = where (관계부사)
This is the office **in which** Moris works.
= This is the office **where** Moris works. (= This is the office **and** Moris works **here**.)

⑤ 관계 대명사의 생략

(1) 목적격 관계대명사
목적격 관계대명사는 생략할 수 있다.
하지만, <전치사 + 목적격 관계대명사> 구조에서는 목적격 관계대명사이더라도 생략할 수 없다.

This is the girl **(whom)** I went out with. 얘가 내가 사귀었던 여자애다.
= This is the girl **with whom** I went out.
The fruit **(which)** I like the most is a watermelon. 내가 가장 좋아하는 과일은 수박이다.

(2) <주격 관계대명사 + be동사>를 생략 = 분사
I know the man **(who is)** looking at the computer screen.
나는 컴퓨터 스크린을 보고 있는 남자를 안다.

I visited Janet's house **(which is)** located in the suburbs.
나는 외곽에 위치한 재닛의 집을 방문했다.

GRAMMAR PRACTICE

A 다음 두 문장을 관계대명사를 이용하여 한 문장으로 만든 후, 생략 가능한 부분은 괄호 ( )로 표시하세요.

1. I met a woman. + The woman is seated on the bench.
   = _____

2. All the products will be packaged and shipped promptly. + You ordered all the products.
   = _____

3. Yesterday I visited a garden. + The garden is full of beautiful flowers and trees.
   = _____

4. People live in large cities. + People are busy every day.
   = _____

5. This is automatically deducted from the selling price. + The selling price is charged to the customer.
   = _____

B 보기 중 알맞은 것을 고르세요

1. The contract clearly specifies the date ---------- which the items should be delivered.
   (A) by   (B) for   (C) against   (D) with

2. Please identify yourself and the speaker to ---------- you'd like to direct your question.
   (A) which   (B) whom   (C) that   (D) what

3. The new program ---------- have developed for 5 years is believed to be the most significant advancement in the field.
   (A) who   (B) we   (C) that   (D) which

4. Tomorrow, the annual conference will take place at the Nova Plaza Hotel, ---------- opened just two weeks ago.
   (A) where   (B) when   (C) that   (D) which

5. The director decided to leave the company ---------- he had worked for twenty years to start a business of his own.
   (A) which   (B) that   (C) where   (D) what

VOCA package 포장하다　ship 발송하다　objectively 객관적으로　deduct 공제하다　selling price 판매가　specify 명시하다　identify 확인하다, 밝히다　significant 중요한, 상당한, 의미심장한　advancement 진보, 발전　take place 열다, 개최하다　start a business of one's own 자기 자신의 사업을 시작하다

GRAMMAR POINT

⑥ 관계부사

관계대명사가 <접속사 + 대명사>의 역할을 한다면, 관계부사는 <접속사 + 부사>의 역할을 한다. 따라서 관계부사 뒤에는 완전한 절이 온다.

선행사	관계부사
시간 day, year, time	when
이유 the reason	why
장소 place, building	where
방법 the way	how * the way와 how는 함께 쓸 수 없음

The reason why I'm calling you is to invite you to a Christmas party.
내가 너에게 전화한 이유는 너를 크리스마스 파티에 초대하고 싶어서이다.

I tried to figure out the way how the washing machine works. (X)
→ I tried to figure out **the way** the washing machine works. (O)
= I tried to figure out **how** the washing machine works. (O)
그는 세탁기가 어떻게 작동하는지 알아내려고 노력했다.

⑦ 복합관계사

(1) 복합관계사의 종류

whoever/whomever 누구나, 누구든지	whenever 언제 ~하든 상관없이
whichever 어떤 것이든지	wherever 어디에 ~하든 상관없이
whatever 무엇이든지	however 어떻게 ~하든 상관없이

(2) 복합관계사가 이끄는 절

복합관계사가 이끄는 절은 명사절과 부사절로 쓰인다. 따라서 문장에서 주어, 목적어의 자리에 올 수 있으며, 부사절일 때는 '~한다 할지라도'라는 의미의 양보절로 쓰인다.

① 명사절로 사용된 경우

Whoever (= Anyone who) comes will be welcome. (주어) 누가 오든지 환영할 것이다.

You may choose ***whichever*** (= anything that) you like. (목적어)
네가 좋아하는 것은 무엇이든지 고르면 된다.

② 부사절로 사용된 경우

Wherever you go, ***whatever*** you do, I will be right here waiting for you.
네가 어디를 가든지, 무엇을 하든지, 나는 여기서 너를 기다릴 것이다.

③ **However + 형용사/부사 + S2 + V2, S1 + V1**

복합 관계부사이자 접속사로 사용되는 however의 어순은 기억해두어야 한다.

However rich he may be, he can't buy it. 그가 아무리 부자라고 해도 그는 그것을 살 수 없다.
(=No matter how)

GRAMMAR PRACTICE

A 주어진 표현들을 적절히 배열하여 문장을 완성하세요.

1. live / many people / where
   Most large cities, _____, cause a lot of pollution.
2. stocks / buy / you / when
   This is the right time _____.
3. Linda first / met / he / when
   Tony still remembers the day _____.
4. can buy / we / some food / more cheaply / where
   There must be a place _____.
5. for work / now / you're always late / why
   Do you understand the reason _____?

B 두 문장의 의미가 같도록 빈칸에 알맞은 복합관계사를 넣으세요.

1. Give it to **anyone who** wants it. = Give it to _____ wants it.
2. Give it to **anyone whom** you like.= Give it to _____ you like.
3. You are allowed to do **anything that** you like. = You are allowed to do _____ you like.
4. **Anyone who** arrives first will leave with the prize money. = _____ arrives first will leave with the prize money.
5. **No matter how** humble it may be, there is no place like home.
   = _____ humble it may be, there is no place like home.

C 보기 중 알맞은 것을 고르세요.

1. Many healthcare centers and medical organizations regularly hold campaigns -------- donors are invited to donate blood.
   (A) which (B) that (C) where (D) what
2. -------- you do in order to lose weight, we believe that you will succeed sooner or later.
   (A) What (B) Whatever (C) However (D) That
3. We will hire -------- has several years of direct past experience in this field and truly enjoys working with people.
   (A) whomever (B) whoever (C) wherever (D) however
4. Because Tomas has made a lot of money, he can buy -------- he likes.
   (A) whatever (B) whoever (C) however (D) whenever

GRAMMAR IN SENTENCE

▶ 의미 단위로 문장을 끊어 읽고, 해석하세요.
단, 경우에 따라 명사구 또는 명사절은 { }, 형용사구 또는 형용사절은 [ ], 부사구 부사절은 ( )로 표시하세요.

1. We are a reliable organization which provides job to the right people.

2. We must give adequate compensation to farmers whose lands are seized.

3. Awards are given to students who maintained a perfect attendance record.

4. Residents should refrain from playing musical instruments which disturb other people.

5. Most of the people who lag behind schedule have to pay a penalty.

6. This request is for a position that needs to be filled due to the resignation of the present director.

7. Please find copies of all your outstanding accounts that are past due over 30 days.

8. Thousands have taken these courses, which are available through private organizations across Canada.

9. We are an organization which is reliable in terms of offering jobs to people who are appropriate for them.

10. The notice stated that only students that are members of the band will be allowed to use the practice room.

 **Outro**

관계사

관계대명사

접속사 + 대명사

관계대명사 앞에 나온 명사를 선행사라고 하고, 선행사가 사람이면 who를, 사물이면 which를 쓴다. 관계대명사는 절과 절을 연결하는 '접속사+ 대명사' 역할을 한다. 관계대명사가 이끄는 문장은 선행사를 꾸미는 역할을 하므로 형용사절이다.

격 \ 선행사	사람	사물
주격	who, that	which, that
소유격	whose	whose, of which
목적격	who, whom, that	which, that

관계부사

접속사 + 부사

두 문장을 연결하는 '접속사 + 부사' 역할을 한다.
불완전한 절을 이끄는 관계대명사와는 달리 관계 부사는 완전한 절을 이끈다.

선행사	관계부사
시간 day, year, time	when
이유 the reason	why
장소 place, building	where
방법 the way	how ★ the way와 how는 함께 쓸 수 없음

복합관계사

관계사에 -ever를 붙인 것이 복합관계사이다. '~든지 (상관없이)'라는 뜻으로 명사절을 이끌 수도 있고, '~한다 할지라도'라는 뜻으로 부사절을 이끌 수도 있다.

복합 관계대명사 = 선행사 + 접속사 + 대명사	복합 관계부사 = 선행사 + 접속사 + 부사
whoever/whomever 누구나, 누구든지 whichever 어떤 것이든지 whatever 무엇이든지	whenever 언제 ~하든 상관없이 wherever 어디에 ~하든 상관없이 however 어떻게 ~하든 상관없이

ACTUAL TEST 5

A 보기 중 맞는 것을 고르세요.

1 The hotel dining room will be closed between seven ------- eleven o'clock.
   (A) or
   (B) if
   (C) and
   (D) yet

2 Managers were called in to receive advice on -------- will take care of the problems they are encountering with the current project.
   (A) who
   (B) how
   (C) that
   (D) where

3 Bob Dillon can receive his master's degree this semester --------- he has completed his courses and completed his thesis.
   (A) now that
   (B) therefore
   (C) unless
   (D) accordingly

4 We will give prospective consumers a good impression -------- they will be able to have easy access to our website.
   (A) as
   (B) although
   (C) in spite of
   (D) because of

5 The manager had already approved the week's work schedule; ---------- he accepted Mr. Carton's request for sick leave.
   (A) nevertheless
   (B) so as
   (C) despite
   (D) although

6 ------- he moved into the position of vice president in December, Mr. Clinton has been focusing on spreading Olive's name in the international market.
   (A) Since
   (B) Unless
   (C) Accordingly
   (D) Meanwhile

7 -------- the new shopping center in Atlanta opens, the new bus terminal will not be operational.
   (A) During
   (B) Rather
   (C) Until
   (D) By

8 Most teens start off working in fields ------- pay minimum wage and require little skill.
   (A) who
   (B) whose
   (C) what
   (D) that

9 Unfortunately, the person ------- trade skills are needed to solve these problems is off today.
   (A) who
   (B) whom
   (C) whose
   (D) that

10 Due to employee complaints, the company has adopted a new benefits program -------- will begin at the end of the fiscal year.
   (A) that
   (B) such
   (C) when
   (D) until

B 보기 중 맞는 것을 고르세요.

Questions 11-16 refer to the following magazine review.

Book Review Section: A Guide to Eating Right by Joe Kimberly

Review by Contributor Jeff Montaya

Joe Kimberly's newest book, *A Guide to Eating Right* explores the complexities of the food choices **11** ------- we encounter every day.

Millions of copies of the book have **12** ------- sold, and last week it was nominated for the National Literature Award, **13** ------- is the most prestigious award in the country.

The success of this book is **14** ------- due to the simplicity of his message. He gives readers straight facts on health and nutrition as well as various tips on **15** ------- to eat well.

Copies of *A Guide to Eating Right* by Brent Henley **16** ------- available at McMaster's Bookstore for $35.00.

11 (A) if
(B) that
(C) who
(D) where

12 (A) yet
(B) hardly
(C) ever
(D) already

13 (A) that
(B) what
(C) which
(D) when

14 (A) likely
(B) likeness
(C) like
(D) likes

15 (A) how
(B) why
(C) what
(D) wherever

16 (A) is
(B) are
(C) was
(D) has been

잉글리쉬앤 그래머 MASTER

실전편

 코스

Unit 16 가정법
Unit 17 비교
Unit 18 강조와 도치

6코스

5코스

4코스

UNIT 16 가정법

◎ GRAMMAR POINT

① 가정법의 개념

가정법이란 '내가 학생이 아니라면 그 직업에 지원을 할 텐데'(=If I were not a student, I would apply for the position.)에서와 같이 어떠한 특정 사실에 대한 반대를 가정할 때 사용한다. 즉, 현재 내가 학생이어서 어떤 직업에 지원을 못하고 있을 때 이렇게 가정을 할 수 있다. 가정법은 주로 if절과 주절이 함께 쓰이며 독특한 시제를 사용한다. 가정법은 미래의 일어날 확률이 낮은 일에 대한 가정을 하는 가정법 미래와 현재의 사실을 반대로 가정하는 가정법 과거, 과거의 사실을 반대로 가정하는 가정법 과거완료로 나뉜다.

② 가정법의 형태

(1) 가정법 미래: 미래의 사실을 가정할 때

> If + 주어 + should + 동사원형 ~, 주어 will/can/may + 동사원형
> If + 주어 + should + 동사원형 ~, 명령문

If it **should rain** tomorrow, **please call** me. 내일 비가 오면 나에게 전화해.

(2) 가정법 현재: 현재나 미래에 대한 막연한 가정

> If + 주어 + 현재 동사 ~, 주어 will/can/may + 동사원형
> If + 주어 + 현재 동사 ~, 명령문

If you **love** me, I **can do** everything for you.
당신이 나를 사랑하다면 나는 당신을 위해 무엇이든지 할 수 있다.

If you **meet** Jenny tomorrow, **please give** her this book.
내일 Jenny을 만나면 이 책을 그녀에게 주세요.

(3) 가정법 과거: 현재의 일을 가정할 때 사용

> If + 주어 + 과거 동사 (were) ~, 주어 + would/could/might + 동사원형

If I **were** you, I **would call** him now. 내가 너라면 그에게 지금 전화하겠다.
If I **were** a bird, I **could fly** in the sky. 내가 새라면 하늘을 날 수 있을 텐데.
If we **had** a calculator, we **could work** a lot quicker.
우리가 계산기가 있다면, 일을 훨씬 더 빨리 할 수 있을 텐데.

(4) 가정법 과거 완료: 과거의 일을 가정할 때 사용

> If + 주어 + had + p.p. ~, 주어 + would/could/might/should + have + p.p.

If I **had had** your phone number, I **could have called** you last night.
나에게 네 전화번호가 있었더라면, 어젯밤에 네게 전화를 했을 텐데.

If we **had taken** your advice, we **would have saved** a lot of time.
우리가 너의 충고를 받아들였었다면, 시간을 많이 절약할 수 있었을 텐데.

GRAMMAR PRACTICE

A 괄호 안에서 알맞은 것을 고르세요.

1. If you (should find, found) any problem with our product, please call our customer service representative immediately.
2. If you (will finish, finish) the report, please let me know.
3. If Ms. Curry (were, had been) there, she could have helped you.
4. We (could see, must see) you more often if we lived near your house.
5. If you (should change, changed) your mind, just call us to discuss other options.
6. If he (made, makes) a mistake, Tony will try to conceal it.
7. If I (am, were) a graduate student, I could apply for the position.
8. If I won the lottery, I (will quit, would quit) my job first.
9. If it should snow tomorrow, I (canceled, will cancel) my trip.
10. If you (should have, had) any further questions regarding your purchase, please contact a service representative

B 보기 중 알맞은 것을 고르세요.

1. If Mr. Smith had taken the plane instead of a train, he ---------- at the meeting on time.
   (A) could arrive
   (B) could have arrived
   (C) could have been arrived
   (D) had arrived
2. If various types of public transportation were available, people ---------- their cars much less frequently.
   (A) use
   (B) used
   (C) could use
   (D) are using
3. If the computer malfunction had not been reported quickly, we ---------- the technical support we needed this morning.
   (A) will not receive
   (B) cannot receive
   (C) would not have received
   (D) had received
4. If the work ---------- with the building codes, it will have to be removed or rebuilt.
   (A) complies
   (B) does not comply
   (C) complied
   (D) didn't comply
5. ---------- the company moves to California, it can easily find highly motivated, qualified and experienced workers ready to work for it.
   (A) So
   (B) Wherever
   (C) Whom
   (D) If

VOCA representative 담당직원 conceal 숨기다 be likely ~할 것 같은 frequently 자주 malfunction 기능장애 code 규정 highly 상당히, 매우 motivated 의욕이 있는 qualified 자격이 있는

GRAMMAR POINT

(5) 혼합 가정법

이미 발생한 과거의 일이 현재에 영향을 미칠 때 쓰는 표현이다. 종속절은 가정법 과거 완료를, 주절은 가정법 과거의 형식을 따른다. 주절에 now, today 등의 부사가 오는 것이 특징이다.

> If + 주어 + had + p.p. ~, 주어 + would/could/might/should + 동사원형

If I **had saved** money, I **would be** rich now. 돈을 절약했더라면 나는 지금 부자일 텐데.

③ If 대용어구

without, unless, as long as, if 외에도 조건이나 단서를 달아 가정할 때 쓸 수 있는 표현들이 있다. 이러한 if 대용어구를 알아보도록 한다.

(1) Without = But for = Except for = Barring = If not for: ~이 없다면/~이 없었다면

without, but for, except for, barring 등은 if it were not for(가정법 과거: ~이 없다면) 및 if it had not been for(가정법 과거 완료: ~이 없었다면)의 의미이다. if절을 한층 간략하게 나타낼 수 있는 대용어구이다.

① 가정법 과거: ~이 없다면

If it were not for water, nothing could live. 물이 없으면 아무것도 살 수 없다.
= **Were it not for** water, nothing could live. (도치구문)
= **If not for** water, nothing could live.
= **But for** water, nothing could live.
= **Except for** water, nothing could live.
= **Barring** water, nothing could live.
= **Without** water, nothing could live.

② 가정법 과거 완료: ~이 없었다면

If it had not been for your help, I couldn't have done it.
너의 도움이 없었더라면 나는 그 일을 할 수 없었을 텐데.
= **Had it not been for** your help, I couldn't have done it. (도치구문)
= **If not for** your help, I couldn't have done it.
= **But for** your help, I couldn't have done it.
= **Except for** your help, I couldn't have done it.
= **Barring** your help, I couldn't have done it.
= **Without** your help, I couldn't have done it.

(2) Unless = If ~ not: ~하지 않는다면

We will go on a picnic **if** it **doesn't** rain tomorrow. 내일 비가 오지 않으면 우리는 소풍 갈 것이다.
= We will go on a picnic **unless** it rains tomorrow.

GRAMMAR PRACTICE

A 다음 문장의 의미가 같도록 빈칸을 넣으세요.

1. **If it were not for** water, nothing could live. 물이 없으면 아무것도 살 수 없다.

    = _____ _____ _____ _____ water, nothing could live.

    = _____ _____ _____ water, nothing could live.

    = _____ _____ water, nothing could live.

    = _____ _____ water, nothing could live.

    = _____ water, nothing could live.

    = _____ water, nothing could live.

2. **If it had not been for** your help, I couldn't have finished the project.

    = _____ _____ _____ _____ _____ _____ your help, I couldn't have finished the project.

    = _____ _____ _____ your help, I couldn't have finished the project.

    = _____ _____ your help, I couldn't have finished the project.

    = _____ _____ your help, I couldn't have finished the project.

    = _____ your help, I couldn't have finished the project.

    = _____ your help, I couldn't have finished the project.

3. Let me tell her **if** you **don't** have to tell her yourself.

    = Let me tell her _____ you have to tell her yourself.

B 괄호 안에서 알맞은 것을 고르세요.

1. If you had taken my advice, you (could have made, could make) a lot of money now.

2. (Without, With) air, all living things would die.

3. (Provides, Providing) that you were here now, I would be happy.

4. (Barring, But) your help, I couldn't have finished the report.

5. If I had won the lottery, I (could be, could have been) rich now.

◎ GRAMMAR POINT

(3) Provided = Providing = Supposing ~라면

Provided (that) all your work is done, you may go home. 일이 다 끝나면 당신은 집에 가도 좋다.

(4) as if = as though 마치 ~인 것처럼

Dan always talks **as if** he were a genius. Dan은 그가 마치 천재인 것처럼 말한다.
John acted **as though** he had been a king. John은 마치 그가 왕인 것처럼 행동했다.

(5) I wish 가정법

① I wish 가정법 과거 = I wish 주어 과거동사 ~라면 좋을텐데

I wish that John **agreed**.
= I'm sorry that John doesn't agree.
John이 동의하면 좋았을 텐데.

② I wish 가정법 과거 = I wish 주어 has p.p. ~라면 좋았을텐데

I wish I had attended the meeting.
= I'm sorry that I didn't attend the meeting.

(6) It's time 가정법 : It's time 주어 과거동사 ~해야 할 때이다

It's time you went to bed. It's almost 1:00 a.m now. 자러 가야 할 시간이다. 지금 거의 새벽 1시다.

(7) in case (that) ~한 경우에 대비해서

in case S+V는 주절이 in case S+V보다 시간상으로 선행한다는 점에서 if와 다르므로 서로 바꾸어 사용할 수 없고 가정의 의미는 가지고 있다.

Get the figures printed out **in case** the system crashes.
시스템이 다운될 수도 있으니 수치를 출력해 두어라.

(8) 그 밖의 if 대용어구

As long as ~하는 한	On the condition (that) ~라면
In the event (that) ~한 경우에 대비해	Considering~ ~을 고려하면, ~라는 점을 감안하면
Given~ ~을 고려하면, ~라는 점을 감안하면	

As long as you love me, I can do everything for you.
나를 사랑해 주는 한 나는 당신을 위해 모든 것을 할 수 있다.

GRAMMAR PRACTICE

A 주어진 문장과 의미가 통하도록 빈칸에 알맞은 가정법 문장을 쓰세요.

1. I am sorry that I don't have my own car.

    = I wish _____.

2. I am sorry that I didn't study harder for the test.

    = I wish _____.

3. In fact, Mr. Lee is not an expert.

    = _____ as if _____.

4. In fact, they don't know each other.

    = _____ as if/though _____.

5. In fact, she didn't live in Hawaii.

    = _____ as though _____.

B 괄호 안에서 알맞은 것을 고르세요.

1. We'll buy everything you manufacture (providing, provide) the price is right.

2. I will pardon him (in case, provided that) he acknowledges his fault.

3. Give me a call (in the case, in case) you need some help.

4. (Suppose, Supposing) it were true, what would happen?

5. (Given, Giving) good weather, the thing can be done.

6. (Consider, Considering) his age, he sees and hears very well.

7. (Providing that, Suppose that) all your work is done, you may go home.

8. (In case, As long as) stores don't accept credit cards, tourists should bring cash or traveler's checks.

9. (Provided, Unless) you finish your homework on time, I will give you some gifts.

10. It is expected that sales will increase dramatically (in case, provided that) the store advertises on the Internet.

GRAMMAR IN SENTENCE

▶ 의미 단위로 문장을 끊어 읽고, 해석하세요.
단, 경우에 따라 명사구 또는 명사절은 { }, 형용사구 또는 형용사절은 [ ], 부사구 부사절은 ( )로 표시하세요.

1. If Mr. Smith had taken the plane instead of a train, he could have arrived at the meeting on time.

2. If various types of public transportation were available, people would use their cars much less frequently.

3. If the computer malfunction had not been reported quickly, we would not have received the technical support we needed this morning.

4. If the work does not comply with the building codes, it will have to be removed or rebuilt.

5. If the company moves to California, it can easily find highly motivated, qualified and experienced workers ready to work for it.

6. If you had taken my advice, you could make a lot of money now.

7. Without air, all living things could die.

8. Providing that you were here now, I would be happy.

9. Barring your help, I couldn't have finished the report.

10. If I had won the lottery, I could be rich now.

 **Outro**

가정법

	조건절(if절)	주절	의미
가정법 미래	If + 주어 + should + 동사원형	주어 + will/can/may + 동사원형 ………………… 명령문	미래에 더한 강한 의심이나 일어날 것 같지 않은 일을 가정
가정법 현재	If + 주어 + 현재 동사	주어 + will/can/may + 동사원형	현재나 미래에 대한 막연한 가정
가정법 과거	If + 주어 + 과거 동사	주어 + would/could/might + 동사원형	현재의 사실을 반대로 가정
가정법 과거 완료	If + 주어 + had + p.p.	주어 + would/should/could/might + have + p.p.	과거의 사실을 반대로 가정

UNIT 17 비교

GRAMMAR POINT

① 원급 비교

'~만큼 …한', '…와 같은'처럼 어떤 대상을 다른 동등한 대상과 비교해 말할 때는 형용사나 부사의 원급을 이용할 수 있다.

(1) 원급 비교: as + 원급 + as
원급 비교인 as와 as 사이에는 반드시 형용사나 부사의 원급을 사용한다.

> 2형식 불완전 자동사 + as + **형용사** + as
> 일반 동사 + as + **부사** + as

He **is as smart as** his brother. 그는 그의 형만큼 영리하다.
Matt **worked as quickly as** I expected. Matt는 내가 예상했던 것처럼 빨리 일을 했다.

(2) the same ~ as 구문은 '…와 ~이 똑같다'는 의미이다.
just as ~ as : as ~ as를 강조할 때는 앞에 부사 just를 쓸 수 있다.

Justine is **the same** age **as** Anna. Justine은 Anna와 나이가 같다.
Everyone is **just as** busy **as** you. 사람들은 모두 너만큼 바쁘다.

(3) 배수 비교
twice, three times 등과 같은 표현이 as ~ as 구문과 함께 쓰이면 배수 비교를 나타낸다.

Their house is about **three times** as big as ours. 그들의 집은 우리 집보다 약 3배 크다.
= Their house is **three times** bigger than ours.

② 비교급

형용사의 원뜻에 '좀 더'란 의미를 추가해 어떤 대상이나 상황과 비교할 때 이용되는 것이 바로 비교급이다.

(1) 비교급 만들기
- **1음절 단어:** -er를 붙인다. ▶ higher, easier
- **2음절 이상 단어:** more를 붙인다. ▶ more diligent, more beautiful
* many/much(▶ more)나 good/well(▶ better)의 비교급 같이 불규칙적으로 변하는 경우는 따로 기억해 두어야 한다.

(2) 비교급 ~ than
비교급과 than의 짝을 맞추는 문제가 많이 나온다.

He has **more** money **than** you have. 그는 당신이 가진 것보다 더 많은 돈을 갖고 있다.
This box is **heavier than** the other one. 이 상자는 다른 것보다 무겁다.

(3) 비교급 강조 표현
부사 much, far, even, still, a lot(훨씬 ~한)은 비교급 앞에서 비교급을 수식하여 강조한다.

He has **much more** money **than** you have. 그는 당신이 가진 것보다 훨씬 더 많은 돈을 갖고 있다.

GRAMMAR PRACTICE

A 괄호 안에서 알맞은 것을 고르세요.

1. John is as (diligent, diligently) as Henry.

2. I answered the difficult question as (good, well) as I could.

3. K-Mart has been as (reliable, reliably) as Walmart.

4. The store was as (crowd, crowded) this morning as it usually is.

5. I'm just as (qualified, more qualified) as him.

6. Nobody was (much, more) surprised than us.

7. He is more worried about his health (as, than) I am.

8. The meal was (little, less) expensive than I had expected.

9. This building is (much, more) taller than I had expected.

10. Everest is (higher, the highest) than every other mountain.

B 어법상 틀린 문장은 바르게 고치고, 틀린 부분이 없으면 O로 표시하세요.

1. Clothes are a lot of cheaper than before.

2. The red one is far older than the blue one.

3. This box is more heavier than the other one.

4. The demand among teenagers for the new line of products is greater than last year.

5. For most people, health and happiness are more much important than money.

VOCA   reliable 신뢰할 수 있는, 믿을 수 있는   crowded 혼잡한, 만원인

◎ GRAMMAR POINT

③ 최상급
형용사의 원뜻에 '제일, 가장'이란 의미를 추가해주는 것이 바로 최상급이다.

(1) 최상급 만들기
- **1음절 단어:** the -est를 붙인다. ▶ the largest, the biggest
- **2음절 이상 단어:** the most를 붙인다. ▶ the most intelligent, the most difficult
* many/much(▶ most)나 good/well(▶ best)의 최상급 같이 불규칙적으로 변하는 경우는 따로 기억해 두어야 한다.

(2) 최상급을 알려주는 신호들
최상급은 셋 이상을 비교할 때 쓰이므로 반드시 비교 대상이 셋 이상 있어야 한다. 주로 <in + 단수 명사>, <of + 복수 명사>, <among + 복수 명사> 또는 경험을 나타내는 '관계대명사절'이 함께 쓰인다.

You are **the best** man **in the world.** (최상급 ~ in + 장소)
네가 이 세상에서 최고의 남자다.

(3) 최상급 강조 표현
부사 much(훨씬), by far(훨씬), the very(바로 그), 서수(~번째로) 등이 최상급을 수식하여 강조한다.

Tom is **the second tallest** boy in his class. Tom은 그의 반에서 두 번째로 크다.
　　　　　(두 번째로 키가 제일 큰)

④ 주의해야 하는 특수한 비교급

(1) 비교급 앞에 the가 오는 경우
기본적으로 비교급 앞에는 the를 붙이지 않는 것으로 되어 있지만 예외적으로 the가 붙는 경우가 있으므로 이들은 따로 기억해 두어야 한다.

① **of the two**가 있는 문장에서는 비교급 앞에 the를 쓴다.

Of the two applicants, Justine is **the more qualified** for the job.
두 명의 지원자 중에서, Justine이 그 일에 더 적격이다.

② **the** 비교급 ..., **the** 비교급 ~: …하면 할수록 더욱 ~하다

The more we have, **the more** we want. 우리는 더 많이 가질수록, 더 많이 원한다.

(2) 라틴어 비교급
보통 -ior형으로 끝나는 형용사 뒤에는 than 대신에 to를 쓴다.

inferior to ~보다 열등한	**superior to** ~보다 우수한
junior to ~보다 나이가 아래인	**senior to** ~보다 나이가 위인
prior to ~보다 앞선	**prefer A to B** A를 B보다 선호하다

We should look over the report **prior to** the meeting. 회의 전에 우리는 보고서를 검토해야 한다.

GRAMMAR PRACTICE

A 괄호 안에서 알맞은 것을 고르세요.

1. He is (tallest, the tallest) boy in our class.
2. Bill Gates was (richer, the richest) of all Americans.
3. This is (better, the best) movie that I have ever seen.
4. This is the (single, most) tallest building in Asia.
5. Everest is (the highest, high) mountain in the world.
6. Of the two students, Matt is (taller, the taller).
7. The (warm, warmer) the weather is, the better I feel.
8. The more electricity you use, the (higher, highest) your bill will be.
9. This car is (better, superior) to that one.
10. The more (expensive, expensively) the hotel is, the better the service is.

B 어법상 틀린 문장은 바르게 고치고, 틀린 부분이 없으면 O로 표시하세요.

1. It is most delicious food that I have ever eaten.
2. She is the most smart girl of all the students.
3. Of the two candidates, Beth Lyon is more qualified for the position.
4. This novel of his is inferior to the previous one.
5. Cancelations or amendments must be made no later than 5 days prior than arrival.

VOCA   cancelation 취소   amendment 변경   no later than 늦어도 ~까지   arrival 도착

GRAMMAR IN SENTENCE

▶ 의미 단위로 문장을 끊어 읽고, 해석하세요.
단, 경우에 따라 명사구 또는 명사절은 { }, 형용사구 또는 형용사절은 [ ], 부사구 부사절은 ( )로 표시하세요.

1. Clothes are a lot cheaper than before.

2. The red one is far older than the blue one.

3. This box is much heavier than the other one.

4. The demand among teenagers for the new line of products is greater than last year.

5. For most people, health and happiness are much more important than money.

6. It is the most delicious food that I have ever eaten.

7. She is the smartest girl of all the students.

8. Of the two candidates, Beth Lyon is the more qualified for the position.

9. This novel of his is inferior to the previous one.

10. Cancelations or amendments must be made no later than 5 days prior to arrival.

 **Outro**

비교

비교급의 형태

원급 비교	두 가지를 비교하여, 차이가 없을 때
	as 형용사/ 부사 as
비교급 비교	두 가지를 비교하여, 차이가 있을 때
	형용사/부사 + -(i)er, more(less) + 형용사/부사
최상급 비교	세 가지 이상을 비교하여, 최고의 것을 나타낼 때
	the + 형용사/부사 + -(i)est, the most(least) + 형용사/부사

비교급, 최상급을 이용한 중요 표현

형태	의미	예
비교급 ~ than	~보다 ~하다	A basketball is **bigger than** a baseball. 농구공이 야구공보다 크다.
the 최상급 in 장소 (of 복수명사)	가장 ~한	Mike is **the tallest** boy **in his class**. Mike가 교실에서 가장 크다.
the 비교급, the 비교급	~할수록 더욱 ~하다.	**The sooner, the better.** 빠르면 빠를수록 더 좋다.
Of the two, the 비교급	둘 중에서 ~가장 ~한	**Of the two students**, Mike is **the taller** one. 두 명의 학생중에서 Mike 더 크다.
rather than	~보다	It's is really a matter of style **rather than** content. 그것은 내용 보다는 스타일의 문제이다.
other than	~ 이외에	Many people have middle names **other than** their first and last names. 많은 사람들이 성과 이름 외에 중간 이름을 갖고 있습니다.
no longer	더이상	It turns out that the claim is **no longer** true. 그러나 이것이 더 이상 사실이 아니라는 것이 밝혀졌다.
no later than	늦어도 ~까지	Return to the bus **no later than** 11 o'clock. 11시 전까지 버스로 돌아오세요.
more than	~ 이상	There are **more than** 60,000 pizzerias in the U.S. alone. 미국에만 60,000개 이상의 피자 가게가 있습니다.
less than	~ 이하	In **less than** two weeks, I've gained 4 kg! 그러나 2주도 되지 않아서, 4킬로그램이나 쪘어!

UNIT 18 강조와 도치

GRAMMAR POINT

① 가정법 도치

가정법 구문에서 조건절의 if를 생략하면 주어와 동사의 위치가 바뀌게 된다.

미래(현재)	If + 주어 + **should** + 동사원형 ~, 주어 will/can/may + 동사원형/ 명령문 (도치) → **Should** + 주어 + 동사원형 ~, 주어 will/can/may + 동사원형 / 명령문
과거	If + 주어 + **과거 동사(were)** 보어~, 주어 + would/could/might + 동사원형 (도치) → **Were** + 주어 + 보어~, 주어 + would/could/might + 동사원형
과거 완료	If + 주어 + **had + p.p.** ~, 주어 + would/could/might/should + have + p.p. (도치) → **Had** + 주어 + **p.p.** 주어 + would/could/might/should + have + p.p.
혼합 가정법	If + 주어 + **had + p.p.** ~, 주어 + would/could/might + 동사원형 (도치) → **Had** + 주어 + **p.p**. 주어 + would/could/might + 동사원형

If it should rain tomorrow, please call me. 내일 비가 오면 나에게 전화해.
→ (도치) **Should it rain** tomorrow, please call me.

If I were you, I would call him now. 내가 너라면 지금 그 남자한테 전화하겠어.
→ (도치) **Were I** you, I would call him now.

If I were a bird, I could fly in the sky. 내가 새라면 하늘을 날 수 있을 텐데.
→ (도치) **Were I** a bird, I could fly in the sky.

If we had taken your advice, we would have saved a lot of time.
→ (도치) **Had we taken** your advice, we would have saved a lot of time.
우리가 너의 충고를 받아들였었다면, 시간을 많이 절약할 수 있었을 텐데.

If I had saved money, I **would be** rich now. 돈을 절약했더라면 나는 지금 부자일 텐데.
→ (도치) **Had I saved** money, I would be rich now.

② 유도부사 there 동사 + 주어

'~가 있다' 는 뜻으로 뒤의 명사의 수에 맞추어 be 동사의 수를 정한다.

> **There** + 동사(be동사, remain, exist, live) +**명사**
> 　　　　　　　　단수동사　　단수주어
> 　　　　　　　　복수동사　　복수주어

There are so many **countries** to visit in the world. 세상에는 방문할 나라들이 아주 많다.

GRAMMAR PRACTICE

A 다음을 가정법 도치 문장으로 바꾸세요.

1. If you **should change** your mind, just call us to discuss other options.

   (도치) → _____

2. **If I were** a graduate student, I **could apply** for the position.

   (도치) → _____

3. **If I had won** the lottery, I **would have called** you first.

   (도치) → _____

4. **If** you **had listened** to my advice, you **would** not **be** in danger **now (today)**.

   (도치) → _____

5. **If I had had** your phone number, I could have called you last night.

   (도치) → _____

B is 와 are 중에서 알맞은 것을 넣으세요.

1. There _____ a tree in the garden.
2. There _____ many people on the street.
3. There _____ some heavy equipment in the area.
4. There _____ many books on the table.
5. There _____ some information which will become public.

C 괄호 안에서 알맞은 것을 고르세요.

1. (Should, Will) anybody call me, tell that person my cell phone number.
2. (Have, Had) Mr. Simpson been more careful, he wouldn't have fallen down on the street.
3. I (could buy, could have bought) you anything that you want were I a billionaire.
4. I will never forgive you (should, could) you do it again.
5. (Have, Had) I had no work to do, I could have gone to see you at the party.

VOCA cell phone 핸드폰   fall down 쓰러지다, 넘어지다   billionaire 억만장자

GRAMMAR POINT

③ So / Neither 동사 주어

상대방의 의견에 동의하는 표현인 So do I, Neither do I 등은 동사 주어의 어순으로 도치해서 사용한다.

A : I like apples. 나는 사과를 좋아해.
B : So do I. 나도 좋아해.

A : I can't swim. 나는 수영을 못해.
B : Neither can I. 나도 못해.

④ 강조를 위한 도치

① 부정어 도치

부정어구 도치는 부정어(not, never, no, no sooner, no long, not only, no more, no + 비교) 혹은 준 부정어(little, few, hardly, rarely, barely, scarcely, seldom) 문두에 위치하면 도치가 된다.

He had **no sooner** received the letter **than** he turned pale.
   scarcely   **when**
   hardly   **before**

= **No sooner** had he received the letter **than** he turned pale.
 Scarcely   **when**
 Hardly   **before**

그는 편지를 받자마자 얼굴이 창백해졌다.

② 보어의 도치

The church is on the hill. → On the hill is the church. 언덕 위에 교회가 있다.

③ 부사의 도치

The snow came down. → Down came the snow. 눈이 내렸다.

⑤ It ~that 강조 구문

I met the woman at the restaurant yesterday.
→ It was **I** that met the woman at the restaurant yesterday. (I 강조)
→ It was **the woman** that I met at the restaurant yesterday. (the woman) 강조
→ It was **at the restaurant** that I met the woman yesterday. (at the restaurant) 강조
→ It was **yesterday** that I met the woman at the restaurant. (yesterday 강조)

⑥ 동사를 강조하는 do

I do love you. 나는 너를 사랑한다.

GRAMMAR PRACTICE

A 다음 문장을 보기와 같이 동의하는 표현으로 바꾸세요.

> 보기) Jane : I am a student.
> David : So am I
> = Jane is a student, as is David. Jane은 David와 마찬가지로 학생입니다.
>
> Laura : I am not a student.
> Alex : Neither am I
> = Laura is not a student , nor is Alex. Laura는 학생이 아니며 Alex도 아닙니다.

1. Jane : I went to school yesterday.
   David : So did I.

2. Laura : I didn't do my homework last night.
   Alex: Neither did I.

3. Jane : I can swim in the sea.
   David : So can I.

B 다음 문장을 부정어 도치 강조 구문으로 바꾸세요.

1. I have never seen such a beautiful sunset.
   → _____

2. I seldom have time to read books these days.
   → _____

3. Austin had no sooner returned home than it began to rain.
   → _____

C 다음 문장을 It ~ that 강조 구문으로 바꾸세요.

> Albert gave a presentation at the monthly meeting yesterday at 10 am.

1. Albert 강조
   → _____

2. a presentation 강조
   → _____

3. at the monthly meeting 강조
   → _____

GRAMMAR IN SENTENCE

▶ 의미 단위로 문장을 끊어 읽고, 해석하세요.
단, 경우에 따라 명사구 또는 명사절은 { }, 형용사구 또는 형용사절은 [ ], 부사구 부사절은 ( )로 표시하세요.

1. Should anybody call me, tell that person my cell phone number.

2. Had Mr. Simpson been more careful, he wouldn't have fallen down on the street.

3. I could buy you anything that you want were I a billionaire.

4. I will never forgive you should you do it again.

5. Had I had no work to do, I could have gone to see you at the party.

6. Jane was planning to travel to Europe, as was David.

7. Laura won't go on a picnic tomorrow, nor will Alex.

8. Seldom do I have time to read books these days.

9. No sooner had he returned home than it began to rain.

10. Never did I think that one of my friends would be successful as a singer.

강조와 도치

가정법 도치

가정법 구문에서 조건절의 if를 생략하면 주어와 동사의 위치가 바뀌게 된다.

미래 (현재)	If + 주어 + **should** + 동사원형 ~, 주어 will/can/may + 동사원형/ 명령문 (도치) → **Should** + 주어 + 동사원형 ~, 주어 will/can/may + 동사원형 / 명령문
과거	If + 주어 + 과거 동사**(were)** 보어~, 주어 + would/could/might + 동사원형 (도치) → **Were** + 주어 + 보어~, 주어 + would/could/might + 동사원형
과거 완료	If + 주어 + **had + p.p.** ~, 주어 + would/could/might/should + have + p.p. (도치) → **Had** + 주어 + **p.p**. 주어 + would/could/might/should + have + p.p.
혼합 가정법	If + 주어 + **had + p.p.** ~, 주어 + would/could/might + 동사원형 (도치) → **Had** + 주어 + **p.p**. 주어 + would/could/might + 동사원형

ACTUAL TEST 6

A 보기 중 맞는 것을 고르세요.

1 If she ---------- up earlier than usual not to miss the plane, Hillary could have participated in the annual conference in New York.
(A) wake
(B) woke
(C) has waken
(D) had woken

2 Read the operation manual carefully and then call the customer service representative ------- you experience any problems with Philips shaver.
(A) had
(B) will
(C) should
(D) has

3 If the drinking water ------- the standard, this water can be associated with little of this risk and be considered safe.
(A) meet
(B) to meet
(C) had meet
(D) meets

4 I would have picked you up at the airport ------- you notified me of your arrival in Chicago in advance.
(A) had
(B) have
(C) if
(D) provided

5 ------- I known you invited family members and friends for my birthday party, I would have cooked dinner and cleaned my room.
(A) had
(B) have
(C) if
(D) provided

6 -------- had the vice president left the office than his employees started talking about him.
(A) No sooner
(B) As soon as
(C) No longer
(D) No later than

7 As the best salesperson this year, William Rutherford received ------- bonus among the employees in the company.
(A) the higher
(B) the highest
(C) high
(D) highly

8 Under the new rules, pizza will be served with less sodium, and more whole grains and a -------- selection of fruits and vegetables will be available.
(A) widen
(B) widest
(C) widely
(D) wider

9 Ms. Frazier prefers to travel around the world by herself rather -------- with a tour group.
(A) to
(B) as
(C) than
(D) among

10 One of the possible conclusions is that the success of today's insurance companies depends much -------- on the business strategies.
(A) more
(B) many
(C) well
(D) than

B 보기 중 맞는 것을 고르세요.

Questions 11-16 refer to the following news article.

The next time your baby or toddler comes down with a cold, there will be **11** ------- relief available **12** ------- far as medicine goes. The government has warned parents that over-the-counter cough and cold products should not be used to treat children **13** ------- than 2 years of age. Serious and potentially life-threatening side effects such as deaths and rapid heart rates **14** ------- on rare occasions.

The Food and Drug Administration stated that the medicines have not proven to be safe or **15** ------- in children under 2.

Officials are now evaluating the risks of use by kids aged 2 to 11 and should have their decision by spring. Parents are asked to be **16** ------- more careful when choosing cold products for their babies.

11 (A) few
(B) many
(C) various
(D) little

12 (A) as
(B) much
(C) how
(D) very

13 (A) as
(B) more
(C) most
(D) less

14 (A) have reported
(B) have been reported
(C) has been reported
(D) has reported

15 (A) effect
(B) effected
(C) effective
(D) effectively

16 (A) best
(B) lots
(C) much
(D) very

MINI TEST 3

A 보기 중 맞는 것을 고르세요.

1 We give you three options for delivery on most items unless they're either heavy ------- fragile.
(A) both
(B) or
(C) neither
(D) but

2 -------- I had some trouble understanding the immigration official at the airport, my trip to Italy was pleasant.
(A) Despite
(B) In spite of
(C) Although
(D) Even

3 Now, the online system can track sales records far ---------- than a printed list.
(A) more easily
(B) easiest
(C) easy
(D) easier

4 This new device is ---------- as reliable as the current one, so don't worry about the malfunctioning of the system.
(A) much
(B) far
(C) just
(D) a lot

5 The recent survey results indicated that ---------- competition has led to higher ticket prices and reduced choices among airlines during the past 15 years.
(A) least
(B) less
(C) fewer
(D) a few

6 Of these two applicants, Mr. Luke is the ---------- qualified to work on our confidential project.
(A) better
(B) much
(C) too
(D) very

7 Employees --------- would like to contribute to the public charity drive are invited to place their donations in the charity box in Ms. Lee's office.
(A) if
(B) that
(C) whom
(D) whose

8 The new bathroom fixtures will be installed next Wednesday -------- the old ones are removed this week.
(A) after
(B) although
(C) because
(D) since

9 ------- the weather improves this afternoon, we will have to cancel the workshop and the seminar.
(A) Without
(B) Unless
(C) As a result of
(D) While

10 -------- the artists of the sculptures in the exhibition may be, they certainly have a keen sense of beauty.
(A) Who
(B) Whoever
(C) What
(D) Whatever

B 보기 중 틀린 것을 고르세요.

1 All special (A)[orders] must (B)[be] approved, completed, and (C)[deliver] by a shift member (D)[within] 48 hours of receiving the order.

2 Many tourists recommend stopping (A)[at] beautiful Albert Park, (B)[which] one can get some rest and (C)[enjoy] a picnic (D)[with] family members.

3 The UN's World Health Organization's job (A)[is] (B)[to] make the world a (C)[healthiest] place to live (D)[in].

4 (A)[Nationally], (B)[while] the past two years, (C)[the rate] of increase of the average full-professor salary compared to (D)[that of] the average assistant professor decreased substantially.

5 The factory supervisors believe (A)[there it is] every (B)[indication] (C)[that] products have (D)[been manufactured] at the highest level of quality.

6 (A)[For] his convenience, Mr. Lee decided (B)[to rent] a house (C)[in] the city (D)[rather buying] a house in the country.

7 Ms. Lambert will (A)[receive] an award (B)[for creating] a business plan (C)[considers] original, innovative (D)[and] unique with good ideas for the future of the company.

8 Buyers (A)[who] will stay for a week (B)[may] stay at the hotel outside the city, (C)[except] they (D)[request] accommodations downtown.

9 (A)[In addition to] both (B)[candidates] have the (C)[required] educational backgrounds, Ms. Johnson has (D)[far] more experience.

10 Ms. Brown is going to (A)[study] in the office (B)[until] late at night (C)[due to] she has a test for (D)[promotion] tomorrow.

MINI TEST 3

C 보기 중 맞는 것을 고르세요.

Questions 1-6 refer to the following article.

School has always been **1**. ------- important means of **2**. ------- the wealth of tradition from one generation to the next. This applies today to an even **3**. ------- degree than in former times. **4**. ------- modern development of economic life, the family as bearer of tradition and education **5**. -------. The continuance and health of human society are therefore in a **6**. ------- higher degree dependent on the school than formerly.

1
(A) much
(B) little
(C) most
(D) the most

2
(A) transfer
(B) transfers
(C) transferring
(D) transferred

3
(A) high
(B) higher
(C) highest
(D) highly

4
(A) Through
(B) Without
(C) In
(D) Along

5
(A) have weakened
(B) have been weakened
(C) has weakened
(D) has been weakened

6
(A) still
(B) many
(C) more
(D) further

Questions 7-12 refer to the following e-mail.

To: steve.taylor@email.com

Subject: Board Meeting on February 28

Steve, is there any possibility **7** ------- you could reschedule the regular board meeting? I have just received an invitation to attend a conference in Shanghai during the last week of February. The Shanghai conference is sponsored by the Hong Kong Spindle Corporation. It is our **8** ------- customer in Asia and purchases many of our components for its automated spindle monitoring systems. Managers from other companies **9** ------- may be interested in our products will be attending the conference. It's too good an opportunity **10** -------. Please let me know **11** ------- you can help in this matter.

I am available during the third week of February and the first week in March. If you tell me you can't reschedule, then I'll try to figure out **12** ------- I can do about the meeting.

---

7 (A) who
    (B) that
    (C) which
    (D) what

8 (A) well
    (B) better
    (C) more
    (D) best

9 (A) that
    (B) whom
    (C) which
    (D) whose

10 (A) passed up
    (B) to passing up
    (C) to pass up
    (D) passing up

11 (A) although
    (B) because
    (C) since
    (D) whether

12 (A) which
    (B) that
    (C) what
    (D) who

FINAL TEST

A 보기 중 맞는 것을 고르세요.

1 Access to the Children's Memorial Hospital may be difficult for the next few months because the parking lot ---------.
(A) is renovating
(B) is being renovated
(C) has been renovating
(D) renovated

2 When making a nomination for the service award, please consider organizations --------- programs primarily benefit women and children in need.
(A) which
(B) what
(C) whose
(D) who

3 In addition to holiday specials, customers can purchase ------- they are looking for with ease.
(A) that
(B) what
(C) who
(D) which

4 Carl McGuire is a vice president for New York Telephone, --------- he has worked for 30 years.
(A) which
(B) where
(C) who
(D) that

5 Tommy Electronics, Inc. provides innovative products ------- revolutionize business operations for our customers worldwide.
(A) who
(B) whom
(C) whose
(D) that

6 All the money Mr. Fetzer earns each month in commissions on sales ------- to his account 30 days after the last day of the month.
(A) credited
(B) are credited
(C) is credited
(D) credits

7 After the inspection ---------, all the management of our factory was pleased to get a good result.
(A) had completed
(B) had been completed
(C) will be completed
(D) is completing

8 The new sales plan --------- after receiving the analysis of the customer survey responses.
(A) has been modified
(B) has modified
(C) modified
(D) were modified

9 Please ask your customers to confirm their billing addresses before receiving their -------- by credit card.
(A) paying
(B) payment
(C) payable
(D) paid

10 If the computer malfunction had not been reported quickly, we --------- the technical support we needed today.
(A) will not receive
(B) cannot receive
(C) would not have received
(D) had received

B 보기 중 틀린 것을 고르세요.

1 (A)[After] the new employees (B)[have completed] (C)[them] orientation and training, they will (D)[be assigned to] their respective departments.

2 All (A)[the] money Mr. Robinson (B)[earns] each month in commissions on sales (C)[are credited] (D)[to] his account 45 days after the last day of the month.

3 According (A)[to recent] survey, online (B)[shoppers] buy (C)[from] small and large e-businesses (D)[alike].

4 Joseph's films (A)[have] received (B)[highly] praise for (C)[his] portrayals of multidimensional characters (D)[and] funny, true-to-life human interactions.

5 (A)[Thousands of] high school students (B)[are held] back every year, mainly (C)[so] they need (D)[help with] developing ideas for reading or writing as well as analyzing long essay.

6 The Public Relations Department (A)[has received] a couple of (B)[e-mails which] customers (C)[complain about] the poor customer service (D)[at] our movie theater.

7 (A)[A wide range] of skiing opportunities exist (B)[within] a short (C)[distant] (D)[of] the Hampshire campus.

8 I should inform (A)[to you] that our store policy (B)[prohibits] (C)[refunds] or exchanges (D)[on] sale items.

9 Before (A)[retiring] from NJT today, Benjamin (B)[was] a manager for New Jersey Telephone, (C)[where] he worked (D)[since] 40 years.

10 Mr. Smith will (A)[be reprimanded] for having given (B)[inaccurately] and questionable (C)[information] to overseas buyers (D)[at the] last conference.

FINAL TEST

C 보기 중 맞는 것을 고르세요.

Questions 1-6 refer to the following letter.

April 10th

Family Medical Services
1649 East Lake Avenue
Brookings, NY 84325

To **1**. ------- It May Concern:

Recently, I **2**. ------- another notice for payment from your Billing Department.

I **3**. ------- you a copy of the statement from my credit card company showing the amount of $30 for my blood tests once again. Please note that this charge **4**. ------- on March 15; my balance **5**. ------- on March 30.

Please **6**. ------- to this letter by calling me at (815)-881-5595.

Sincerely,
Ann Lauren
Ann Lauren

1. (A) Who
   (B) Whom
   (C) What
   (D) That

2. (A) am receiving
   (B) will receive
   (C) receive
   (D) have received

3. (A) have been sent
   (B) was being sent
   (C) am sending
   (D) was sent

4. (A) will be made
   (B) was made
   (C) have made
   (D) was making

5. (A) was paid
   (B) paid
   (C) is paying
   (D) has paid

6. (A) respond
   (B) contact
   (C) call
   (D) answer

Questions 7-12 refer to the following notice.

O'Hare International Airport Security Update

Due to increased security **7** ------- at O'Hare International Airport, be aware of the following precautionary measures.

All non-ticketed individuals will **8** ------- from passing the security barriers. All ticketed passengers may be subject to hand searches of all carry-on items. Passengers will be asked for their cooperation; passengers may not approach, touch, or in any way interfere with the security agent **9** ------- the search. If any **10** ------- occurs, agents may be asked to escort passengers to a security office.

There may be pat-down and sensor-wanding by same-gender security agents if there is a need as **11** ------- by metal detector sensors.

For a complete **12** ------- of passenger regulations and rights, please visit us online at www.bghairport.com or contact your local airline branch or travel agency.

---

7 (A) standard
(B) standards
(C) standardize
(D) standardized

8 (A) bar
(B) have barred
(C) be barring
(D) be barred

9 (A) throughout
(B) during
(C) along
(D) with

10 (A) interfere
(B) interfered
(C) interference
(D) interfering

11 (A) display
(B) displaying
(C) displayed
(D) displays

12 (A) list
(B) lists
(C) listing
(D) listed

잉글리쉬앤 그래머 MASTER

정답 및 해설

3코스
2코스
1코스

실전편

UNIT 01 : 명사

GRAMMAR PRACTICE p.13

A
1. manager
2. property
3. advance
4. president
5. construction
6. decision
7. appreciation
8. promotion
9. valuables
10. resignation

B
1. In spite of his **denial** that he robbed the bank, the man was found guilty.
2. O
3. Company officials have taken steps to obtain **approval** from the U.S. Food and Drug Administration.
4. Our **specialty** is creating multilevel work arrangements by widening floor spaces.
5. It is a matter of regret that the long continued **negotiation** have finally proved a failure.

GRAMMAR PRACTICE p.15

A
1. baggage
2. great news
3. goods
4. discounts
5. Advertising
6. access
7. information
8. furniture
9. sources
10. a refund

B
1. Jane should ask our parents and teachers for good **advice**.
2. Starting next month, you will receive **a monthly issue** of New Scientist journal.
3. The woman is looking for a restaurant with outdoor **seating**.
4. O
5. The **luggage** had never been used before and was in perfect condition.

GRAMMAR PRACTICE p.17

A
1. the same
2. the best
3. the report
4. an effort
5. the end

B
1. 2
2. 3
3. 1
4. 4
5. 5

C
1. 2
2. 1
3. 4
4. 3
5. 5

GRAMMAR PRACTICE p.19

A
1. products
2. delivery
3. productivity
4. production
5. information
6. account
7. application
8. safety
9. products
10. productivity

B
1. The visitors are in the underground **parking** lot.
2. O
3. Our goal is to provide customer **satisfaction** and to ensure that customers return over and over again.
4. The **Accounting** Department has paid all of the monthly invoices.
5. O

GRAMMAR IN SENTENCE p.20

1. These results / suggest {that dogs / have / the capacity [to empathize / with humans]}.
   ▶ 이러한 결과들은 / 나타내는 것이다 {개들이 / 가지고 있다 / 능력을 / [공감할 수 있는] / 인간과}
   해석 이러한 결과들은 개들이 인간과 공감할 수 있는 능력을 지녔다는 사실을 나타내는 것이다.

2. Our specialty / is creating / multi-level work arrangements (by widening / floor space).
   ▶ 우리의 전문 분야는 / 것이다 / 만드는 / 다단계 작업 배치를 / (넓힘으로써 / 바닥 공간을)
   해석 우리의 전문 분야는 바닥 공간을 넓혀 다단계 작업 배치를 만드는 것이다.

3. Anybody [who visits / our company] / should contact / the information desk (for identification).
   ▶ 누구나 다 [방문하는 / 저희 회사를] / 연락을 해야만 한다. / 안내 데스크에 / (신원 확인을 위해)
   해석 저희 회사를 방문하는 모든 분들은 신원 확인을 위해 안내 데스크에 연락하여야 합니다.

4. The company / increases / incentives (in an effort [to encourage / employees]).
   ▶ 회사는 / 증가시킨다. 장려금을 (노력의 일환으로 [격려하는 / 직원들을])
   해석 회사는 직원들을 격려하는 노력의 일환으로 장려금을 증가시킨다.

5. You / should finish / the report (by the end of this month).
   ▶ 당신은 / 끝내야만 한다. / 보고서를 / (이번 달 말까지)
   해석 당신은 이번 달 말까지 보고서를 끝내야만 한다.

6. Please send / copies of academic transcripts / or certificates and a letter of reference (along with a complete application form).
▶ 발송하세요. / 성적표 사본 / 또는 수료증 사본과 추천서를 (완전한 지원서와 함께)
해석 완전한 지원서와 함께 성적표 사본 또는 수료증 사본과 추천서를 발송하세요.

7. The bank branch / will open / (once inspectors / have verified {that we have complied with all safety regulations}).
▶ 은행 지점은 / 문을 열 것이다 / (일단 감사원이 확인하면 / {우리가 준수했는지를 모든 보안 규정을})
해석 우리가 모든 보안 규정을 준수했는지 감사원이 확인하고 난 뒤에야, 은행 지점은 문을 열 것이다.

8. They / have reformed / their business regulations (to promote foreign investment).
▶ 그들은 / 개정했다 / 그들의 사업 규정을 (장려하기 위해 / 해외 투자를)
해석 그들은 해외 투자를 장려하기 위해 사업 규정을 개정했다.

9. Our goal / is / {to complete customer satisfaction / and / to ensure / that they / return (over and over again)}.
▶ 우리의 목표는 / 것이다 / {완전한 고객 만족이고 / 고객들이 다시 오도록 하는 / (몇 번이고)}
해석 우리의 목표는 완전한 고객 만족이고 고객들이 몇 번이고 다시 오실 수 있도록 하는 것입니다.

10. The emphasis / of this annual contest / is / a part of the government's promotion strategy.
▶ 주목할 점은 / 이 연례 경연에 / 것이다 / 정부의 홍보 전략의 일부라는
해석 이 연례 경연에 주목할 점은 정부의 홍보 전략의 일부라는 것이다.

UNIT 02 : 대명사

GRAMMAR PRACTICE p.23

A
1. she 2. our 3. him 4. Her 5. mine

B
1. his 2. your 3. her 4. his 5. itself

C
1. Hello, Ms. Choi. When **we** last talked in February, you were waiting to hear back about a job you had applied for.
2. O
3. Our trainer, Mr. Lee, will be transferring to **our** new Singapore office in August, and I think you would be the perfect person to replace him.
4. Please give **me** an e-mail or a give me a call to let me know if you're available.
5. O

GRAMMAR PRACTICE p.25

A
1. itself 2. anything 3. himself
4. myself 5. itself

B
1. that 2. Those 3. those
4. those 5. Those

C
1. We are finally going to post pictures of all our employees participating in the past year's various company events on **our** company web-site.
2. If you have pictures of **yourself** and fellow staff members at an outside activity, please forward them to me.
3. Otherwise, I will hire a professional photographer and have **him** come around in the next few weeks.

GRAMMAR PRACTICE p.27

A
1. little 2. Some 3. are
4. are 5. Any 6. most
7. possess 8. A few 9. documents
10. designs

B
1. some 2. any 3. any
4. any, some 5. some

GRAMMAR PRACTICE p.29

A
1. One, another 2. One, the other
3. One, Another, The other 4. the other
5. another

B
1. others 2. the others 3. other
4. others 5. other

C
1. each other 2. each other 3. one another
4. one another 5. each other

GRAMMAR IN SENTENCE p.30

1. (When we / (last) talked / in February), you / were waiting / (to hear back about a job [you had applied for]).
 ▶ (우리가 / (마지막으로) 얘기 했을 때 / 2월에), / 당신이 / 기다리고 있었죠. / (소식을 듣기 위해 / 일자리에 관한 / [당신이 지원했던])
 해석 우리가 마지막으로 2월에 얘기 했을 때, 당신이 지원했던 일자리에 관한 소식을 듣기 위해 기다리고 있었죠.

2. (If you didn't take that job), I thought / you might like to know / {that we are in need of a trainer / here.}
 ▶ (만약 그 일자리를 잡지 않았다면), 저는 생각합니다. / 당신이 알고 싶어 할 거라고 / {우리가 트레이너를 필요로 하고 있다는 소식을 / 이곳에서}
 해석 만약 그 일자리를 잡지 않았다면, 우리가 이곳에서 트레이너를 필요로 하고 있다는 소식을 알고 싶어 할 거라 생각합니다.

3. Our trainer, Mr. Lee, / will be transferring to our new Singapore office in August, and I think you / would be / the perfect person [to replace him].
 ▶ 우리 트레이너인 이 씨는 / 전근을 가게 됩니다. / 새로 생긴 싱가포르 사무소로 / 8월에. 그래서 저는 생각합니다. 당신이 / 가장 적합한 사람이란 / [그를 대신할]
 해석 우리 트레이너인 이 씨는 8월에 새로 생긴 싱가포르 사무소로 전근을 가게 됩니다. 그래서 저는 당신이 그를 대신할 가장 적합한 사람이란 생각이 듭니다.

4. Those [who are responsible for the conference] will arrive here at 10 o'clock.
 ▶ 사람들은 [이 컨퍼런스에 책임이 있는] / 도착할 것이다 / 10시까지 / 이곳에.
 해석 이 컨퍼런스에 책임이 있는 사람은 이곳에 10시까지 도착할 것이다.

5. The board / has shown / little of the interest (in funding / for facility expansion).
 ▶ 이사회는 / 보였다 / 거의 관심이 없는 (자금 지원에 / 시설 확장에 대한)
 해석 이사회는 시설 확장에 대한 자금 지원에 관심을 거의 보이지 않았다.

6. Any information [that RBC receives through its web site] / will be deemed / to be non-confidential.
 ▶ 정보는 무엇이라도 [RBC가 / 입수하는 / 그들의 웹사이트를 통해] / 간주 될 것이다 / 기밀사항으로.
 해석 그들의 웹사이트를 통해 RBC가 입수하는 정보는 무엇이라도 기밀사항으로 간주될 것이다.

7. Our company / did / all of the architectural designs (for this restaurant).
 ▶ 우리 회사가 / 했다 / 모든 건축 디자인을 / (이 레스토랑을 위해서)
 해석 우리 회사가 이 레스토랑을 위해서 모든 건축 디자인을 했다.

8. Some people / say American beef is safe, but others / say it / could cause / some disease.
 ▶ 몇몇 사람들은 / 말한다. / 미국산 소고기가 안전하다고 하지만 다른 사람들은 / 말한다. 그것이 / 야기 시킬 수 있다고 / 어떤 질병을
 해석 몇몇 사람들은 미국산 소고기가 안전하다고 말하지만, 다른 사람들은 그것이 어떤 질병을 야기 시킬 수 있다고 한다.

9. We / have / 12 students in class. Five / are from Japan, and the others / are from Korea.
 ▶ 우리 / 있다 / 12명의 학생들이 / 학급에. 5명은 / 일본인이고 나머지는 / 한국인이다.
 해석 우리 학급에는 12명의 학생들이 있다. 5명은 일본인이고 나머지 모두는 한국인이다.

10. (Thanks to my special experience / in Tokyo), I / understand / Japanese and their working style / better than others.
 ▶ (나의 특별한 경험 덕분에 / 도쿄에서) 나는 / 이해한다. 일본인들과 그들의 업무 스타일을 / 다른 사람들보다
 해석 도쿄에서의 나의 특별한 경험 덕분에 다른 사람들보다 더 잘 일본인들을 이해하고 그들의 업무 스타일을 파악할 수 있습니다.

UNIT 03 : 동사

GRAMMAR PRACTICE p.33

A
1. respond to
2. speak
3. strange
4. possible
5. worth
6. capable
7. available
8. perfect
9. happened to
10. agreed with

B
1. (C) 2. (A) 3. (C) 4. (D) 5. (B)

GRAMMAR PRACTICE p.35

A
1. access
2. provides
3. with
4. deal
5. resembles
6. disclose
7. contact
8. approached
9. gave
10. from

B
1. adequate compensation to farmers.
2. our patients with the best service.
3. us all mail coming to the new address.

C
1. (D) 2. (D)

GRAMMAR PRACTICE p.37

A
1. sleep
2. throw
3. repaired
4. delivered
5. to deliver
6. advised
7. helped
8. cross
9. require
10. carry

B

1. Mr. Jackson is a music teacher, and likes to hear the students **sing** happily.
2. He made the students **bring** their instruments yesterday.
3. O
4. O
5. Therefore, the teacher encouraged the students **to practice** after school.

GRAMMAR PRACTICE p.39

A

1. discontinue 2. run 3. show
4. press 5. affect 6. go
7. go 8. use 9. admire
10. be able to

B

1. Parents should take care of their children.
   = Parents <u>ought to</u> take care of their children.

2. Albert can't help falling in love with Anna.
   = Albert <u>cannot but</u> fall in love with Anna.

C

1. (C) 2. (D) 3. (D)

GRAMMAR IN SENTENCE p.40

1. Experts / predict {that the unemployment rate / will fall / next year}.
▶ 전문가들은 / 예상하고 있다 / {실업률은 / 하락할 것으로 / 내년에}
해석 전문가들은 내년의 실업률은 하락할 것으로 예상하고 있다.

2. Some of the participants / (actually) become very famous / and even make appearances (on TV shows).
▶ 그 참석자들 중 몇몇은 / (실제로) 유명해져서 / 출연하기도 합니다(TV 쇼에)
해석 그 참석자들 중 몇몇은 실제로 유명해져서 TV쇼에 출연하기도 합니다.

3. The secretary (at the law firm) / answers telephones / and schedules clients' appointments.
▶ 비서는 (법률 사무소에) / 전화를 받고 / 고객의 약속을 잡는다.
해석 법률 사무소의 비서는 전화를 받고 고객의 약속을 잡는다.

4. Interest rates / were expected to remain high (for the remainder of the year).
▶ 금리가 / 예상했다 / 상승세를 유지할 것으로 (올해 나머지 기간 동안에는)
해석 금리가 올해 나머지 기간 동안에는 상승세를 유지할 것으로 예상했다.

5. The American diplomat / will arrive (in Seoul next week) / (to hold talks with the President).
▶ 미국 외교관은 / 도착할 것이다 (서울에 다음주) / (대통령과 회담을 열기 위해)
해석 미국 외교관은 다음 주에 대통령과 회담을 열기 위해 서울에 도착할 것이다.

6. The Wendy's restaurant / will offer / customers / special discounts (next month) / (if they make a reservation online)
▶ Wendy's 레스토랑은 / 제공한다. / 고객들에게 / 특별 할인을 (다음 달에) / 온라인으로 예약할 경우
해석 Wendy's 레스토랑은 다음 달에 고객들이 온라인으로 예약할 경우 특별 할인을 제공한다.

7. (To prepare them for the test), the College Board / will provide / students with free test preparation materials online.
▶ (시험을 준비할 수 있도록 하기 위하여), 칼리지보드는 / 제공한다. / 학생들에게 / 무료 시험 준비 자료를 온라인에
해석 칼리지보드는 학생들이 시험을 준비할 수 있도록, 무료 시험 준비 자료를 온라인에 제공한다.

8. Please, complete / the application form (in as much detail as possible) and return it (to the address shown above).
▶ 작성하라 / 지원서를 (가능한 상세히) 그리고 다시 보내라 그것을 (위의 주소로)
해석 지원서를 가능한 상세히 작성하셔서 위의 주소로 다시 보내 주세요.

9. Next week, / Mike will forward his e-mail to a professor of the Chemistry department / to get related information / directly.
▶ 다음 주에 / Mike는 / 전달할 것이다 / 그의 이메일을 / 화학과 교수님께 / 관련 정보를 얻기 위하여 / 직접
해석 직접 관련 정보를 얻기 위하여 다음 주에 Mike는 그의 이메일을 화학과 교수님께 전달할 것이다.

10. This warranty / does not cover / any damage incurred due to alternations, modifications, accidents, or damage resulting from excess power.
▶ 이 보증서는 / 보상하지 않는다. / 어떤 손상 [때문에 생기는 교체, 변경, 사고 혹은 과전압으로 생긴 피해]
해석 이 보증서는 교체, 변경, 사고로 인한 피해 혹은 과전압으로 생긴 피해는 보상하지 않는다.

ACTUAL TEST ❶ p.42

A

1. (D) 2. (C) 3. (D) 4. (B) 5. (C) 6. (B)
7. (C) 8. (C) 9. (A) 10. (D)

B

11. (D) 12. (A) 13. (B) 14. (C) 15. (B) 16. (D)

A

1. The Executives kept on arguing about the difficult problem for many hours, and then they finally made a -------.
   (A) decide
   (B) decisions
   (C) decisive
   (D) decision

   해석 임원들은 어려운 문제에 대해 여러 시간 동안 토론하고 나서 마침내 결론을 내렸다.
   해설 부정관사 a 다음에는 가산명사의 단수가 와야 한다. 그러므로 정답은 (D) decision이다.
   어휘 **decide** 결정하다, 결론을 내리다 **decisive** 결정적인, 결정하는

2. This scientific journal will provide a very persuasive ------- to all the readers interested in the field.
   (A) argue
   (B) arguing
   (C) argument
   (D) argumental

   해석 이 과학 잡지는 그 분야에 관심이 있는 모든 독자들에게 매우 설득력 있는 논리를 제공할 것이다.
   해설 a very persuasive argument는 <관사+부사+형용사+명사>의 형태이다. 동명사는 명사와 동사 역할을 동시에 할 때만 쓰므로, 명사 자리에는 원래의 명사만을 넣어야 한다.
   어휘 **scientific** 과학의 **journal** 잡지, 정기간행물 **persuasive** 설득력 있는 **argumental** 논쟁상의

3. The device will come on the market within the next year as an ------- to existing computer systems.
   (A) attachments
   (B) attach
   (C) attaching
   (D) attachment

   해석 이 장치는 기존의 컴퓨터 시스템에 부착되어 내년 중 시판될 것입니다.
   해설 부정관사 an 다음에는 명사가 와야 한다.
   어휘 **device** 장비, 장치 **attachment** 애착, 부착, 첨부물

4. Our ------- at World Architects is designing and building homes to your exact specifications, tastes, and needs.
   (A) special
   (B) specialty
   (C) specialize
   (D) especially

   해석 World Architects에서 저희의 전공 분야는 당신의 정확한 요구사항과 취향 그리고 필요에 따라 집을 디자인하고 건축합니다.
   해설 빈칸은 our의 수식을 받으면서 문장에서 주어자리이다. 선택지 중 명사 형태는 B밖에 없다. 문장의 끝에 and를 중심으로 같은 형태의 단어들이 연결된 specifications, tastes, and needs에 주목한다.
   어휘 **specialty** 전문 **specification** 상세 내역서 **taste** 취향, 입맛 **specialize** ~을 전문으로 다루다

5. Although she is having hard time working on the project, Stacy can also feel a sense of accomplishment once she finishes -------.
   (A) she
   (B) her
   (C) hers
   (D) herself

   해석 Stacy는 프로젝트를 수행하느라 어려움을 겪고 있지만, 일단 끝내면 성취감도 맛볼 수 있을 것이다.
   해설 타동사 finish의 목적어 자리에 올 수 있는 것은 목적격 her, 재귀대명사 herself 또는 소유대명사 hers이다. 빈칸에는 her project에 대한 소유대명사로 그녀의 것을 끝낸다는 의미가 적합하므로 정답은 (C)이다.
   어휘 **have hard time ~ing** ~하느라 어려움을 겪다 **a sense of accomplishment** 성취감 **once** 일단 ~하면(접속사)

6. People who took the exam are not permitted sell exam information of any sort, nor should they share their answers with -------.
   (A) other
   (B) others
   (C) some
   (D) any

   해석 시험을 친 사람들은 어떤 형태로든 시험 정보를 팔아서는 안 되며, 다른 사람들과 정답을 공유해서도 안 된다.
   해설 불특정한 다른 사람들을 나타낼 때는 others가 적합하다.

7. To prepare for the annual report, Ashley Newhall is gathering design materials by -------.
   (A) she
   (B) her
   (C) herself
   (D) hers

   해석 연간 보고서를 준비하기 위하여 Ashley Newhall 씨는 혼자서 디자인 자료들을 모으고 있다.
   해설 '혼자서'라는 의미의 재귀대명사의 관용적 용법은 by oneself이다. 그러므로 herself가 적합하다.
   어휘 **annual** 매년의, 연례의

8. Either the city council or the city administration will have to declare ------- support for the proposed park.
   (A) it
   (B) it's
   (C) its
   (D) itself

   해석 시 의회 또는 시 행정당국은 공원 건의안을 지원하기로 공표해야 할 것이다.
   해설 빈칸에는 either ~ Administration을 받는 소유형용사가 와야 하는데 either A or B가 'A나 혹은 B'라는 의미이고 각각 단수명사를 연결했으므로 its 가 필요하다. it's는 it has나 it is의 줄임말로 쓰인다.
   어휘 **council** 의회 **administration** 행정부 **declare** 선언하다, 발표하다 **proposed** 제안된, 건의된

9. Some of the participants actually ------- very famous and even make appearances on TV shows.

(A) become
(B) allow
(C) require
(D) take

해석 그 참석자들 중 몇몇은 실제로 유명해지거나 TV쇼에 출연하기도 합니다.

해설 빈칸 뒤에는 famous 를 보어로 취하는 불완전 자동사 자리이다. 그러므로 정답은 become이다.

어휘 **participant** 참석자 **appearance** 출연, 나타남

10. To prepare them for the test, the college board will ------- students with free test preparation materials online, starting in spring 2025.

(A) give
(B) send
(C) offer
(D) provide

해석 칼리지보드는 학생들이 시험을 준비할 수 있도록, 2025년 봄부터 연습 문제 동영상 자료를 온라인에 무료로 제공한다.

해설 빈칸 뒤를 살펴보면, students with free test preparation materials는 someone with something 의 구조로 되어 있다. 그러므로 3형식 동사인 provide 가 적합하다. give, send, offer은 4형식 동사이므로 with가 없어야 쓸 수 있다.

B

Questions 11-16 refer to the following email.

Dear Tom Johns,

Hello. my name is Lisa Hudson and I made a **11.** ------- at your bed and breakfast for three nights next week. I **12.** ------- fly to Chicago next week, but unfortunately, my flight was canceled. I still want to stay at **13.** ------- place when I get to Chicago. Could you let **14.** ------- know if there is a room available from the 20th to the 22nd? Also, I still need the pick-up service. My flight will **15.** ------- there at 1 pm next Thursday. I am sorry to cause you trouble. Please **16.** ------- me when you get this email. Thank you.

Tom Johns 씨에게

안녕하세요, 제 이름은 Lisa Hudson이고, 다음주부터 3일 동안 당신 숙박시설에 예약을 했습니다. 다음 주에 비행기로 시카고에 도착을 할 예정이었는데 안타깝게도 제가 타려는 비행기가 취소되었습니다. 내일 시카고에 가면 당신 숙박 시설을 여전히 이용할 생각입니다. 20일부터 22일까지 이용 가능한 방이 있는지 말씀해 주시겠어요? 그리고 공항에서 픽업 서비스가 필요합니다. 제가 타고 가는 비행기가 오후 1시에 그곳에 도착을 합니다. 피해를 드려 죄송합니다. 이 이메일을 받으시면 연락을 주세요. 고맙습니다.

어휘 **bed and breakfast** 아침 식사를 제공하는 숙박 시설, 민박집
be supposed to ~하기로 되어 있는 **unfortunately** 유감스럽게도, 안타깝게도 **pick-up service** 공항에서 특정 장소까지 교통편을 제공하는 서비스 **cause a trouble** 피해를 주다

11.
(A) reserve
(B) reserved
(C) reserving
(D) reservation

해설 부정관사 a 다음에는 셀 수 있는 명사의 단수가 와야 하며, '예약을 하다'라는 의미로 make a reservation 이 적합하다.

12.
(A) was supposed to
(B) was supposing to
(C) supposed to
(D) suppose

해설 '~하기로 되어 있었다'. 라는 의미로 was supposed to 동사원형이 적합하다.

13.
(A) you
(B) your
(C) yours
(D) yourself

해설 at ------- place에서 명사 place를 수식하는 소유격이 필요한 자리이므로 정답은 your이다.

14.
(A) I
(B) my
(C) me
(D) myself

해설 Could you let ------- know에서 let이 사역동사이므로 'let+목적어+동사원형'으로 씁니다. 그러므로 정답은 me이다.

15.
(A) visit
(B) arrive
(C) contact
(D) take

해설 나의 비행기가 오후 1시에 그곳에 도착을 한다는 의미로 자동사인 arrive 가 적합하다.

16.
(A) reply
(B) respond
(C) react
(D) call

해설 빈칸 뒤에 목적어 me 가 있으므로, 나에게 연락을 해 달라고 하는 의미의 타동사 call 이 적합하다.

UNIT 04 : 형용사

GRAMMAR PRACTICE p.47

A
1. serious 2. proper 3. broad
4. complimentary 5. considerable 6. available
7. comparable 8. affected

B
1. O
2. This book will provide very **persuasive** argument.
3. O
4. The **proper** safety precaution was not taken.
5. He is **responsible** for all the legal affairs of the company.

C
1. (A) 2. (B)

GRAMMAR PRACTICE p.49

A
1. deep 2. great 3. safe
4. competitive 5. happy 6. open
7. impractical 8. satisfactory 9. happy
10. full

B
1. (A) 2. (B) 3. (D) 4. (C) 5. (B)

GRAMMAR PRACTICE p.51

A
1. considerate 2. industrious 3. industrial
4. numerous 5. timely 6. considerable
7. confidential 8. Industrial 9. successful
10. economic

B
1. ③ 형용사, Alex는 일간지를 정기구독하고 있다.
    ④ 부사, 이 건물의 에스컬레이터는 하루에 세 번 점검됩니다.
2. ③ 형용사, 나의 상관은 바른 대답을 했다.
    ② 동사, 나의 상관은 잘못을 시정했다
3. ③ 형용사, 각 분기별 수익은 주주들에게 거의 보고되지 않는다.
    ④ 부사, 판매 수익은 분기별로 주주들에게 보고된다.
4. ③ 형용사, 그는 객관적으로 관찰했다.
    ① 명사, Lucas 씨는 자신의 목표를 달성했다.
5. ① 명사, 원작은 미술관에 보관되어 있다.
    ③ 형용사, 그 건설 사업은 원안대로 추진될 것이다.

GRAMMAR PRACTICE p.53

A
1. Most 2. Many 3. A few
4. little 5. All

B
1. many 2. division 3. thousands
4. employees 5. great deal

C
1. Three **hundred** people applied for the position.
2. O
3. About three **thousand** people gathered for the rally.
4. O
5. All of the employees **had** gone home by that time.

GRAMMAR IN SENTENCE p.54

1. Wickham / was not / the only city [affected by the heavy snow].
▶ Wichham만이 / 아니었다. / 유일한 도시가 / [폭우의 영향을 받은]
해석 Wichham만이 폭우의 영향을 받은 유일한 도시가 아니었다.

2. Their reviews / turned out / to be something [helpful (for his writing career)].
▶ 그들의 평론은 / 밝혀졌다 / 무언가 인 것으로 / [도움이 되는 (그의 작가 경력에)]
해석 그들의 평론은 그의 작가 경력에 무언가 도움이 되었다.

3. He / didn't have / any plans / of coming back (in the foreseeable future).
▶ 그는 / 없었다. 계획이 / 돌아올 (가까운 장래에)]
해석 그는 가까운 장래에 돌아올 계획이 없었다.

4. All the management / mentioned that everything [possible] / should be done (to protect / the workers / from accidents).
▶ 모든 경영진은 / 언급했다 모든 것 [가능한] / 되어야만 한다고 / (보호하기 위하여 / 직원들을 / 사고로부터)
해석 모든 경영진은 직원들을 사고로부터 보호하기 위하여 온갖 수단을 다 해야 할 것이라고 언급했다.

5. A new contract [with a pharmaceutical company] / made / all employees / happy.
▶ 새로운 계약이 [제약회사와의] / 만들었다 / 전 직원을 / 기쁘게
해석 제약회사와의 새로운 계약이 전 직원을 기쁘게 만들었다.

6. The whole audience [in the auditorium] / thought / Dr. William's address / very impressive.
▶ 모든 청중들은 [강당에 있는] / 생각했다 / William 박사님의 연설이 / 매우 감명 깊다고
해석 강당에 있는 모든 청중들은 William 박사님의 연설이 감명 깊다고 생각했다.

7. The mediator / said {that the woman / had never been cooperative} / (throughout the meeting).
▶ 중재자는 / 말했다 / {그 여인은 / 협조적인 적이 없었다고} / (회의 동안)
해석 중재자에 의하면 그 여인은 회의 동안 협조적인 적이 없었다고 한다.

8. Industrial pollution / is derived / (principally) / from plants [that refine and manufacture / basic metals].
▶ 산업 오염은 / 발생한다. / (주로) / 공장으로부터 [정제하고 제조하는 / 기초 금속 물질을]
해석 산업 오염은 주로 기초 금속 물질을 정제하고 제조하는 공장에서 발생한다.

9. The results / of last month's study / made / the researchers / happy.
▶ 결과는 / 지난달 연구의 / 만들었다 / 연구원들을 / 기쁘게
해석 지난달의 연구 결과는 연구원들을 기쁘게 만들었다.

10. (In both America and Europe), / the fast food market / has become / increasingly full.
▶ (미국과 유럽에서) / 패스트푸드 시장이 / 되었다. / 점차 포화 상태가
해석 미국과 유럽에서 패스트푸드 시장이 점차 포화 상태가 되었다.

UNIT 05 : 부사

GRAMMAR PRACTICE   p.57

A
1. necessarily
2. adequately
3. completely
4. consistently
5. significantly
6. exclusively
7. accurately
8. extremely
9. Simply
10. aggressively

B
1. The director conducted an **extremely** successful on-site training session.
2. Construction was **temporarily** suspended.
3. O
4. Flight attendants are trained to react **calmly** to any emergency.
5. Make sure your seatbelt is **securely** fastened.

GRAMMAR PRACTICE   p.59

A
1. The man often goes fishing.
2. My puppy always makes me smile.
3. David never cries.
4. Sometimes Susan plays the piano on Saturday.
Susan sometimes plays the piano on Saturday.
5. They are usually made of plastic.

B
1. usually
2. still
3. approximately
4. hardly
5. nearly

C
1. We are **always** busy at this time of the year.
2. Because it is the most durable model, it **hardly** ever needs repairs.
3. O
4. Austin has opened three new offices in California for in **nearly** six months.
5. Although she spent many months researching, Julia **still hasn't** finished the project.

GRAMMAR PRACTICE   p.61

A
1. very
2. even
3. enough
4. just
5. much
6. kind enough
7. enough money
8. so
9. too
10. sensitive

B
1. I had **just** gotten in town when I realized it was a national holiday.
2. I want to try lunch at the new restaurant **near** the ice cream shop.
3. O
4. There were **too many** people and there wasn't enough space between the tables.
5. O

GRAMMAR PRACTICE   p.63

A
1. widely
2. highly
3. lately
4. moreover
5. however
6. nonetheless
7. hardly
8. However
9. closely
10. late

B
1. consequently
2. otherwise
3. however
4. therefore
5. meantime

GRAMMAR IN SENTENCE   p.64

1. (Because it is the most durable model), it (hardly ever) needs / repairs.
▶ (이 모델은 가장 내구성이 강한 모델이므로), / (거의) 필요로 하지 (않습니다.) / 수리를
해석 이 모델은 가장 내구성이 강한 모델이므로, 거의 수리를 필요로 하지 않습니다.

2. Austin / has opened / three new offices (in California / for nearly six months).
▶ Austin / 열었다 / 3개의 새로운 사무실을 (캘리포니아에 / 약 6개월 동안에)
해석 Austin 약 6개월 동안에 3개의 새로운 사무실을 캘리포니아에 열었다.

3. (Although she / spent / many months researching), Julia (still didn't) finished the project.
▶ (그녀는 / 보냈지만 / 몇 달을 조사하는 데에) Julia는 / (아직도 못했다) / 마치지 / 그 프로젝트를
해석 Julia는 조사하는 데에 몇 달을 보냈지만, 아직도 그 프로젝트를 마치지 못했다.

4. People / are moving / into this area; consequently, / housing / is becoming scarce.
▶ 사람들이 / 이사를 오고 있다 / 이 지역으로 ; 그 결과로, 집이 / 부족해지고 있다.
해석 이 지역으로 사람들이 이사를 오고 있다. 그 결과로, 집이 부족해지고 있다.

5. All items (in the exhibition) / are for sale (unless otherwise marked).
▶ 작품들은 (전시회에) / 구매가 가능하다 (다른 표시가 없는 한)
해석 다른 표시가 없는 한 전시회에 나와 있는 작품들은 구매가 가능하다.

6. I / didn't receive / the details of your order yet; therefore, send me an email (as soon as possible).
▶ 나는 / 아직 받지 못했습니다 / 세부적인 사항들을 ; 그러므로, 이메일을 보내주세요. (가능한 한 빨리)
해석 세부적인 사항들을 아직 받지 못했습니다. 그러므로 가능한 한 빨리 이메일을 보내주세요.

7. I / will be in touch with her / soon; meantime, don't let her know I'm here.
▶ 제가 / 연락을 할 것입니다 그녀에게 / 곧; 그동안에. 알리지 마세요. 그녀에게 제가 이곳에 있다는 것을
해석 제가 곧 그녀에게 연락을 할 것입니다. 그동안에 제가 이곳에 있다는 것을 그녀에게 알리지 마세요.

8. Ms. Simpson / has served / her neighbors (all her life) and is (highly) respected / by people.
▶ Simpson씨는 / 봉사를 했다 / 이웃을 위해 (일생을) (매우) 존경을 받고 있다 / 사람들로부터
해석 Simpson씨는 일생을 이웃을 위해 봉사를 했고, 사람들로부터 매우 존경을 받고 있다.

9. The fire alarms / are so sensitive / that they're (always) being set off / by cigarette smoke.
▶ 화재경보기는 / 매우 민감해서 / (항상) 경보를 발한다. / 담배 연기에도
해석 화재경보기는 매우 민감해서 항상 담배 연기에도 경보를 발한다.

10. Flight attendants / are trained / to react (calmly) / to any emergency.
▶ 비행기 승무원들은 / 훈련을 받는다. / 대응하는 (침착하게) / 어떤 비상사태에라도

해석 비행기 승무원들은 어떤 비상사태에라도 침착하게 대응하는 훈련을 받는다.

UNIT 06 : 전치사

GRAMMAR PRACTICE   p.67

A
1. at, in   2. in, in   3. on   4. on, in   5. at

B
1. Regarding   2. on   3. Considering
4. On   5. at

C
1. without studying hard.
2. after finishing my homework.
3. before going to bed.
4. about moving to another city.
5. without using a washing machine.

GRAMMAR PRACTICE   p.69

A
1. Due to   2. by   3. during
4. throughout   5. for   6. During
7. between   8. among   9. because of
10. in spite of

B
1. He has worked as an assistant manager **for** 30 years now.
2. Drinks will be provided **during** the recess.
3. Please send me the information **by** Monday.
4. He has to work overtime **until** 9:00 pm tonight.
5. O

GRAMMAR PRACTICE   p.71

A
1. above   2. along   3. In addition to
4. near   5. in front of   6. instead of
7. besides   8. barring   9. along
10. Aside from

B
1. along   2. through   3. up
4. down   5. into

GRAMMAR PRACTICE p.73

A
1. advance   2. detail   3. beyond
4. in   5. out of   6. at
7. observance   8. under   9. at
10. on

B
1. Today, sugar is used **in** bulk in a lot of food products.
2. O
3. The agreement will automatically be terminated **upon** the death of the resident.
4. O
5. If you're not happy with your books, return them within 10 days **at** our expense.

GRAMMAR IN SENTENCE p.74

1. Some students / will run (on the playground / in the afternoon).
▶ 어떤 학생들은 / 달리기를 할 것이다 (운동장에서 / 오후에)
해석 어떤 학생들은 오후에 운동장에서 달리기를 할 것이다.

2. The bus / stops (at the bus stop / every 20 minutes).
▶ 버스가 / 멈춘다. (20분마다 / 버스 정류장에).
해석 버스가 20분마다 버스 정류장에 멈춘다.

3. (Regarding this matter), both parties / has concurred.
▶ (이 문제에 대하여), 양 측은 / 합의를 했다.
해석 이 문제에 대하여, 양 측은 합의를 했다.

4. (Considering his age), William is strong / and looks young.
▶ (나이를 고려하면), William은 힘도 세고, / 젊어 보인다.
해석 나이를 고려하면, William은 힘도 세고, 젊어 보인다.

5. The agreement will (automatically) be terminated (upon the death / of the resident).
▶ 계약은 (자동적으로) 만료될 것이다 (사망 시에 / 거주자의)
해석 계약은 거주자의 사망 시에 자동적으로 만료될 것이다.

6. (If you're not happy with your books), return them (within 10 days / at our expense).
▶ (책이 마음에 들지 않으시면) 반송하세요. / (10일 이내에) / 저희의 비용으로)
해석 책이 마음에 들지 않으시면 10일 이내에 반송하시면, 반송비는 저희가 부담합니다.

7. (In order to meet the deadline), we / should proceed (at the pace of the fastest).
▶ (마감일을 맞추기 위해서), 우리는 / 진행해야한다 (가장 빠른 속도로)
해석 마감일을 맞추기 위해서, 우리는 가장 빠른 속도로 진행해야 한다.

8. The National Bank / will be closed (in observance of a public holiday).
▶ 국립은행은 / 문을 닫을 것이다 (공휴일을 준수하여)
해석 국립은행은 공휴일을 준수하여 문을 닫을 것이다.

9. Many police officers / have stood (guard all / along the street).
▶ 많은 경찰이 서있다 (경비를 하며 모두 / 길을 따라)
해석 많은 경찰이 길에 쫙 깔려 경비하고 있다.

10. (Aside from the minor corrections [Christina is working on]), the booklet / is almost ready / for the event.
▶ (제외하면 약간의 수정작업을 [Christina가 하는 중인]) 책자는 / 거의 준비되었다. / 행사를 위해
해석 Christina가 하는 약간의 수정작업을 빼면 행사를 위해 책자는 거의 준비되었다.

ACTUAL TEST 2 p.76-77

A
1. (D)   2. (C)   3. (D)   4. (B)   5. (B)   6. (A)
7. (B)   8. (A)   9. (B)   10. (A)

B
11. (A)   12. (C)   13. (B)   14. (D)   15. (C)   16. (A)

A

1. All of the participants will be asked to complete a ------- survey about the effectiveness of the session.
(A) briefed
(B) briefest
(C) briefly
(D) brief

해석 모든 참석자들은 그 과정의 효율성에 대한 간단한 설문 조사를 완성하도록 요청받을 것이다.
해설 관사 a와 명사 survey 사이에는 형용사 brief가 가장 적합하다.
어휘 **participant** 참석자 **complete** 완성하다 **brief** 간단한 **survey** 설문 조사 **effectiveness** 효율성 **session** 과정

2. Flight attendants must ensure that ------- of the passengers is properly seated prior to takeoff.
(A) every
(B) all
(C) each
(D) much

해석 비행기 승무원들은 이륙하기 전에 각각의 승객들이 제대로 착석했는지 확인해야만 한다.
해설 of the와 함께 쓸 수 있으며, 대명사 역할을 하면서 단수 동사 is를 써야 하는 것은 each이다.
어휘 **flight attendant** 승무원 **ensure** 확인하다 **passenger** 승객 **properly** 적절하게 제대로 **prior to** ~이전에, ~에 앞서 **takeoff** 이륙

3. According to a recent survey, the abundance of college graduates makes the job market very -------.
(A) competition
(B) compete
(C) competing
(D) competitive

해설 최근 조사에 따르면, 대학 졸업생이 많아지는 것은 구직 시장의 경쟁을 매우 치열하게 한다.

해설 본동사는 makes인 5형식 동사이므로 the job market은 목적어, 빈칸은 목적보어가 필요하다. 그러므로 형용사인 competitive 가 정답이다.

어휘 abundance 풍부, 다수   competition 경쟁   compete 경쟁하다   competitive 경쟁적인

4. It is absolutely necessary that all the researchers wear ------- glasses and gloves while in the laboratory.
(A) protect
(B) protective
(C) protecting
(D) protected

해설 실험에 있는 동안 모든 연구원들은 보호용 안경과 장갑을 무조건 착용해야 한다.

해설 빈칸은 명사인 glasses and gloves를 수식하는 형용사자리이다.

어휘 absolutely 절대적으로, 무조건

5. The two laundry detergents showed in the study were found to be ------- effective.
(A) equal
(B) equally
(C) equality
(D) equaled

해설 연구에서 두 개의 세제는 동등하게 효과가 있고 경제적이라는 것이 판명됐다.

해설 be동사와 형용사 effective 사이에는 부사 equally가 적합하다.

어휘 detergent 세제

6. Charles Raven has had ------- 15 years of experience in marketing and he is a marketing manager for a medium-sized company in South Carolina.
(A) nearly
(B) currently
(C) completely
(D) closely

해설 Charles Raven은 마케팅 분야에서 거의 15년 동안 일한 경력을 가지고 있으며, 현재는 South Carolina 소재 중소기업에 마케팅 부장으로 일하고 있다.

해설 숫자 앞에는 about, nearly, approximately 등을 써서 '약, 대략'의 의미를 나타낸다.

7. Dick Martins is ------- interested in returning to Atlanta, which is his hometown, and he would like to move to a larger city.
(A) especial
(B) especially
(C) exceptional
(D) exceptionally

해설 Dick Martin은 보다 큰 도시로 옮기고 싶을 뿐만 아니라, 특히 그의 고향인 Atlanta로 돌아가고 싶어 한다.

해설 be동사와 과거 분사(interested) 사이에는 부사가 와야 하는데, 문맥상 '특별히, 특히'라는 의미의 especially가 적합하다.

어휘 especial 특별한   exceptional 예외적인

8. After interviewing the candidates, heads of each department will ------- make a decision tomorrow.
(A) finally
(B) final
(C) finance
(D) financial

해설 후보자들에 대한 인터뷰를 한 후에, 각 부서의 부장들은 내일 마침내 결정을 내릴 것이다.

해설 조동사(will)와 동사원형(make) 사이에는 부사인 (A) finally가 정답이다. 부사는 동사구를 수식할 수 있다.

어휘 candidate 후보자   make a decision 결정하다

9. A dinner reception will be held at Hall's Guesthouse and Restaurant starting at 6:00 p.m. ------- Saturday, June 20th.
(A) from
(B) on
(C) in
(D) to

해설 저녁 만찬이 홀 게스트하우스 앤 레스토랑에서 6월 20일 토요일 오후 6시에 열립니다.

해설 특정한 날 앞에는 on이라는 전치사가 쓰인다. 따라서 Saturday, June 20th 앞에는 on이 적합하다.

10. Our company will deliver items ------- three days of the date the order is placed.
(A) within
(B) sometime
(C) nearby
(D) during

해설 우리 회사는 주문 날짜로부터 3일 이내에 물품을 배송합니다.

해설 문맥상 ------- three days는 '3일 이내에'란 의미가 되어야 한다. 어떤 기간 '이내에'라고 할 때는 <within + 기간>을 쓰므로 (A)가 정답이다.

B

Questions 11-16 refer to the following notice.

Attention! Movie Lovers!

When a movie becomes very 11. -------, we often sell out all our tickets for a show.
12. -------, we recommend that in order to get a ticket, you use our ticket reservation system. This system is 13. ------- by phone, through the Internet or by stopping 14. ------- our box office location. To reserve your ticket, select the movie, the time, and how 15. ------- tickets you will purchase. For very large groups, we recommend you talk to a service agent by phone. This way, you will be sure to receive all your tickets 16. ------- the same area.

영화 애호가들 여러분!

영화가 매우 인기 있게 되면, 티켓은 종종 매진됩니다. 따라서 티켓을 구하실 때는 티켓 예약 시스템을 이용하시기를 권장합니다. 이 시스템은 전화나 인터넷을 이용하셔도 되고 매표소에서 이용하실 수도 있습니다. 티켓을 예약하시려면 영화, 시간, 구입 매수를 선택해 주십시오. 많은 수의 단체 예약은 티켓 예매 담당 직원에게 전화하십시오. 그렇게 하시면 티켓을 모두 인접한 좌석의 것으로 받으실 수 있습니다.

어휘 **popular** 인기 있는, 평판 좋은 **popularity** 인기, 평판 **populate** 거주시키다 **reservation** 예약 **available** 이용 가능한 **availability** 유효성, 유용성 **box office** 매표소 **agent** 담당자

11.
(A) popular
(B) popularity
(C) popularly
(D) populate

해설 동사 become은 불완전 자동사로서 보어가 와야 한다. 보어 자리에는 형용사인 popular가 적합하다.

12.
(A) However
(B) Nevertheless
(C) Therefore
(D) For example

해설 '영화가 매우 인기 있게 되면, 티켓은 종종 매진됩니다. 따라서 티켓을 구하실 때는 티켓 예약 시스템을 이용하시기를 권장합니다.'라는 의미로 Therefore 이 가장 적합하다.

13.
(A) avail
(B) available
(C) availability
(D) availably

해설 be동사는 불완전 자동사로서 보어가 와야 한다. 보어 자리에는 형용사인 available이 적합하다.

14.
(A) in
(B) on
(C) of
(D) at

해설 ------- our box office location는 '매표소에서'라는 의미로 특정 장소 앞에는 at을 쓴다.

15.
(A) much
(B) lots
(C) many
(D) every

해설 how ------- tickets에서 tickets 를 수식하는 수량형용사가 필요하다 tickets는 가산명사의 복수 형태이므로 함께 쓸 수 있는 수량 형용사는 many이다. much는 불가산 명사와 lots는 명사이며 lots of 또는 a lot of 가 가산명사의 복수 또는 불가산 명사와 쓸 수 있으며, every는 가산명사의 단수와 함께 쓸 수 있다.

16.
(A) in
(B) through
(C) to
(D) from

해설 ------- the same area.는 '같은 지역(구역)에서'라는 의미이므로 area 앞에는 장소를 나타내는 in이 가장 적합하다.

MINI TEST 1   p.78-81

A
1. (D) 2. (B) 3. (A) 4. (D) 5. (D) 6. (C)
7. (B) 8. (C) 9. (D) 10. (B)

B
1. (A) 2. (C) 3. (A) 4. (B) 5. (D) 6. (B)
7. (C) 8. (D) 9. (B) 10. (B)

C
1. (A) 2. (C) 3. (A) 4. (B) 5. (D) 6. (C)
7. (A) 8. (B) 9. (C) 10. (A) 11. (D) 12. (D)

A

1. The recent increase in sales taxes will result in a ------- in employee benefits.
(A) reduced
(B) reducing
(C) reduces
(D) reduction

해석 최근의 판매세 증가는 직원 복지를 감소시킬 것이다.
해설 부정관사 a 뒤는 명사자리이며, 전치사와 전치사 사이에는 명사가 나와야하므로 답은 reduction이다.
어휘 **result in** ~의 결과를 낳다 **employee benefit** 직원복지혜택

정답 **227**

2. Professional and cultural organizations can be ------- of information about scholarships.
(A) source
(B) sources
(C) sourcing
(D) sourced

해석 전문 직업이나 문화 관련 기관들은 장학금에 대한 정보의 출처가 될 수 있다.
해설 source는 '출처, 근원'이란 의미의 가산 명사이다. 의미상 주어가 복수이므로 sources라고 복수형을 취해야 한다.
어휘 **professional** 직업의, 전문직의, 직업적인, 프로의
source 출처, 근원, 원천   **scholarship** 장학금, 학문

3. Heather stated that her deep love of nature has been ------- main motivation for producing such brilliant works of art.
(A) her
(B) hers
(C) she
(D) herself

해석 Heather 씨는 그녀의 자연에 대한 사랑을 그녀의 훌륭한 작품의 동기라고 언급했다.
해설 빈칸에 들어올 Ms. Heather에 대한 알맞은 소유격은 her이다.
어휘 **motivation** 동기

4. Because his secretary was out of the office yesterday, Mr. Shannon had to take his calls by -------.
(A) he
(B) his
(C) him
(D) himself

해설 비서가 어제 부재중이어서 Mr. Shanon 는 스스로 모든 전화를 받아야 했다.
해설 '그 스스로 전화를 받았다'라는 자연스러운 문맥을 만들기 위해서는 by oneself(스스로, 혼자서)라는 표현을 써야 한다. 따라서 by 다음에 온 빈칸에는 재귀대명사 (D) himself 가 와야 한다.
어휘 **be out of the office** 부재중이다

5. We have already received ------- membership packet in the mail since last year.
(A) few
(B) whole
(C) many
(D) every

해설 우리는 작년 이래로 모든 회원용 소포를 우편으로 받았다.
해설 few와 many는 가산명사의 복수와 함께 쓸 수 있다. 단수명사 packet를 수식할 수 있는 형용사는 every이다.

6. The Health Care Institute prepares graduates to make ------- contributions to society.
(A) valuably
(B) values
(C) valuable
(D) value

해석 Health Care Institute는 졸업생들이 사회에 가치 있는 공헌을 하도록 준비시킨다.
해설 contribution은 명사이므로 명사를 수식하는 형용사 valuable이 가장 적합하다.
어휘 **health care** 건강관리   **prepare** 준비하다   **graduate** 졸업생
valuable 가치 있는   **contribution** 공헌, 기여

7. It is extremely important to enter your personal information ------- to be eligible for this sweepstakes.
(A) correct
(B) correctly
(C) corrected
(D) correction

해석 이 경품 행사에 참가할 자격을 받으려면 귀하의 개인 신상을 정확하게 기입하는 것이 매우 중요합니다.
해설 타동사 enter의 목적어(information)가 나와 있는 상태에서 그 뒤에 빈칸이 있는 형태이므로 동사 enter를 수식하는 부사가 필요한 자리이다.
어휘 **extremely** 매우   **eligible** 자격이 있는   **sweepstakes** (여러 사람이 건 돈을 한 사람 혹은 여러 사람이 휩쓰는) 경품행사

8. In spite of several attempts, Ms. Gilbert has not ------- been able to talk to any customers service representatives over the phone.
(A) still
(B) ahead
(C) yet
(D) already

해석 수차례의 시도에도 불구하고, Gilbert씨는 고객 서비스 담당 직원과 아직 전화연결을 할 수 없었다.
해설 has yet to는 '아직 ~않다'라는 뜻으로 쓰인다.
어휘 **attempt** 시도   **be able to 동사원형** ~ 할 수 있다   **customer service representative** 고객 서비스 담당 직원

9. Please ------- us for more information about special Saturday classes and other options.
(A) comply
(B) look
(C) respond
(D) contact

해석 토요일 특강 및 기타 프로그램에 대한 자세한 내용은 문의 주시기 바랍니다.
해설 us를 목적어로 취하는 타동사 자리이다. 전치사가 필요없는 타동사 (D) contact가 정답이다.
어휘 **option** 선택   **comply with** 따르다, 순응하다   **look** 자동사
respond to 응답하다

10. Employees enrolled in Applied Research in Business can fully ------- in group activities.
(A) participating
(B) participate
(C) had participated
(D) participant

해설 기업 응용 연구 과정에 등록한 직원들은 전적으로 그룹 활동에 참여할 수 있다.

해설 조동사 can 뒤에는 본동사가 와야 하며, 이때 동사원형을 써야 한다. 부사 fully는 종종 조동사와 본동사 사이에 쓰이며, 본동사를 찾는 데 함정으로 이용되기도 한다. 그러므로 동사원형인 participate가 적합하다.

어휘 enroll 등록하다 fully 전적으로 participate in ~에 참가하다 group activity 그룹 활동

B

1. Parents of young (A)[child] have to (B)[deal with] the commercial (C)[influence] of television every time they take them (D)[to] a supermarket or toy store.

정답 (A) child → children

해설 어린 아이들의 부모들은 그들의 아이들과 함께 수퍼마켓이나 장난감 가게에 갈 때마다 텔레비전의 상업적 영향을 잘 처리해야만 한다.

해설 상식적으로 한 아이에게 부모가 여럿 있을 수 없다. 따라서 여러 아이들의 여러 부모님들이 맞으므로 child의 복수형 children으로 바꿔야 한다.

2. (A)[An] e-mail will be sent (B)[to you] to confirm the (C)[cancel] of your registration (D)[for] the international business course.

정답 (C) cancel → cancellation

해설 이메일은 국제 비즈니스 과정 등록 취소를 확인하기위해 당신에게 보내어 질 것입니다.

해설 the 명사 of 명사, cancel의 명사는 cancellation이다.

3. Each regional manager (A)[handle] all health and social care complaints (B)[for] their respective districts (C)[so that] they (D)[become] familiar with local issues and services.

정답 (A) handle → handles

해설 각 지역 관리자는 지역사회의 문제점들과 서비스에 대해 정통해지기 위해 그들 각자가 담당하고 있는 지역의 모든 보건 그리고 사회 보장제도에 대한 불만사항들을 다룬다.

해설 each / every 다음에는 3인칭 단수 동사가 사용된다.

4. Jennifer (A)[plans] to apply (B)[hers] experience in the field of environmental science (C)[as] an undergraduate (D)[toward] an advanced degree in environmental law.

정답 (B) hers → her

해설 Jennifer은 환경법에서 높은 점수를 따기 위해 대학생으로서 환경과학 분야에서 그녀의 경험을 적용시킬 계획이다.

해설 she의 소유격은 her이며 소유대명사는 hers이다. 여기서는 소유격이 필요하므로 her로 고쳐야 한다.

5. The new restaurant will (A)[be open] (B)[for business] (C)[near] the N&H Department Store (D)[on] the beginning of next month.

정답 (D) on → at

해설 새로운 음식점이 다음 달 초에 N&H 백화점 근처에서 영업을 시작할 것이다.

해설 '~초에'를 의미하는 숙어로 at the beginning of를 쓴다.

6. The new product design (A)[has not] generated (B)[many] interest (C)[from] consumers (D)[judging by] the survey results.

정답 (B) many → much

해설 새로운 제품 디자인은 고객들의 흥미를 유발하지 못하였다는 것이 조사에 의해 판명되었다.

해설 many는 무조건 뒤에 복수명사가 와야 한다. interest는 불가만 명사이므로 much로 바꿔야 정답이다.

7. I (A)[ran into] (B)[an] acquaintance of (C)[me] from my former company (D)[on] the street.

정답 (C) me → mine

해설 나는 길에서 전 직장에서 알던 사람을 우연히 만났다.

해설 '내 친구'는 a friend of mine이다. '아는 사람'도 an acquaintance of mine으로 표현하면 된다.

8. Ms. Cruise will (A)[play] the (B)[title role] in the film, (C)[which] is an (D)[adapting] of the play, The Merchant of Venice.

정답 (D) adapting → adaptation

해설 Cruise씨는 희곡 베니스의 상인을 개작한 영화에서 주연을 맡았다.

해설 관사와 전치사 of 사이에는 명사가 와야 한다. 따라서 동명사 adapting을 adaptation으로 바꿔야 한다.

9. The law firm (A)[met] yesterday and (B)[discussed about] the (C)[implications] of a (D)[recent] high court decision regarding a paint manufacturer.

정답 (B) discussed about → discussed

해설 그 법률 회사는 한 페인트 제조사에 관한 최근 고등 법원의 판결이 의미하는 바를 어제 만나서 논의 했다.

해설 discuss는 타동사로 전치사를 취하지 않는다.

10. (A)[To join] the member's club, (B)[completely] one of the forms (C)[by] the cash register and submit it (D)[to] the customer service desk.

정답 (B) completely → complete

해설 클럽에 가입하려면, 현금 계산기 옆에 있는 양식을 작성하여 고객 서비스 창구에 제출하라.

해설 적절한 품사 자리를 묻는 문제로 명령문이므로 동사의 원형이 와야 한다.

C

Questions 1-6 refer to the following e-mail.

Date: April 15

Subject: Revised Office Policies: Meeting

As of May 1, we will **1.** ------- some new office policies on safety and evacuation procedures. We will be holding a meeting **2.** ------- April 20th at 3:00 p.m. **3.** ------- the main auditorium. It is necessary that all employees **4.** ------- the meeting as we will be going over a number of important policy changes.
If you have any questions or concerns, please **5.** ------- them to Amy Jermons by e-mail at amyj@mail.org or by telephone at 654-1230. Thank you for your **6.** -------.

5월 1일부터 안전과 대피 과정에 관한 새 회사 정책을 실행할 것입니다. 주 강당에서 4월 20일 오후 3시에 회의가 열릴 예정입니다. 다수의 중요한 정책 변화에 대해 논의할 예정이므로 모든 직원들은 회의에 꼭 참석해야 합니다.
문의사항이 있으시면 이메일 주소 amyj@mail.org나 전화 654-1230으로 Amy Jermons에게 연락하시기 바랍니다. 협조해 주셔서 감사합니다.

어휘 implement 실행하다 evacuation 피난, 대피 procedure 진행, 절차 auditorium 강당 a number of 다수의

1.
(A) implement
(B) implementing
(C) implemented
(D) implementation

해설 적절한 동사 형태를 고르는 유형이다. new office policies가 목적어로서 타동사(implement)가 능동태가 되어야 한다. 조동사 will 다음에는 동사원형을 써야한다.

2.
(A) from
(B) in
(C) on
(D) of

해설 '------- April 20th'에서 특정일 앞에는 전치사 on을 쓴다.

3.
(A) in
(B) on
(C) above
(D) below

해설 '------- the main auditorium'는 주강당에서 라는 의미로 장소 안에서 이루어진다는 의미로 전치사 in을 쓴다.

4.
(A) participate
(B) attend
(C) take part
(D) go

해설 회의(meeting)에 '참석하다.'라는 의미의 타동사가 필요한 자리이다. attend는 타동사이며, 참석하다의 의미의 자동사로는 participate in, take part in 그리고 가다는 go to 로 써야한다.

5.
(A) reply
(B) deal
(C) respond
(D) direct

해설 please ------- them에서 them 을 목적어로 취할 수 있는 타동사 자리이다. reply to= respond to 응답하다, deal with 거래하다로 자동사이며, direct A to B 로 타동사인 direct 가 정답이다.

6.
(A) cooperate
(B) cooperative
(C) cooperation
(D) cooperatively

해설 전치사 for 뒤에는 명사를 써야한다. 그러므로 협조해 주셔서 감사합니다. 라는 의미로 cooperation 이 적합하다.

Questions 7-12 refer to the following flyer.

David Lucas will be performing live!

Finally, David Lucas **7.** ------- that he can give a truly great performance.

☐ Venue: World Music Store	☐ Dates: Friday, December 20 to Sunday, December 22
☐ Time: 7:00 P.M.	☐ Cost: $50 adults / $20 children under fifteen

To purchase tickets in **8.** -------, send a personal check or money order to the World Music Store **9.** ------- Wednesday, December 4. You can **10.** ------- by credit card by calling 1-800-123-1234. Any remaining tickets will be sold on a first-come, first-served basis **11.** ------- the evening of each performance.
Cash will be the only **12.** ------- form of payment on these evenings.

David Lucas가 실황으로 공연할 것입니다!

마침내 David Lucas가 진정 훌륭한 공연을 제공할 수 있다는 것을 실제로 보여드릴 것입니다.

☐ 장소: World Music 스토어	☐ 날짜: 12월 20일(금)부터 12월 22일(일)
☐ 시간: 오후 7시	☐ 요금: 성인 50달러 / 15세 미만 아동 20달러

미리 티켓을 구입하기 위해서, 12월 4일 수요일까지 월드 뮤직 스토어로 가계수표 또는 우편환을 발송하세요. 귀하는 1-800-123-1234번으로 전화하셔서 신용카드로 지불하실 수 있습니다. 남아있는 티켓은 공연 당일 저녁에 선착순으로 판매될 것입니다.
현금은 공연 당일 저녁에 유일하게 수납되는 지불 종류입니다.

어휘 **perform live** 실황으로 공연하다　**live** (부사) 실황으로, 생방송으로　**demonstrate** 해보이다　**venue** 장소　**adult** 성인　**in advance** 미리, 사전에　**personal check** 가계수표　**money order** 우편환　**on a first come, first served basis** 선착순으로　**acceptable** 받아들일 수 있는

7.
(A) will demonstrate
(B) demonstrated
(C) has demonstrated
(D) demonstrates

해설 David Lucas ------ that he can give a truly great performance.에서 전체적인 내용으로 보아 앞으로 있을 공연에 관한 내용이므로 미래시제를 써야한다. 그러므로 정답은 will demonstrate이다.

8.
(A) advancement
(B) advance
(C) advanced
(D) advancing

해설 '미리'라는 의미의 전치사 관용어 구는 in advance이다.

9.
(A) for
(B) in
(C) by
(D) at

해설 send a personal check or money order to the World Music Store ------ Wednesday, December 4.에서 12월 4일 수요일까지라는 의미이므로 by가 적합합니다.

10.
(A) pay
(B) be paid
(C) paying
(D) have paid

해설 'You can ------ by credit card'에서 신용카드로 지불할 수 있다는 의미로 pay가 적합하다.

11.
(A) at
(B) on
(C) for
(D) in

해설 ------ the evening of the performance.에서 공연날 저녁이라는 의미이므로 전치사 in을 써야 합니다.

12.
(A) accept
(B) accepted
(C) accepting
(D) acceptable

해설 명사 form을 수식하는 것은 형용사 acceptable (받아들일 수 있는)

UNIT 07 : 수일치

GRAMMAR PRACTICE　p.85

A
1. washes　2. am　3. is　4. goes　5. applicants
6. is　7. have　8. is　9. are　10. is

B
1. Either a bus or a taxi **is** available at the airport.
2. Neither my parents nor my sister **likes** pork.
3. I met a woman who **works** for the department store.
4. Our top priority for the remainder of the year **is** revenue growth.
5. O

GRAMMAR PRACTICE　p.87

A
1. were　2. is　3. is　4. is　5. were
6. is　7. is　8. has　9. are　10. is

B
1. There **were** a demonstration, a discussion and a presentation yesterday.
2. The clerks in this store **work** overtime every Monday.
3. What the president said **was** true.
4. Eating breakfast everyday **is** good for your health.
5. O

GRAMMAR IN SENTENCE　p.88

1. There were / a demonstration, a discussion and a presentation (yesterday).
▶ 있었다. / 실연, 토론, 발표가 (어제).
해설 어제 실연, 토론, 발표 등이 있었다.

2. {What we want to know} / is / if Ann will come to the party / tomorrow.
▶ {우리가 알고 싶은 것은} / 이다 / Ann이 파티에 오는지 / 내일
해석 우리가 알고 싶은 것은 Ann이 내일 파티에 오는지의 여부이다.

3. Half of the students / were receiving / less than 50% / on tests.
▶ 절반의 학생들은 / 받았다 / 50% 미만을 / 시험에서
해석 절반의 학생들은 시험에서 50% 미만을 받았다.

4. The clerks [in this store] / work overtime / (every Monday).
▶ 점원들은 [이 상점에서] / 야근을 한다 / (월요일마다)
해석 이 상점의 점원들은 월요일마다 야근을 한다.

5. {Eating breakfast} / everyday / is good for your health.
▶ {아침 식사를 하는 것은} / 매일 건강에 좋다.
▶ 아침 식사를 매일 하는 것은 건강에 좋다.

6. (Since it was a holiday), the number of cars / on the road / was (noticeably) reduced.
▶ (연휴이기 때문에) 자동차의 수가 / 길에 다니는 / (확연히) 줄었다.
해석 연휴이기 때문에 길에 다니는 자동차의 수가 확연히 줄었다.

7. The next item (on today's meeting agenda) is our company's expansion into Asia.
▶ 다음 항목은 (오늘 회의 안건의) /이다 / 우리 회사의 아시아로의 확장
해석 오늘 회의 안건의 다음 항목은 우리 회사의 아시아 확장입니다.

8. Residents adjacent to the airport have filed a lawsuit because of the noise.
▶ 공항 주변에 사는 주민들은 소음 때문에 소송을 제기했다.
해석 공항 주변에 사는 주민들은 소음 때문에 소송을 제기했다.

9. Not only exam results but also class participation / is included / in the score.
▶ 시험 결과뿐만 아니라 수업 참여도 / 포함된다 / 점수에
해석 시험 결과뿐만 아니라 수업 참여도 점수에 포함된다.

10. Anyone [with an interest in classical music] is welcome to attend / this event.
▶ 사람은 누구나 [고전 음악에 관심이 있는] / 참석할 수 있다 / 이 행사에
해석 고전 음악에 관심이 있는 사람은 누구나 이 행사에 참석할 수 있다.

UNIT 08 : 시제

GRAMMAR PRACTICE p.91

A
1. goes
2. walking
3. taking
4. broke
5. will travel

B
1. will have
2. was
3. is
4. will go
5. was driving

C
1. I **will be checking** in at the airport next Sunday morning.
2. O
3. Our company **introduced** the new system last month.
4. I **am** studying hard now to study abroad.
5. Next month, the Marketing Department **will implement** a strategy to increase the company's revenue.

GRAMMAR PRACTICE p.93

A
1. has introduced
2. have risen
3. has been playing
4. had lived
5. will have been repaired

B
1. arrived
2. have been working
3. haven't finished
4. will have been
5. had broken

C
1. I **called** the technician about fixing this machine yesterday.
2. The detective **has looked** into the accident thoroughly since last month.
3. O
4. O
5. O

GRAMMAR PRACTICE p.95

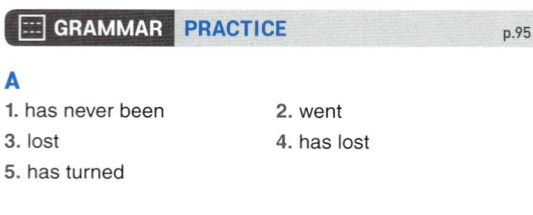

A
1. has never been
2. went
3. lost
4. has lost
5. has turned

B
1. will have introduced
2. has attracted
3. work
4. has spent
5. wire

C
1. I've **been** to the museum when I was a child.
2. The Interview schedules will be set shortly after we **review** the applications.
3. O
4. O
5. I **forgot** my appointment with the doctor yesterday.

GRAMMAR PRACTICE p.97

A
1. will come
2. will have
3. had been
4. got
5. fill

B
1. work
2. finish
3. wear
4. be
5. take

C

1. The teacher asked that all students **submit** their reports by noon.
2. O
3. When I **arrived** at the airport, the plane had already departed.
4. Before he joined our company, he **had** already worked at an advertising agency for 5 years.
5. O

GRAMMAR IN SENTENCE p.98

1. Early retirement packages / are (usually) available (for long working employees).
▶ 조기 퇴직 혜택은 / (대개) 이용이 가능하다 / (장기근속 직원들에 대하여)
해석 조기 퇴직 혜택은 장기근속 직원들은 대개 이용이 가능하다.

2. (Before he joined our company), he / had already worked (in an advertising agency / for 5 years).
▶ (그가 우리 회사에 입사하기 전에), 그는 이미 일을 했었다 (광고사에서 / 5년 동안).
해석 그가 우리 회사에 입사하기 전에 그는 이미 광고사에서 5년 동안 일을 했었다.

3. Regulations / require that all passenger trains / maintain / low speeds (as they pass / through towns).
▶ 규정은 요구한다 / 모든 여객 열차는 / 유지해야 한다 / 낮은 속도를 / (그들이 통과할 때 / 마을을)
해석 규정에 따르면 모든 여객 열차는 마을을 통과할 때 서행해야 된다.

4. Interview schedules / ll be set / (shortly after we / review / the applications).
▶ 인터뷰 스케줄이 / 잡힐 것이다 / (직후에 우리가 / 검토하다 / 원서를)
해석 지원서를 검토하는 즉시 인터뷰 스케줄이 잡힐 것이다.

5. I / called / the technician (about fixing this machine yesterday).
▶ 나는 / 전화했다 / 기술자에게 (고쳐달라고 / 복사기를 / 어제)
해석 나는 어제 기술자에게 복사기를 고쳐달라고 전화했다.

6. The detective / have looked into the accident (thoroughly / since last month).
▶ 형사는 / 조사하고 있다 / 그 사건을 (철저히 / 지난달부터)
해석 형사는 지난달부터 그 사건을 철저히 조사하고 있다.

7. He will have met his girlfriend (for two years / by the end of this month).
▶ 그는 / 만날 것이다 / 자신의 여자 친구를 / (2년 동안 / 이번 달 말이 되면)
해석 이번 달 말이 되면 그는 자신의 여자 친구를 만난 지 2년이 된다.

8. The technician / has been fixing / the computer (since this morning).
▶ 그 기술자는 / 수리하고 있다 / 그 컴퓨터를 (오늘 아침부터)
해석 그 기술자는 오늘 아침부터 그 컴퓨터를 수리하고 있다.

9. (By the time we get to the cinema), the film / will have started.
▶ (우리가 극장에 들어갈 때쯤에는) 영화는 / 시작해 있을 것이다.
해석 우리가 극장에 들어갈 때쯤에는 영화는 시작해 있을 것이다.

10. (Next month), the marketing department / will implement / a strategy / to increase the company's revenue.
▶ (다음 달에) 마케팅 부서는 / 이행할 것이다 / 전략을 / 회사의 수입을 증가시키는 .
해석 다음 달에 마케팅 부서는 회사의 수입을 증가시키는 전략을 이행할 것이다.

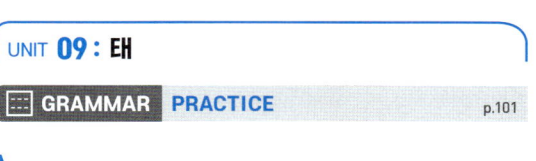

GRAMMAR PRACTICE p.101

A

1. held
2. was held
3. was given
4. will be served
5. was wounded

B

1. The president **is respected** by all the employees.
2. Your sister **has been seen** at the party before.
3. O
4. All my friends will **be invited** to my housewarming party.
5. All the proceeds will **be used** to acquire more properties.

C

1. I was given a novel I wanted to read yesterday (by her).
   A novel I wanted to read was given to me (by her).
2. The loan payments must be sent to the Nations Bank by the fifteenth of this month.
3. Mr. Wilson is considered one of the best public speakers because his speech is powerful as well as impressive (by people).
4. An exhibition of Erica's paintings and sculptures has been held at the BACO Gallery in New York (by them).
5. Maintenance equipment that is not in use in the warehouse should be locked (by them).

GRAMMAR PRACTICE p.103

A

1. All employees are required to wear protective equipment in the workplace (by them).
2. All visitors are required to present their identification (by the company).
3. Heavy rains are expected to continue throughout the day (by them).
4. Guests dining at this restaurant on weekends are advised to make a reservation (by them).
5. He was heard to shout "Watch out!" by someone.

B
1. My parents allowed me to throw a party.
2. I encouraged him to write poems.
3. A teacher made the boy read the book.
4. The professor advised Tony to study a foreign language.
5. They heard children laughing (laugh) loudly in the classroom.

C
1. in   2. at   3. at   4. with   5. with

GRAMMAR PRACTICE p.105

A
1. expired   2. were dealt with   3. with
4. in   5. in

B
1. as   2. for   3. to   4. of   5. from

C
1. O
2. The annual Christmas dinner **will take place** on Friday, December 20th at 6:00 p.m.
3. Every attendee **is asked** to drop their name in the Secret Santa Box in your office.
4. Names **will be drawn** by Lisa Ring on December 10th and your partner's name will be placed in your mailbox.
5. O

GRAMMAR PRACTICE p.107

A
1. The matter is discussed everyday (by them).
2. The matter will be discussed tomorrow (by them).
3. The matter was discussed yesterday (by them).
4. The matter has been discussed since yesterday (by them).
5. The matter will have been discussed by tomorrow (by them).
6. The matter had been discussed (by them) when I arrived there.
7. The matter is being discussed now (by them).
8. The matter was being discussed (by her) when I arrived there.

B
1. 평서문 You did your homework last night.
   평서문 수동태 Your homework was done last night.
   의문문 수동태 Was your homework done last night?
2. When were these pictures taken by you?
3. The dishes were washed by whom.
   By whom were the dishes washed?
4. Let the window be opened.
5. Let your homework be done.

GRAMMAR IN SENTENCE p.108

1. All my friends / will be invited / to my housewarming party.
   ▶ 나의 친구들은 / 초대될 것이다 / 나의 집들이에
   해석 나의 친구들은 나의 집들이에 초대될 것이다.

2. All proceeds / will be used / (to acquire more properties).
   ▶ 모든 수익금은 / 사용될 것이다 / (좀 더 많은 부동산을 취득하기 위하여)
   해석 모든 수익금은 좀 더 많은 부동산을 취득하는 데 사용될 것이다.

3. The roads / were / very dangerous (because they were covered with ice).
   ▶ 길들이 / 매우 위험했다 (때문에 그것들이 얼음으로 덮였기).
   해석 길들이 얼음으로 덮였기 때문에 매우 위험했다.

4. In Japan, / everyone / is dressed (in their new clothes on New Year's Day).
   ▶ 일본에서는 / 모든 사람들이 / 입는다 (새 옷을 새해 첫날에).
   해석 일본에서는 모두 새해 첫날 새 옷을 입는다.

5. It / is rock music [that I was absorbed in (when I was young)].
   ▶ 그것은 / 록 뮤직이다. [내가 몰두했던 (젊었을 때)]
   해석 그것은 내가 젊었을 때 몰두했던 것은 록 뮤직이다.

6. Mr. Mandela / is known (as one of the world's greatest leaders).
   ▶ 만델라는 / 알려져 있습니다 / (세계에서 가장 위대한 지도자 중 한 사람으로서)
   해석 만델라는 세계에서 가장 위대한 지도자 중 한 사람으로 알려져 있습니다.

7. Iraq / used to be known / to the west (by the Greek name, Mesopotamia.)
   ▶ 이라크는 알려져 있었다 / 서구 국가에 (그리스 이름인 메소포타미아로).
   해석 이라크는 서구 국가에 그리스 이름인 메소포타미아로 알려져 있었다.

8. Mr. Wilson / is considered / one of the best public speakers (because his speech is powerful as well as impressive).
   ▶ Wilson 씨는 / 간주된다. / 최고의 대중연설가 중의 한명으로 (그의 연설은 힘이 있고 감동적이기 때문에)
   해석 Wilson 씨의 연설은 힘이 있고 감동적이기 때문에 최고의 대중연설가 중의 한명으로 간주된다.

9. An exhibition [of Erica's paintings and sculptures] / has been held / at the BACO Gallery in New York.
   ▶ 전시회가 [Erica의 그림과 조각에 대한] / 열렸다 / BACO 갤러리에서 뉴욕에
   해석 Erica의 그림과 조각 전시회가 뉴욕의 BACO 갤러리에서 열렸다.

10. Maintenance equipment [that is not in use] / should be stored / in the warehouse.
▶ 수리 장비는 [사용되지 않는] / 보관되어야 한다 / 창고에
해석 사용되지 않는 수리 장비는 창고에 보관해야 한다.

ACTUAL TEST 3   p.110-111

A
1. (A) 2. (D) 3. (D) 4. (B) 5. (C) 6. (A)
7. (B) 8. (D) 9. (B) 10. (D)

B
11. (B) 12. (A) 13. (B) 14. (C) 15. (A) 16. (C)

A

1. Building a factory ------- a good way to offer local residents more job opportunities efficiently.
(A) is
(B) are
(C) has
(D) have

해석 공장을 설립하는 것은 지역 주민들에게 더 많은 일자리를 효율적으로 제공할 수 있는 좋은 방법이다.
해설 동명사가 주어로 오면 단수동사를 씁니다. building a factory의 building이 주어이므로 적합한 동사는 is입니다.
어휘 **local** 지역의 **resident** 주민 **job opportunity** 일자리 기회 **efficiently** 효율적으로

2. Our customer service representatives ------- you with a registration number and free coupons on drinks.
(A) provision
(B) providing
(C) provides
(D) provide

해석 고객 서비스 담당 직원이 등록 번호와 음료수에 대한 무료 쿠폰을 드립니다.
해설 주어가 복수인 representatives 이므로 복수 동사인 provide를 넣어야 합니다.
어휘 **customer service representatives** 고객 서비스 담당 직원 **registration number** 등록 번호

3. A number of middle school students in the city ------- in the special event held by Dell this weekend.
(A) participates
(B) are participated
(C) is participating
(D) are participating

해석 도시의 많은 중학생들이 이번 주말에 Dell에 의하여 개최되는 특별행사에 참석할 것이다.
해설 주어가 middle school students 로 복수이므로 복수 동사인 are participating을 써야합니다. a number of는 '많은'의 의미이며, participate in은 자동사이므로 수동태로 쓸 수 없습니다.
어휘 **middle school students** 중학생 **special** 특별한 **hold** 개최하다

4. The board of directors ------- sometime next week to discuss the renovation of the Dows building.
(A) to convene
(B) will convene
(C) convening
(D) convened

해석 이사회는 Dows 빌딩의 수리를 의논하기 위하여 다음 주 중에 회의를 소집할 것이다.
해설 next week는 미래 시제와 함께 쓴다. 그러므로 will convene이 가장 적합하다.
어휘 **board of directors** 이사회 **convene** ~을 모으다, 소집하다 **renovation** 수리, 혁신

5. Best Buys ------- a mutually amicable purchasing agreement with Happy Electronics Trade for over 3 years.
(A) has
(B) had
(C) has had
(D) will have

해석 Best Buys는 Happy Electronics Trade와 3년간 상호 우호 판매 계약을 맺어 왔다.
해설 for over 3 years는 3년 전부터 지금까지의 기간을 나타내므로 현재완료 시제가 적합하다.
어휘 **mutually** 상호적으로 **amicable** 우회의

6. Researchers at the University of Chicago ------- that the tea has the potential to cure diabetes.
(A) believe
(B) believes
(C) is believing
(D) are believed

해석 시카고 대학의 연구원들은 차(tea)는 당뇨병을 치료하는 잠재력을 갖고 있다고 생각한다.
해설 주어가 researchers로 복수이므로 정답은 (A) believe이다. believe는 that 절을 목적어로 취한다.
어휘 **researcher** 연구원 **potential** 잠재력 **cure** 고치다, 치료하다 **diabetes** 당뇨병

7. After the committee ------- discussing the contract, they moved onto the next item.
(A) finishes
(B) had finished
(C) has finished
(D) will have finished

해석 위원회는 계약에 대해 이야기를 마친 후 다음 항목으로 넘어갔다.
해설 주절이 과거시제로 moved 이므로 접속사 after 이 이끄는 종속절은 과거완료가 적합하다. 과거보다 먼저 있었던 사실은 과거완료로 쓴다.
어휘 **committee** 위원회 **contract** 계약

정답 **235**

8. Mr. Taylor ------- a short speech after dinner to express his appreciation for the retirement gift yesterday.
(A) delivers
(B) delivered
(C) is delivered
(D) has delivered

해석 어제 Taylor 씨는 저녁식사 후에 퇴임 선물에 감사를 표하는 짧은 연설을 했다.

해설 yesterday 와 함께 쓸 수 있는 것은 과거시제입니다. 그러므로 정답은 (B) delivered입니다.

어휘 **give a speech** 연설하다　**express one's appreciation** 감사를 표하다　**retirement gift** 은퇴 선물

9. The client's request to revise the contracts ------- considerable problems for the legal department since last week.
(A) is caused
(B) has caused
(C) will cause
(D) is causing

해석 고객이 계약서 수정을 요구해 왔기 때문에 법무부서는 심각한 문제에 봉착했다.

해설 since last week는 '지난주 이후로 줄 곳'이라는 의미로 since 과거시점은 현재완료 시제와 써야합니다. 그러므로 정답은 (B) has caused입니다.

어휘 **considerable**은 상당한, 중요한, 심각한　**legal** 합법적인, 법률의

10. Because of the heavy traffic jam, the film ------- by the time we got to the cinema.
(A) has been started
(B) started
(C) is starting
(D) had started

해석 심한 교통 체증 때문에 우리가 극장에 들어갈 때쯤에는 영화는 시작해 있을 것이다.

해설 극장에 들어가면 이미 영화는 상영 중이라는 의미이므로 과거와 현재와 미래를 포함하는 시제인 미래 완료와 써야 한다.

어휘 **traffic jam** 교통체증

B

Questions 11-16 refer to the following article.

The Mentor Language Study School **11.** ------- a problem with student work levels. From the middle of the term this year, the average student **12.** ------- at least one homework assignment every week. Half of the students **13.** ------- less than 50% on tests. The teachers decided that something had to **14.** ------- to help the students want to study.

The manager suggested that the teachers **15.** ------- a class award system. Every class of students who completed their homework assignments and received over 85% on tests would **16.** ------- a pizza party at the end of the term. Within 3 weeks, student work levels improved by 70%.

Mentor 언어 학습 학교는 학생 학습 수준과 관련하여 문제점을 가지고 있습니다. 올해 학기 중간부터 학생들은 평균적으로 매주 최소 한 가지씩의 과제를 하지 않고 있었습니다. 학생들의 절반이 시험에서 중간 점수도 받지 못했습니다. 교사들은 학생들의 학구열을 높이기 위해 무엇인가 해야 한다고 결정했습니다.
관리자는 교사들에게 학과 시상 제도를 시행하도록 제안했습니다. 모든 수업에서 과제를 완수하고 시험에서 85점 이상의 성적을 받는 학생들은 학기 말에 피자 파티를 상으로 받게 됩니다. 3주 만에 학생 학업 수준은 70%가 향상되었습니다.

어휘 **term** 학기　**homework assignment** 과제　**class award system** 학과 시상 제도

11.
(A) have had
(B) has had
(C) have
(D) had had

해설 주어가 The Mentor Language Study School로 고유명사이므로 단수 취급을 한다. 그러므로 has had가 적합하다.

12.
(A) was missing
(B) were missing
(C) was missed
(D) were missed

해설 주어가 the average student이므로 단수이고, miss는 자동사이다. 그러므로 was missing이 가장 적합하다.

13.
(A) receive
(B) receives
(C) was receiving
(D) were receiving

해설 문맥의 흐름으로 볼 때 과거 시제와 함께 써야한다. Half of the students ------- less than 50% on tests.에서 학생 절반이 중간 점수도 받지 못했다는 의미로 주어가 복수인 students 이므로 were receiveing 이 가장 적합하다.

14.
(A) do
(B) did
(C) be done
(D) done

해설 조동사인 had to 뒤에는 동사원형이 와야 하고 빈칸 뒤에 목적어가 없으므로 be done 이 적합하다.

15.
(A) begin
(B) began
(C) begun
(D) was beginning

해설 The manager suggested that the teachers에서 ------ a class award system. 주절의 동사가 요구 주장 명령 제안에 해당되는 suggest 이므로 that 절 이하에는 should 가 생략된 동사원형을 써야 한다.

16.
(A) received
(B) receives
(C) receive
(D) receiving

해설 조동사 would 다음에는 동사원형이 와야 한다.

UNIT 10 : 부정사

GRAMMAR PRACTICE p.115

A
1. good for health to exercise every day.
2. important to be polite to others.
3. very difficult to answer this question.
4. imperative to finish the project on time.
5. important to be kind to our guests.
6. essential to wear protective clothing.
7. possible to use the machine.
8. impossible to finish the project on time.
9. difficult to stay up all night.
10. possible to complete the assignment.

B
1. Jenny decided to study Spanish because she wanted **to travel** to Mexico.
2. O
3. The purpose of this study is **to investigate** the correlation between age and learning ability.
4. The doctor advised his patients **to take** vitamin C daily.
5. O

GRAMMAR PRACTICE p.117

A
1. ② 예정
   사장님이 우리의 새 공장을 다음 주에 방문하실 것이다.
2. ③ 의무
   6시까지 그것을 마쳐주셔야 해요.
3. ① 가능
   거리엔 아무도 보이지 않았다.
4. ④ 의도
   성공하고자 한다면 열심히 일해야 한다.
5. ⑤ 운명
   그는 다시는 그의 고향으로 돌아가지 않았다.

B
1. (In order / so as) To win the contest,
2. (in order) to participate in the seminar.
3. (in order / so as) to get 20% off your airfare.
4. smart enough to solve
5. too cold to sleep

C
1. It's time **to get** ready to go back to school now!
2. I had the opportunity **to learn** many things through them.
3. The workshop will be a chance **to familiarize** oneself with some of the new technologies.
4. O
5. An employee has a right **to receive** at least one month's notice of dismissal or intention to leave.

GRAMMAR PRACTICE p.119

A
1. promised to keep in touch with me.
2. plans to stay here for a month.
3. struggled to make ends meet.
4. afford to buy a sports car.
5. to manage to meet the deadline..

B
1. allowed   2. to go   3. to reach
4. submit   5. of

C
1. Alex persuaded his son **to change** his mind.
2. My parents allowed me **to participate** in the festival.
3. O
4. This book is too difficult **for you** to read.
5. It was very foolish **of you** to do that.

GRAMMAR PRACTICE p.121

A
1. able   2. likely   3. willing
4. liable   5. diversify   6. supposed
7. to hit   8. expected   9. willing
10. reluctant

B
1. The manager is **supposed** to hold the meeting this afternoon.
2. Jack is **likely** to pass the exam this time.
3. O
4. A lot of people were **eager** to give their help to the organization.
5. The teacher let students **look** around the museum.

GRAMMAR IN SENTENCE p.122

1. Jenny / decided / to study Spanish (because she / wanted / to travel to Mexico).
   ▶ Jenny는 / 결심했다 / 공부하기로 / 스페인어를 (멕시코를 여행하고 싶어서)
   해석 Jenny는 멕시코를 여행하고 싶어서 스페인어를 공부하기로 결심했다.

2. My plan / {is to travel / around Italy / (in the near future) and visit / historical sites}.
   ▶ 나의 계획은 / {여행하는 것이다 / 이탈리아를 / (가까운 미래에) / 방문하는 것이다. / 유적지를}
   해석 나의 계획은 가까운 미래에 이탈리아를 여행하며 유적지를 둘러보는 것이다.

3. The purpose of this study / is to investigate / the correlation (between age and learning ability).
   ▶ 이 연구의 목적은 / 조사하는 것이다. / 상관관계를 (나이와 학습능력에 관한)
   해석 이 연구의 목적은 나이와 학습능력에 관한 상관관계에 대한 것이다.

4. The doctor / advised / his patients / to take / vitamin C / (daily).
   ▶ 의사는 / 조언했다 / 그의 환자에게 / 복용하라고 / 비타민 C를 / (매일)
   해석 의사는 환자에게 비타민 C를 매일 복용하라고 조언했다.

5. My grandparents / made / it / possible / for me / to rest (comfortably).
   ▶ 나의 조부모님께서는 / 해 주셨다 / 나를 / 쉴 수 있도록 (편히)
   해석 나의 조부모님께서는 나를 편히 쉴 수 있도록 해 주셨다.

6. The airport construction project / will help / the company / diversify.
   ▶ 공항 건설 사업은 / 도움이 될 것이다. / 그 회사가 / 다각화하는 것에
   해석 공항 건설 사업은 그 회사의 사업 다각화에 도움이 될 것이다.

7. Climate change / is likely to hit / some nations / (more than others).
   ▶ 기후 변화는 / 더 큰 타격을 줄 가능성이 있다 / 일부 국가에 / (다른 국가보다)
   해석 기후 변화는 다른 국가보다 일부 국가에 더 큰 타격을 줄 가능성이 있습니다.

8. This year, over 1000 people / are expected to visit / the ski festival.
   ▶ 올해는 1000명이 넘는 사람들이 / 방문할 것으로 예상됩니다 / 스키 축제를.

9. I / had the opportunity / to learn / many things (through them).
   ▶ 저는 / 기회가 되었습니다 / 배울 수 있는 / 많은 것을 (그들을 통해)
   해석 저는 그들을 통해 많은 것을 배울 수 있는 기회가 되었습니다.

10. An employee / has a right [to receive / at least one month's notice / of dismissal or intention to leave].
    ▶ 직원은 / 권리가 있다 / [받을 / 최소 한 달 전에 / 해고나 권고사직 통보를]
    해석 직원은 해고나 권고사직 통보를 최소 한 달 전에 받을 권리가 있다.

UNIT 11 : 동명사

GRAMMAR PRACTICE p.125

A
1. Investing
2. Helping
3. Swimming
4. Exercising
5. listening
6. speaking
7. writing
8. going
9. walking
10. achieving

B
1. Please quit **worrying** about me.
2. Both riding a bicycle and **taking** a walk every day are good for your health.
3. O
4. On hot summer days, people often feel like **eating** ice cream.
5. The teacher summarized a long report by **giving** its main ideas.

GRAMMAR PRACTICE p.127

A
1. to cook, cooking
2. playing
3. smoking
4. avoid
5. to tell, telling

B
1. to lock
2. seeing
3. studying
4. to sell
5. fighting

C
1. Mr. Johnson decided to discontinue **smoking** yesterday.
2. Although she is busy, Ms. Lee will continue **to study** English.
   Although she is busy, Ms. Lee will continue **studying** English.
3. Jane suddenly started **eating** the leftovers.
   Jane suddenly started **to eat** the leftovers.
4. O
5. O

GRAMMAR PRACTICE p.129

A
1. developing
2. development
3. shipping
4. organization
5. organizing
6. introduction
7. introducing
8. expansion
9. expanding
10. having

B
1. We cannot be too careful **in choosing** books.
2. O
3. I've been working for five years in the **marketing** division at Intel.
4. O
5. When a celebrity appears in an **advertisement**, people want to buy that product.

GRAMMAR PRACTICE p.131

A
1. to preserving 2. tidying 3. to jogging
4. at 5. to speaking 6. to preventing
7. to broaden 8. to building 9. to enhance
10. to perform

B
1. Ms. Ruppert recommends that we seek legal advice before **signing** any agreement.
2. David spends most of his time **preparing** for the entrance exam.
3. O
4. Your suggestion is **worth** considering.
5. Most workers are used to **working** in dangerous environments.

GRAMMAR IN SENTENCE p.132

1. Both riding a bicycle and taking a walk / (every day) / are good / for your health.
▶ 자전거를 타는 것과 산책을 하는 것은 / (매일) 좋다 / 당신의 건강에
해석 매일 자전거를 타는 것과 산책을 하는 것은 당신의 건강에 좋다.

2. The teacher / summarized / a long report (by giving its main ideas).
▶ 그 선생님은 / 요약했다 / 긴 보고서를 (말함으로써 / 주요한 개념들을)
해석 그 선생님은 주요한 개념들을 말함으로써 긴 보고서를 요약했다.

3. (No matter how difficult / it may seem), keep trying / to do your best.
▶ (아무리 어려워 보여도) / 꾸준히 시도해라 / 최선을 다해
해석 아무리 어려워 보여도 꾸준히 최선을 다해 시도해라

4. David / spends / most of his time / preparing (for the entrance exam).
▶ David는 / 보내고 있다 / 대부분의 그의 시간을 / 준비를 하느라 (입학 시험을)
해석 David는 입학시험 준비를 하느라 대부분의 시간을 보내고 있다.

5. Ms. Ruppert / recommends that we / seek / legal advice (before signing any agreement).
▶ Ruppert 씨는 / 추천한다 / 우리가 / 구할 것을 / 법률 자문을 / (어떤 계약서에라도 서명하기 전에).
해석 Ruppert 씨는 어떤 계약서에라도 서명하기 전에 우리가 법률 자문을 구할 것을 추천한다.

6. (When a celebrity / appears / in an advertisement), people / want to buy / that product.
▶ (유명인이 / 나오면 / 광고에), 사람들은 / 구매하고 싶어 한다 / 그 제품을
해석 유명인이 광고에 나오면, 사람들은 그 제품을 구매하고 싶어한다.

7. Dr. Phillips / is seeking to broaden / the research (by conducting a genetic study).
▶ Phillips 박사는 / 넓히려고 한다 / 연구의 범위를 (유전자 연구를 함으로써)
해석 Phillips 박사는 유전자 연구를 함으로써 연구의 범위를 넓히려고 한다.

8. Most of the residents / objected to building / the factory (in this area).
▶ 대부분의 주민들은 / 반대했다 / 짓는 것을 / 공장을 / (이 지역에)
해석 대부분의 주민들은 이 지역에 공장을 짓는 것을 반대했다.

9. The purpose of the program / is / to enhance / the effectiveness of the organization.
▶ 이 프로그램의 목적은 / 이다 / 증진시키는 것 / 그 기관의 효율성을.
해석 이 프로그램의 목적은 그 기관의 효율성을 증진시키는 것이다.

10. This training program / will enable / the employees / to perform better.
▶ 이 훈련 프로그램은 / 해 줄 것이다 / 직원들이 / 일을 더 잘 수행할 수 있도록.
해석 이 훈련 프로그램은 직원들이 일을 더 잘 수행할 수 있도록 해 줄 것이다.

UNIT 12 : 분사

GRAMMAR PRACTICE p.135

A
1. built 2. named 3. wearing
4. invited 5. invited 6. wearing
7. held 8. proposed 9. charged
10. damaged

B
1. (B) 2. (C) 3. (D) 4. (B) 5. (A)

A
1. exciting, excited.
2. impressive, impressed
3. satisfactory, satisfied
4. disappointing, disappointed
5. surprising, surprised

B
1. satisfied   2. skilled   3. qualified
4. limited   5. informed

C
1. (D)   2. (B)   3. (D)   4. (A)   5. (D)

A
1. Being happy
2. Born in April
3. Having been advised to lose weight by his doctor
4. disappointing everybody
5. Having discussed possible measures
6. Not knowing the man at all

B
1. Although I lives next door to her
2. As she has traveled abroad many times,
3. When I arrived at the bus station
4. When you apply for the position
5. Since the library was built in 1990
6. As I didn't know what to say

GRAMMAR PRACTICE p.141

A
1. Judging from his accent
2. Speaking of bears
3. Frankly speaking
4. Compared with last year
5. Strictly speaking

B
1. **Granting that** you were drunk, you are responsible for your conduct.
2. The event was initially scheduled **to be held** in Tokyo in March.
3. O
4. You should be careful **not to get** involved in that complication.
5. O

C
1. (B)   2. (C)   3. (A)   4. (B)   5. (D)

GRAMMAR IN SENTENCE p.142

1. We / live / in a large house [built of stone and brick].
▶ 우리는 / 살고 있다 / [큰 집에 돌과 벽돌로 지은]
해석 우리는 돌과 벽돌로 지은 큰 집에 살고 있다.

2. A man [named Aesop] / wrote / this famous storybook.
▶ 한 사람이 [Aesop이란 이름을 가진] / 썼다 / 이 유명한 이야기책을
해석 Aesop이란 이름을 가진 사람이 이 유명한 이야기책을 썼다.

3. I / know / the girl [wearing / a big straw hat].
▶ 나는 / 알고 있다 / 소녀를 [쓴 / 큰 밀짚모자를
해석 나는 저 큰 밀짚모자를 쓴 소녀를 알고 있다.

4. The workshop [held last month] / was / to increase productivity.
▶ 워크숍은 [지난 주 열린] / 것이었다 / 생산성 향상을 위한.
해석 지난 주 열린 워크숍은 생산성 향상을 위한 것이었다.

5. They / expressed / significant interest / for the newly proposed production schedule.
▶ 그들은 / 표현했다 / 각별한 관심을 / 새롭게 제안된 생산 일정에 대해
해석 그들은 새롭게 제안된 생산 일정에 대해 각별한 관심을 보였다.

6. There / is / a fee [charged for each transaction].
▶ 있다 / 수수료가 / [부과되는 각 거래에]
해석 각 거래에 부과되는 수수료가 있다.

7. We / will be happy to refund or replace / damaged goods (if / they are returned / within 15 days of purchase).
▶ 우리는 / 기꺼이 환불하거나 교체해 줄 것이다 / (손상된 물건에 대해 만약 / 반품이 되면 / 15일 이내에)
해석 만약 15일 이내에 반품이 되면 우리는 기꺼이 손상된 물건에 대해 환불하거나 교체해 줄 것이다.

8. A person [remaining in the building after 10 p.m.] is requested / to lock the door / when he leaves.
▶ 사람은 [남아있는 건물에 10시 이후에] / 요구되어 진다 / 문을 잠글 것 이 나갈 때
해석 10시 이후 건물 안에 남아있는 사람은 나갈 때, 문을 잠가야 한다.

9. Anyone [wanting to apply / for the accounting position advertised] must submit / their resumes and cover letters / by the end of the month.
▶ 사람은 [누구라도 지원하고 싶은] / 광고된 회계 직에 제출하여야 한다 / 이력서와 첨부설명서를 / 월말까지
해석 광고된 회계 직에 지원하고 싶은 사람은 누구라도 이력서와 첨부설명 서를 월말까지 제출하여야 한다.

10. She could figure out the amount of time [required on the job], (since she had had a similar experience).

▶ 그녀는 / 헤아릴 수 있었다 / 시간의 양을 [그 일에 요구되어지는] (그녀는 비슷한 경험을 갖고 있었기 때문에)

해설 그녀는 비슷한 경험을 갖고 있었기 때문에 그 일에 필요한 시간의 양을 헤아릴 수 있었다.

📖 ACTUAL TEST 4
p.144-145

A
1. (D) 2. (B) 3. (A) 4. (C) 5. (D) 6. (A)
7. (B) 8. (D) 9. (B) 10. (A)

B
11. (C) 12. (A) 13. (D) 14. (B) 15. (D) 16. (B)

A

1. In an effort to ------- many travelers, the travel agency has made the cheapest package tour of Europe.
(A) attracting
(B) attractively
(C) attraction
(D) attract

해석 많은 관광객을 유치하기 위한 일환으로 여행사는 가장 싼 유럽 관광용 패키지 상품을 내놓았다.

해설 effort는 to 부정사의 수식을 받는다. 또한 <in an effort to + 동사원형>은 '~을 하기 위한 일환으로'라는 뜻의 관용어구이다.

어휘 travel agency 여행사   package tour 패키지 여행

2. The new system will encourage students ------- their behavior instead of simply punishing them.
(A) modifying
(B) to modify
(C) modify
(D) modified

해석 그 새로운 제도는 단순히 벌을 주는 대신에 학생들이 자신들의 행동을 고치도록 격려할 것이다.

해설 encourage는 목적 보어로 to부정사를 취하는 동사이다.

어휘 modify 고치다, 수정하다   behavior 행동   instead of ~ 대신에

3. Friendly Messenger lets you instantly ------- with your coworkers over long distances all around the world.
(A) communicate
(B) to communicate
(C) communicating
(D) communicated

해석 Friendly Messenger는 멀리 떨어져 있는 당신의 동료와 전 세계에 있는 친구들이나 가족들과 즉시 의사소통을 할 수 있도록 한다.

해설 본동사인 let은 사역동사이므로 목적어 다음 동사원형이 와야 한다. 그러므로 정답은 (A)이다.

어휘 let A 동사원형 A가 ~하도록 해주다
communicate with ~와 의사소통 하다, 연락하다   coworker 동료
all around the world 전 세계에 있는   instantly 즉시

4. Trainers who have completed their daily tasks should spend time ------- manuals on company policies.
(A) read
(B) to read
(C) reading
(D) with reading

해석 하루의 업무를 끝낸 훈련생들은 회사 정책들에 관한 매뉴얼을 읽어야 한다.

해설 spend time ~ing 의 '~하는데 시간을 보내다'라는 의미의 관용구입니다. 그러므로 정답은 reading입니다.

어휘 complete 완료하다, 완성하다   task 직무, 일

5. Terry is used to ------- on the left side of the road because he has lived in Tokyo for a long time.
(A) drive
(B) drove
(C) driven
(D) driving

해석 Terry는 오랫동안 도쿄에 살았기 때문에 왼쪽으로 운전하는 것에 익숙하다.

해설 be used to ~ing는 '~에 익숙하다'라는 의미이며, be used to 동사원형은 '~하기 위해 사용되어 진다'라는 뜻입니다.

어휘 for a long time 오랫동안

6. Every employee should remember that all items ------- directly from the local manufacturer will take an additional two days.
(A) shipped
(B) shipping
(C) ships
(D) was shipping

해석 모든 직원들은 지역 생산자들로부터 바로 선적된 물건들은 2일이 추가로 걸린다는 것을 기억해야 합니다.

해설 items (which were) shipped 가 되어 과거 분사 shipped가 item을 수식하는 형태입니다.

어휘 item 물건   ship 배달하다, 선적하다   local 지역의
manufacturer 생산자   take (시간이) 걸리다   additional 추가의

7. ------- requests for a better work environment, the company decided to renovate the building.
(A) Received
(B) Having received
(C) Having been received
(D) Being received

해설 더 좋은 근무 환경을 만들자는 요청을 받고서, 그 회사는 건물을 수리하기로 결정했다.

정답 **241**

해설 완료 분사 구문은 주절의 시제보다 앞선 시제를 나타내게 된다. 목적어 requests가 있으므로 능동의 의미인 Having Received가 적합하다.

어휘 **work environment** 근무 환경 **renovate** 수리하다

8. Before visitors could enter the ------- parking area, they had to have security passes.
(A) designate
(B) designating
(C) designation
(D) designated

해석 방문객들은 지정된 주차 장소에 들어가기 전에, 보안 카드를 받아야만 했다.

해설 복합명사인 parking area를 수식하는 형용사 역할을 하는 분사가 필요한 자리이며, 의미상 과거분사인 designated 가 와야 합니다.

어휘 **security pass** 보안 카드

9. Emergency rescue teams will conduct an active search of the area for the ------- children.
(A) miss
(B) missing
(C) missed
(D) misses

해석 응급 구조 팀들은 아이들이 행방불명된 지역에 대한 활발한 조사를 진행할 것이다.

해설 잃어버린 이라는 의미의 분사는 missing입니다.

10. ------- customer satisfaction, the fast growing company established a new Customer Service Department last year.
(A) To improve
(B) Improving
(C) Improves
(D) Improved

해석 고객 만족을 증대시키기 위하여, 고속 성장하고 있는 그 회사는 작년에 새로운 고객 서비스 부서를 설립했다.

해설 to부정사의 부사적 용법은 대개 '~하기 위하여'라는 의미로 쓰인다. in order to do와 so as to do도 같은 의미를 나타낸다. 따라서 빈칸에는 To expand가 적합하다.

어휘 **customer service department** 고객 서비스 부서

B
Questions 11-16 refer to following notice.

Attention All Pet Owners!

Do your pets have all their vaccine and immunization shots? Have these records been filed with The Federal Bureau for Animal Control or your local Animal Control Office?

11. ------- your pet safe and healthy is both your and our goal. It is important 12. ------- records of your pet's immunization for international travel purposes, in the event that your pet gets lost, goes missing or becomes ill.

To check on the status of your pet's immunization and vaccine record, or 13. ------- your pet's file, please bring 14. ------- documents of your pet's medical history from a licensed veterinarian to your local Animal Control Office. Mandatory vaccinations and immunizations can also 15. ------- by the Animal Control Office. Please call ahead 16. ------- an appointment for these services.

애완동물을 기르시는 분들은 주목하세요!

여러분의 애완동물은 백신과 면역 주사를 맞았습니까? 이 기록들은 연방동물관리국이나 지역동물관리 사무실에 정식으로 제출되었습니까? 여러분의 애완동물을 안전하고 건강하게 지키는 것은 여러분과 저희의 목표입니다. 해외여행 전이나, 애완동물이 길을 잃거나 실종되거나 아플 경우를 대비해 면역접종기록을 갖고 있는 것이 중요합니다.
애완동물의 면역과 백신 접종기록 상태를 확인하거나 애완동물 파일을 갱신하기 위해, 면허 있는 수의사나 지역 동물관리 사무실에서 발급된 애완동물의 의료기록이 있는 증명서를 가져오십시오. 동물관리 사무실에서 의무 백신과 면역 접종을 받을 수 있습니다. 이러한 서비스를 예약하려면 먼저 전화해주십시오.

어휘 **vaccine** (접종용의) 백신 **immunization** 면역(접종) **shot** 주사 **federal** 연방의 **bureau** 국 (= department) **status** 상태 **certified** 증명된 **licensed** 인가된, 면허를 받은 **veterinarian** 수의사 (= veterinary surgeon) **mandatory** 명령의, 필수의, 의무의 (= obligatory) **book** 예약하다

11.
(A) Keep
(B) Kept
(C) Keeping
(D) Being kept

해설 문장구조 분석을 통해 알맞은 단어의 형태를 고르는 유형이다. 문장의 구조를 분석 할 때 우선적으로 파악해야 하는 것은 주어와 동사이다. 동사인 is를 중심으로 보면 주어에 어떤 요소가 와야 하는지를 알 수 있는데, your pet safe and healthy를 목적어로 취하면서 동시에 주어 노릇을 할 수 있는 것은 부정사나 동명사뿐이다. 현대영어에서는 일반적으로 동명사 주어를 사용한다.

12.
(A) to maintain
(B) to be maintained
(C) to maintaining
(D) maintains

해설 빈칸에는 record를 목적어로 취하는 능동형의 to 부정사가 들어가야 한다. It is important ------ records ~에서 it은 가짜주어 to maintain ~이 진짜 주어이다.

13.
(A) updating
(B) updated
(C) updates
(D) to update

해설 동사인 update의 올바른 형태를 찾는 유형이다. or이라는 접속사가 힌트가 되고 있는데 등위접속사라 불리는 and 나 or의 경우에는 연결되는 단어나 어구가 같은 성질과 형태가 되어야 하기 때문에 이미 등장한 to check과 같은 형태를 유지해야 한다.

14.
(A) certify
(B) certified
(C) certifying
(D) certificate

해설 ------ documents 에서 증명된 서류라는 의미이므로 과거분사형 형용사인 certified 가 적합하다.

15.
(A) provide
(B) have provided
(C) provides
(D) be provided

해설 immunizations can also ------ by the Animal Control Office 에서 조동사 can 다음에는 동사원형이 와야 하고 목적어가 없으므로 수동형으로 써야한다.

16.
(A) book
(B) to book
(C) booking
(D) booked

해설 주동사인 call과 빈칸 이후로 자연스럽게 연결하는 어구를 찾는 유형이다. '~하기 위해'라는 부사적 의미를 지닌 부정사가 정답이 된다. 정답 (B)

MINI TEST 2
p.146-149

A
1. (B) 2. (C) 3. (C) 4. (D) 5. (C) 6. (A)
7. (C) 8. (A) 9. (C) 10. (A)

B
1. (B) 2. (D) 3. (A) 4. (B) 5. (C) 6. (A)
7. (B) 8. (C) 9. (B) 10. (A)

C
1. (C) 2. (A) 3. (D) 4. (A) 5. (D) 6. (B)
7. (A) 8. (A) 9. (C) 10. (C) 11. (D) 12. (D)

A

1. Together they began a ------ study of the funeral industry, and Bob suggested that they publish their findings.
(A) detailing
(B) detailed
(C) details
(D) detail

해석 그들은 함께 장례 산업에 대한 구체적인 연구를 시작했는데 밥은 그들에게 연구결과를 출판하라고 제안했다.

해설 명사인 study를 수식하기 위한 형용사가 필요하다. '상세한'이라는 의미의 형용사화 된 분사는 detailed이다.

어휘 study 연구

2. Despite the recent economic recession, high-technology venture firms keep growing in size, ------ numerous college graduates with degrees in engineering and technology.
(A) hire
(B) hires
(C) hiring
(D) hired

해석 최근 경제 불황에도 불구하고 최첨단 벤처 회사들은 공학과 기술에 학위를 가진 수많은 대학 졸업생들을 고용하면서 규모 면에서 계속 성장하고 있다.

해설 high technology venture firms keep growing in size가 주어와 동사를 갖춘 완전한 절이고, 빈칸 앞에는 접속사가 없는 형태이다. 그러므로 현재 분사나 과거 분사로 시작하는 분사 구문 자리이다. 동사 뒤에 목적어인 numerous college graduates가 있으므로 능동형인 현재 분사가 적합하다.

어휘 economic recession 경기 침체, 경제 불황 keep+-ing 계속 ~하다 graduate 졸업생 degree 학위

3. ------ the chief executive officer, Ms. Lucas has access to confidential information and statistics regarding the company's performance.
(A) To be
(B) Be
(C) Being
(D) Has been

243

해석 최고 경영자로 재직 중인 Lucas 씨는 회사의 업무 성과에 대한 비밀 정보와 통계에 접근할 수 있다.

해설 As she is the chief executive officer, Ms. Lucas has access to confidential information and statistics about the company's performance.에서 종속절의 접속사 as와, 주절의 주어(Ms. Lucas)와 동일한 종속절의 주어(she)를 생략하고 동사 (is)를 분사인 being으로 바꾼 분사 구문이다.

어휘 chief executive officer 최고 경영자(= CEO) have access to ~에 접근할 수 있다 confidential 비밀의 performance 업무 실적

4. The number of freelance writers ------- remarkably in recent years at a significantly faster rate than that of dependent writers.
(A) will increase
(B) are increased
(C) have increased
(D) has increased

해석 자유 계약한 작가들의 수가 소속된 저널리스트들의 수 보다 훨씬 더 빠른 속도로 최근 몇 년간 두드러지게 증가하였다.

해설 in recent years은 '최근 몇 년 동안'이라는 의미로 과거 또는 현재완료 시제와 써야 한다. 또한 주어 the number 이므로 단수형이므로 현재완료형인 (D)has increased 가 정답이다.

어휘 freelance 자유 계약의 significantly 상당히, 두드러지게 rate 비율 dependent 의존적인, 소속된

5. The recent issue of the journal Science, written by famous scientists, ------- by a courier service next week.
(A) will deliver
(B) is delivering
(C) will be delivered
(D) delivers

해석 유명 과학자들에 의하여 쓰여 진 사이언스지 최근호가 다음 주에 배송 될 것이다.

해설 next week는 미래 시제와 함께 써야 하며, deliver은 타동사인데 목적어가 없으므로 수동태를 써야 한다. 그러므로 정답은 (C) will be delivered이다.

어휘 issue 발행물, 호 journal 정기간행물 courier 택배(업자) delivery 배송

6. Our supervisor requested that some equipment ------- from the basement to the newly built warehouse.
(A) be moved
(B) move
(C) is moved
(D) moves

해석 우리 감독관은 몇 몇 기기를 지하에서 새로 지은 창고로 옮길 것을 요청했다.

해설 request와 같이 제안/요청하는 동사가 주절에 쓰여서 that절에 should가 생략된 동사원형인 be moved를 써야한다.

어휘 basement 지하 newly 새로이 warehouse 창고

7. Our flight attendants ------- complimentary beverages once we are airborne.
(A) provides
(B) are provided
(C) will be providing
(D) have provided

해석 비행기가 정상궤도에 이르게 되면 승무원들이 무료 음료를 제공해 드릴 것입니다.

해설 시간과 조건의 부사절에서는 미래 대신 현재시제를 쓰고, 주절에는 미래 시제를 써야한다. 그러므로 조건절인 once we are airborne와 비교해 보면. 주절에는 미래 시제인 will be providing이 적합하다.

어휘 complimentary 무료의 once 일단 ~하면 airborne 이륙하여, (공중에) 떠

8. It is recommended that a driver ------- a minimum of 8 hours of sleep prior to driving on long trips.
(A) obtain
(B) is obtained
(C) obtained
(D) obtaining

해석 운전기사들은 긴 운행 시간 전에 최소한 8시간의 수면을 취할 것이 권고되어진다.

해설 추천을 의미하는 recommend의 영향으로 that 절 안에서는 주어가 3인칭 단수라 할지라도 동사원형을 쓰는 것이 바람직하다. (B)는 수동태이고, (D)는 주동사의 형태가 아니다. (C)는 일반적인 사실에 대한 이야기이므로 과거동사가 올 이유가 없다.

어휘 a minimum of 최소한의 prior to 이전의

9. The company's advisor suggested ------- the releases of the new products due to unfavorable conditions in the market.
(A) postpone
(B) to postpone
(C) postponing
(D) postponed

해석 그 회사의 고문은 시장의 불리한 상황 때문에 신제품 출시를 연기하라고 제안했다.

해설 suggest는 동명사를 목적어로 취한다. 그러므로 정답은 (C) postponing이다.

어휘 suggest 제안하다 postpone 지연하다 release 출시, 발매

10. Failing ------- with the new regulations can lead to serious consequences, including fines and imprisonment.
(A) to comply
(B) complying
(C) complied
(D) to be complied

해석 새 규정에 따르지 않는 것은 벌금과 금고형을 포함하여 심각한 결과를 이끌 수 있다.

해설 fail은 to 부정사를 목적어로 취하며, 자동사로 쓰이므로 수동형으로 쓸 수 없다. 그러므로 정답은 (A) to comply이다.

어휘 comply with ~에 따르다 regulations 규정, 규제 lead to ~로 이끌다 consequences 결과 fine 벌금 imprisonment 감금, 투옥, 금고형

B

1. This year's (A)[annual] Multimedia Art Asia Pacific media arts festival will be (B)[holding] in Brisbane, Australia, (C)[from] October 23 (D)[to] November 10.

   정답 (B) holding → held

   해석 올해의 연례 MAAP 미디어 예술 축제는 2005년 10월 23일부터 11월 10일까지 호주의 Brisbane에서 열릴 것입니다.

   해설 정확한 미래의 시점이 나와 있으므로 미래진행형이 아닌 미래시제이어야 하고 축제는 열리는 것이므로 수동태가 되어야 한다. hold-held-held.

2. (A)[After] hearing and considering the (B)[views of] the members of the union, the executive committee drew up a (C)[report on] the issue that will be (D)[sent it] to the Ministry of Industry and Energy.

   정답 (D) sent it → sent

   해석 노동조합 구성원들의 견해를 듣고 고려한 후에 집행위원회는 산자부에 보낼 문제에 대한 보고서를 작성했다.

   해설 원래의 문장은 SB sent the issue to the ~이다. 이것을 수동태로 고치면 the issue was sent to the~가 되며 본 문장에서는 the issue가 주격관계대명사의 선행사로 사용되었다.

3. Before (A)[clean] the copy machine, the user (B)[should] make sure (C)[that] he (D)[removes] the cord from the outlet.

   정답 (A) clean → cleaning

   해석 사용자는 복사기를 청소하기 전에 연결선을 분리했는지 확인해야 한다.

   해설 주어가 생략됐으므로, 동사의 분사 형태가 와야 한다. 목적어가 있으므로, 능동형인 현재 분사형이 와야 한다.

4. Mr. Thompson (A)[resigned as] the administrative head (B)[in order pursue] other (C)[activities] (D)[for] the local community.

   정답 (B) in order pursue → in order to pursue

   해석 Thompson씨는 지역 사회를 위한 다른 활동을 추구하기 위해서 경영진 자리를 사임했다.

   해설 in order to는 '~하기 위해'라는 의미의 to 부정사의 부사적 용법을 나타내는 표현이다.

5. It is predicted (A)[that] the (B)[representatives] of different (C)[company] all over the world will also (D)[copy] this kind of device.

   정답 company → companies

   해석 전 세계의 다양한 회사들의 대표자들 역시 이와 같은 장치를 모방할 것이라고 예상된다.

   해설 형용사 different 다음에는 앞에 관사가 없으므로 복수형의 명사가 와야 한다.

6. Questions (A)[involve] product (B)[warranties], repair, and pricing (C)[should be] (D)[directed to] Mr. Harrison in Sales.

   정답 (A) involve → involving

   해석 제품 보증과 수리, 가격에 관한 질문들은 판매부서의 Harrison씨에게로 돌려져야 합니다.

   해설 본동사는 should be directed이다. involve는 동사가 아니라 분사 수식어구가 되어야 하므로 정답은 involving이다.

7. Graduate students (A)[interested] in (B)[pursue] careers (C)[in] agriculture are recommended (D)[to] attend the farmer's conference in Maine.

   정답 (B) pursue → pursuing

   해석 농업에 관심 있는 졸업생들은 메인주에서 열리는 농업 세미나에 참석할 것이 권장된다.

   해설 전치사 다음에는 동사의 동명사 형태가 와야 한다.

8. he sales representative (A)[informed] us (B)[that] Mr. Green was (C)[satisfaction] with our (D)[after sales service] and will continue to do business with our company.

   정답 (C) satisfaction → satisfied

   해석 판매 담당자가 Green씨가 우리의 AS에 만족했고, 우리 회사와 계속 거래를 하겠다고 알려주었다.

   해설 be 동사 다음에 형용사 보어가 나와야 한다. 따라서 과거분사 satisfied로 바꿔야 한다.

9. (A)[Applicants] are (B)[reminded obtain] all the necessary personal (C)[documents] to (D)[apply for] any jobs at this company.

   정답 (B) reminded obtain → reminded to obtain

   해석 응시자들에게 이 회사에 응시할 때 모든 필요한 개인 서류를 준비할 것을 상기시켰다.

   해설 '~에게 …할 것을 상기시키다'의 의미로 remind A to do를 쓰므로, reminded와 obtain 사이에 to를 넣어야 한다.

10. The NK Newspaper (A)[allow] readers (B)[to] check for (C)[updated] news at any time (D)[on] their cell phones as a bonus for subscribing.

    정답 (A) allow → allows

    해석 NK Newspaper은 구독에 대한 사은으로 독자들이 휴대폰 상에서 최신 뉴스를 볼 수 있도록 하고 있다.

    해설 NK Newspaper이 3인칭 단수이기 때문에 동사도 단수가 되어야 한다.

C

Questions 1-6 refer to the following letter.

September 10

Karl Leman
Taylor Bay Apartments
335 Waterfront Ave.
San Francisco, CA 10009

To Karl Leman:

I **1.** ------- a tenant in your building on Waterfront Avenue for the past 5years. I have always paid my rent on time, and have never had any issues arise with respect to the level of service offered. However, last month my bathroom sink began **2.** -------, and I immediately called the building manager, who told me she would contact a maintenance person. It took 2 days for a maintenance person to arrive, by which time a significant amount of water **3.** ------- onto the dining room carpet. While I did my best to dry up the water, it has left a permanent stain.

I **4.** ------- the building manager of the stain, and she sent a cleaner to steam clean the carpet. The stain **5.** -------, but I arrived home today to find a bill for

$75.00 for the cleaning services.

I have paid the bill, but would like to ask that I **6.** ------- the full amount (or
have it deducted from next month's rent of $450.00).

Thank you,
Julie Andrews, Apartment 1208

어휘 **tenant** 세입자 **with respect to** ~에 관하여 **leak** 새다 **maintenance** 보수 관리, 정비 **permanent** 영구적인, 불변의 **stain** 얼룩 **deduct** 빼다, 공제하다

1.
(A) am
(B) was
(C) have been
(D) had been

해설 for the past 5years는 지난 5년 동안을 나타내므로 동사는 현재완료를 써야 한다. 그러므로 정답은 (C) have been이다.

2.
(A) leaking
(B) to leaking
(C) leaks
(D) leaked

해설 begin은 to 부정사 또는 동명사를 목적어로 취할 수 있으므로 began leaking 또는 began to leak 이 적합하다.

3.
(A) has leaked
(B) leaks
(C) will have leaked
(D) had leaked

해설 It took 2 days for a maintenance person to arrive, by which time a significant amount of water ------- onto the dining room carpet. 문장에서 해석을 해 보면, 수리공이 도착하는 데는 이틀이 걸렸는데 그동안 상당한 양의 물이 식당 카펫까지 흘렀다는 건 대과거의사건이므로 과거완료를 써야한다. 그러므로 정답은 (D) had leaked이다.

4.
(A) informed
(B) announced
(C) said
(D) mentioned

해설 ------- the building manager of the stain 에서 사람목적어 of 명사의 구조를 취할 수 있는 타동사는 informed이다. announce say mention은 that을 곧장 목적어로 취하거나 to 사람 that 절의 구조로 쓴다.

5.
(A) removes
(B) removed
(C) is removed
(D) was removed

해설 The stain -------, 에서 얼룩이 제거되었다는 의미로 수동형이면서 과거시제를 써야한다. 그러므로 정답은 (D) was removed이다.

6.
(A) refund
(B) be refunded
(C) refunds
(D) refunded

해설 주절에 요구 주장 명령 제안을 나타내는 동사 would like to ask 가 있으므로 that 절이라는 should 생략된 동사원형을 쓴다. 이 때 수동형을 써야 하므로 정답은 be refunded이다.

Questions 7-12 refer to the following advertisement.

> **BRIGHT CLEANETTES: HOME DRY-CLEANING KIT**
>
> Owning wool clothing **7.** ------- a luxury many of us enjoy. However, **8.** ------- it to the dry cleaner's every time can be a money-consuming problem! Now, You don't have to spend much money **9.** ------- your wool clothing. With the new Bright Cleanette Home Dry-Clean Kit, you can **10.** ------- clean wool clothing in your own home. Don't miss out on the quality of wool clothing. Bright Cleanette **11.** ------- you with quality cleaning for less! Also, you can save up to thirty percent by **12.** ------- Bright Cleanette through the catalogue before the end of this month.

가정용 드라이클리닝 세트,
브라이트 클리네트

양모 의류를 소유하는 것은 우리 중 많은 사람들이 즐기는 사치입니다. 그러나 매번 드라이클리닝을 맡기면 돈이 많이 드는 문제가 생깁니다! 이 제, 여러분은 양모로 만든 의류를 세탁하는데 더 이상 돈을 많이 쓸 필요 가 없습니다. 새로운 브라이트 클리네트 가정용 드라이클리닝 세트로 여 러분은 댁에서 양모로 만든 의류를 세탁하실 수 있습니다. 양질의 양모 로 만든 의류를 세탁할 기회를 놓치지 마세요. 브라이트 클리네트는 저 렴한 가격으로 높은 세탁 품질을 제공합니다. 또한, 여러분은 이달 말 전 에 카탈로그를 통해서 브라이트 클리네트를 주문함으로써 30퍼센트까 지 절약할 수 있습니다.

어휘 **dry cleaner's** 세탁소 **money-consuming** 돈이 드는
miss out 기회를 놓치다 **provide A with B** A에게 B를 제공하다
up to+숫자 ~까지

7.
(A) is
(B) are
(C) has
(D) have

해설 양모 의류를 소유하는 것은 우리 중 많은 사람들이 즐기는 사치입니다. 라는 의미로 주어가 동명사인 owning이다, 동명사는 단수 취급을 하 므로 is 가 적합하다.

8
(A) taking
(B) take
(C) taken
(D) took

해설 can be가 동사부이고, ------- it to the dry cleaner's every time 이 주어부로, 주어 역할을 할 수 있도록 만들어주는 형태가 빈칸에 와야 한다. 동명사가 주어 역할을 할 수 있으므로 taking이 적합하다.

9.
(A) clean
(B) to clean
(C) cleaning
(D) cleaned

해설 '~ 하는 데 돈을 쓰다'는 의미의 <spend money+-ing> 구문이다. 그러므로 cleaning이 적합하다.

10.
(A) ease
(B) easy
(C) easily
(D) easier

해설 you can ------- clean wool clothing 에서 조동사와 일반동사 사 이에는 부사가 온다. 그러므로 easily 가 정답이다.

11.
(A) gives
(B) sends
(C) offers
(D) provides

해설 ------- you with quality cleaning에서 빈칸 뒤가 someone with something 의 구조이므로 정답은 3형시 동사 provides이다.

12.
(A) ordered
(B) orders
(C) order
(D) ordering

해설 by는 전치사이므로 뒤에 명사 또는 동명사를 목적어로 취한다. 빈칸 뒤 에 Bright Cleanette이라는 명사구가 있으므로 이를 목적어로 취할 수 있는 동명사가 와야 한다. 그러므로 ordering이 적합하다.

UNIT **13** : 접속사 I

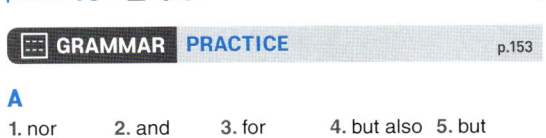

A
1. nor 2. and 3. for 4. but also 5. but

B
1. The movie was interesting **and** exciting.
2. Either visiting us or **calling** us is up to you.
3. O
4. I like **reading** books and listening to music.
5. The teacher as well as the students **has** never read the novel.

C
1. (B) 2. (D) 3. (C) 4. (B) 5. (B)

GRAMMAR PRACTICE   p.155

A
1. that the sun rises in the east.
2. that you are too critical.
3. that the work was worth doing.
4. if you will attend the meeting.
5. whether they will sign the contract.

B
1. **Whether** or not he will serve as the chairman is an important issue.
2. O
3. It is a great relief to know **that** the report is not due until Monday.
4. Please let me know **whether** or not you could help in this matter.
5. **That** Mr. Murphy was elected as the new chairman is quite surprising.

C
1. that   2. whether   3. that
4. if   5. whether

GRAMMAR PRACTICE   p.157

A
1. what   2. What, that   3. that
4. what   5. What   6. That
7. that   8. that   9. What
10. What

B
1. O
2. **Whether** he will go on a business trip next week or not will be decided tomorrow.
3. O
4. The problem is **that** the same mistake has
5. O

GRAMMAR PRACTICE   p.159

A
1. how I should
2. whether to go to the concert
3. when to give
4. what to eat
5. what to wear, how he should behave/how to behave

B
1. how   2. where   3. when
4. who   5. why

C
1. It has not yet been decided **which** department he will be transferred to.
2. O
3. **What** the boss is worried about right now is whether he can pay his employees a salary.
4. Can you show me **where** the concert hall is?
5. O

GRAMMAR IN SENTENCE   p.160

1. The fact [that you've worked as a secretary] will help / find a job.
▶ 사실이 [당신이 비서로 일해 보았다는] / 도움이 될 것입니다 / 일을 구하는 데
해석 비서로 일해 보았다는 사실이 일을 구하는 데 도움이 될 것입니다.

2. {Whether he will go on a business trip next week or not} will be decided / tomorrow.
▶ {그가 출장을 가게 될 지 아닐지는} / 다음 주에 결정될 것이다 / 내일
해석 그가 다음 주에 출장을 가게 될 지 아닐지는 내일 결정될 것이다.

3. This / is not {what we / are used to seeing / this time of the year}.
▶ 이것은 아닙니다 {우리가 / 보는 것이 / 익숙한 것이 / 일 년 중 이맘때에}
해석 이것은 우리가 일 년 중 이맘때 보는 데 익숙한 것이 아닙니다. 한 해 이맘 때 이례 경우입니다.

4. The problem / is {that the same mistake / has been made / many times before}.
▶ 문제는 / 것이다 / {바로 똑같은 실수가 / 저질러졌다는 것이다 / 여러 차례 예전에도}
해석 문제는 바로 똑같은 실수가 예전에도 여러 차례 저질러졌다는 것이다.

5. He / is afraid {that the company / is losing / clients}.
▶ 그는 / 걱정하고 있다 / {회사가 / 잃고 있어서 / 손님을}
해석 그는 회사가 손님을 잃고 있어서 걱정하고 있다.

6. It has not yet been decided {which department / he will be transferred to}.
▶ 아직 결정이 안 되었다. / {어느 부서로 / 그가 / 전근하게 될 지는}
해석 그가 어느 부서로 전근하게 될 지는 아직 결정이 안 되었다.

7. Do you happen to know {why Mr. Johnson / was late / this morning}?
▶ 혹시 아세요 / {왜 Johnson 씨가 / 늦었는 지 / 오늘 아침에}
해석 왜 Johnson 씨가 오늘 아침에 늦었는지 아세요?

8. {What the boss / is worried about right now} is whether he / can pay / his employees / a salary.
▶ {사장이 / 걱정하는 것은 / 지금이다} 그가 / 줄 수 있느냐이다 / 직원들에게 / 월급을
해석 지금 사장이 걱정하는 것은 직원들에게 월급을 줄 수 있느냐이다.

9. Can you / show / me / {where the concert hall is}?
▶ 보여 주시겠어요 / 저에게 / {어디에 콘서트홀이 있는 지}?
해석 어디에 콘서트홀이 있는 지 보여주시겠어요?

10. They / know {how to use / their time / wisely and effectively}.
▶ 그들은 / 알고 있습니다 / {어떻게 / 사용하는 지를 / 자신들의 시간을 / 지혜롭고 효과적으로}
해석 그들은 자신들의 시간을 지혜롭고 효과적으로 사용하는 법을 알고 있습니다.

UNIT 14 : 접속사 II

GRAMMAR PRACTICE p.163

A
1. before
2. While
3. since
4. now that
5. until
6. because
7. Now that
8. By the time
9. Since
10. while

B
1. O
2. **Because** plastic is more durable than wood, it is ideal for window frames.
3. We hired Joe Smith **because** his portfolio was the most unique and innovative among the applicants.
4. **Since** the classroom is poorly lit, students can't take notes.
5. Mobile professionals require access to important company resources **when** they are away from the office.

GRAMMAR PRACTICE p.165

A
1. so that
2. unless
3. In case
4. even though
5. If
6. whereas
7. Although
8. so that
9. Once
10. if

B
1. O
2. **Once** your application has been approved, we will send you a written notification of your acceptance to the program.
3. Please refrain from utilizing our services **if** you object to the terms and conditions of this agreement.
4. O
5. Please let me know this itinerary is to your satisfaction **so that** I can reserve flights.

GRAMMAR PRACTICE p.167

A
1. During, While, Meanwhile, meanwhile
2. Despite, Nevertheless, nevertheless

B
1. In case of
2. If
3. otherwise
4. unless
5. though

C
1. O
2. **In the event of** any problems or complaints, all calls and e-mails will be handled in a timely manner.
3. O
4. Cars have a permit attached to the rear window **while** parked on company property.
5. Reservations are subject to cancelation **unless** confirmed at least 3 days in advance of your arrival.

GRAMMAR IN SENTENCE p.168

1. We / are seriously thinking / we may need to throw a party / for Kennedy (once he gets the chairmanship).
▶ 우리는 / 심각하게 고려하고 있다. / 파티를 열 것에 대하여 / Kennedy를 위해 / (일단 그가 챔피언이 되면)
해석 우리는 Kennedy가 챔피언이 되면 파티를 열 것에 대하여 심각하게 고려하고 있다.

2. (Once your application has been approved), we / will send / you / a written notification of your acceptance / to the program
▶ (당신의 지원서가 승인되면), 우리는 / 보낼 것이다 / 당신에게 / 서면상의 통지서를 / 당신을 수락하는 / 그 프로그램에
해석 당신의 지원서가 승인되면, 우리는 당신에게 그 프로그램에 당신을 수락하는 서면상의 통지서를 보낼 것이다.

3. Please refrain / from utilizing our services (if you object to the terms and conditions of this agreement),
▶ 삼가해 주시기 바랍니다. / 우리 서비스 이용을 / (이 약관에 반대하신다면)
해석 이 약관에 반대하신다면 우리 서비스 이용을 삼가해 주시기 바랍니다.

4. We need to increase our advertising budget (if we hope to expand our customer base).
▶ 우리는 / 늘려야 할 필요가 있다 / 광고 예산을 / (우리의 고객층을 늘리려면) .
해석 우리의 고객층을 늘리려면 광고 예산을 늘려야 할 필요가 있다.

5. (Please) let / me / know / this itinerary / is to your satisfaction (so that I can reserve flights).
▶ 주세요 / 나에게 / 알려 / 이 일정이 / 만족스러운 지를 / (제가 항공편을 예약 할 수 있도록)
[해석] 항공편을 예약할 수 있도록 이 일정이 만족스러운지 알려주세요.

6. (While cleaning out the room), they / found / several umbrellas [which had fallen behind the sofa].
▶ (방을 청소하다가) 그들은 / 찾아냈다 / 여러개의 우산들을 [소파 뒤에 떨어져 있던]
[해석] 방을 청소하다가 그들은 소파 뒤에 떨어져 있던 우산들을 여러 개 찾아 냈다.

7. (In the event of any problem or complaint), all calls and e-mails / will be handled / in a timely manner.
▶ (어떠한 문제점이나 불평 사항이 있는 경우에는) 모든 전화와 이메일은 / 처리될 것이다 / 시기적절하게
[해석] 어떠한 문제점이나 불평 사항이 있는 경우에는 모든 전화와 이메일은 시기적절하게 처리될 것이다.

8. Visitors / should be conscious of health precautions / and should consult / a tropical medical adviser (before traveling to or in India).
▶ 방문객들은 / 건강 예방 조치를 염두에 두어야 하며 / 조언을 구해야만 한다. / 열대 지역 의학 전문가에게 (인도로 여행을 가거나 인도에서 여행을 하기 전에)
[해석] 인도로 여행을 가거나 인도에서 여행을 할 때 방문객들은 건강 예방 조치를 염두에 두어야 하며 열대 지역 의학 전문가에게 조언을 구해야만 한다.

9. Cars have a permit [attached to the rear window] (while parked on company property).
▶ 차들은 / 있어야 한다 / 주차증을 / [뒤쪽 창에 부착된] (회사 소유지에 주차되어 있는 동안)
[해석] 회사 소유지에 주차되어 있는 동안 차들은 뒤쪽 창에 주차증을 부착해야 한다.

10. Reservations are subject to cancellation (unless confirmed / at least 3 days / in advance of your arrival).
▶ 예약은 취소될 수 있다 (확인하지 않으면 / 최소한 3일 전에 / 도착하기)
[해석] 도착하기 최소한 3일 전에 확인하지 않으면 예약은 취소될 수 있다.

UNIT 15 : 관계사

GRAMMAR PRACTICE p.171

A
1. who I was teaching
2. whom I wanted to see
3. whose father is the president of our company.
4. whom everyone respects
5. which describes the performance.

B
1. which provides the job to the right people.
2. whose lands are seized.
3. who have maintained a perfect attendance record.
4. which will disturb other people.
5. who lag behind schedule

C
1. (B) who place
2. (C) which reflects
3. (D) who are

GRAMMAR PRACTICE p.173

A
1. that 2. What 3. what 4. that 5. what

B
1. (B) 2. (D) 3. (A) 4. (B) 5. (B)

C
1. This request is for the position **that** needs to be filled due to the resignation of the present director.
2. Please find the copies of all your outstanding accounts, **which** are past due over 30 days.
3. Thousands have taken these courses, **which** are available through private organizations across Canada.
4. O
5. O

GRAMMAR PRACTICE p.175

A
1. I met the woman (who is) seated on the bench.
2. All the products (which) you ordered will be packaged and shipped promptly.
3. Yesterday I visited the garden (which is) full of beautiful flowers and trees.
4. People (who are) living in large cities are busy every day.
5. This is automatically deducted from the selling price (which is) charged to the customer.

B
1. (A) 2. (B) 3. (B) 4. (D) 5. (C)

GRAMMAR PRACTICE p.177

A
1. where many people live
2. when you buy stocks.
3. when he met Linda first.
4. where we can buy some food more cheaply.
5. why you're always late for work now?

B
1. whoever   2. whomever   3. whatever
4. Whoever   5. However

C
1. (C)   2. (B)   3. (B)   4. (A)

GRAMMAR IN SENTENCE   p.178

1. We / are / the reliable organization [which provides the job / to the right people].
▶ 우리는 / 믿을 수 있는 기관이다 [일을 제공하는 / 적합한 사람에게]
해석 우리는 적합한 사람에게 일을 제공하는 믿을 수 있는 기관이다.

2. We / must give / adequate compensation / to farmers [whose lands are seized].
▶ 우리는 / 반드시 해야 한다 / 충분한 보상을 / 농부들에게 [토지를 수용당한]
해석 우리는 반드시 토지를 수용당한 농부들에게 충분한 보상을 해야 한다.

3. Awards / are given / to students [who have maintained / a perfect attendance record].
▶ 상들이 / 수여된다 / 학생들에게 [유지하는 / 완벽한 출석 기록을]
해석 한 번도 결석한 적이 없는 학생들에게 상을 수여한다.

4. Residents / should refrain / from playing / musical instruments [which will disturb / other people].
▶ 주민들은 / 삼가 해야만 한다 / 연주하는 것을 / 악기를 [다른 사람들을 방해하는]
해석 주민들은 다른 사람들에게 방해되는 악기를 연주하는 것을 삼가 해야만 한다.

5. Most of the people [who lag behind the schedule] have to pay / a penalty.
▶ 대부분의 사람들은 [스케줄에 뒤처진] 지불해야만 한다 / 벌금을
해석 스케줄에 뒤처진 대부분의 사람들은 벌금을 지불해야만 한다.

6. This request / is / for the position [that needs to be filled / due to the resignation of the present director].
▶ 이 요구 사항은 / 것이다 / 직책에 관한 [충원될 필요가 있는 / 현재 이사의 사임 때문에]
해석 이 요구 사항은 현재 이사의 사임 때문에 충원될 필요가 있는 직책에 관한 것이다.

7. Please find / the copies of all your outstanding accounts [that are past due over 30 days].
▶ 확인하세요 / 귀사의 미불 계정 사본을 [30일 이상 연체되어 있는]
해석 30일 이상 연체되어 있는 귀사의 미불 계정 사본을 확인하세요.

8. Thousands / have taken / these courses, which are available / through private organizations / across Canada.
▶ 수천 명이 / 수강했다 / 이 과정들을, 이것은 / 이용할 수 있다 / 사립 기관들을 통해 / 캐나다 전역에 있는
해석 수천 명이 이 과정들을 수강했는데, 이것은 캐나다 전역에 있는 사립 기관들을 통해 이용할 수 있다.

9. We / are / the organization [which is reliable / in terms of offering the job to the person [who would be appropriate for it]].
▶ 우리는 / 기관이다 / 믿을 수 있는 / [면에서 / 제공한다는 / 일을 [적합한 사람에게]]
해석 우리는 적합한 사람에게 일을 제공하는 믿을 수 있는 기관이다.

10. The notice / stated that only students [that are members of the band] will be allowed to use / the practice room.
▶ 공지가 / 되어 있다 / 학생들만 [밴드의 멤버인] 사용할 수 있다고 / 연습실을
해석 밴드의 멤버인 학생들만 연습실을 사용할 수 있다고 공지되어 있다.

ACTUAL TEST 5   p.180-181

A
1. (C)   2. (A)   3. (A)   4. (A)   5. (A)   6. (A)
7. (C)   8. (D)   9. (C)   10. (A)

B
11. (B)   12. (D)   13. (C)   14. (A)   15. (A)   16. (B)

A

1. The hotel dining room will be closed between seven ------- eleven o'clock.
(A) or
(B) if
(C) and
(D) yet
해석 호텔 식당은 개인적인 파티 때문에 7시와 11시 사이에는 문을 닫을 것이다.
해설 between A and B의 구문이므로 빈칸에는 and가 들어가야 한다.
어휘 **dining room** (집·호텔 따위의) 식당

2. Managers were called in to receive advice on ------- will take care of the problems they are encountering with the current project.
(A) who
(B) how
(C) that
(D) where
해석 현재 진행 중인 프로젝트가 직면해 있는 문제점을 누가 해결해야 할지에 대한 조언을 주기 위해 관리자들을 소집했다.
해설 전치사 뒤에 올 수 있는 절은 명사절이며, ------- will take care of the problems ~에서 주어가 없는 불완전한 절이다. 그러므로 누가 해결해야 할지라는 뜻으로 의문대명사 who 가 적합하다.
어휘 **call in** 소집하다   **take care of** 돌보다, 처리하다   **encounter** 직면하다

3. Bob Dillon can receive his master's degree this semester ------- he has completed his courses and completed his thesis.
(A) now that
(B) therefore
(C) unless
(D) accordingly

해석 Bob Dillon은 모든 수업과정을 마쳤고 논문이 통과되었기 때문에 이번 학기에 석사학위를 받을 수 있다.

해설 빈칸은 절과 절을 연결하는 접속사 자리이다. therefore와 accordingly는 부사이므로 부적합하다. '수업과정을 마쳤고 논문이 통과되었기 때문에 석사학위를 받을 수 있다는 의미이므로 '이제 ~이니까'라는 의미의 now that 이 적합하다.

어휘 **Master's degree** 석사학위 **thesis** 논문 **accordingly** 따라서

4. We will give prospective consumers a good impression ------- they will be able to have easy access to our website.
(A) as
(B) although
(C) in spite of
(D) because of

해석 우리는 장래의 고객들이 우리의 웹 사이트에서 쉽게 접근할 수 있기 때문에 좋은 인상을 줄 것이다.

해설 빈칸은 절과 절을 이어주는 접속사 자리이다. in spite of와 because of는 전치사이므로 절과 함께 쓸 수 없다. although는 '그럼에도 불구하고'라는 뜻으로 해석상 부적절하다. '웹 사이트에서 많은 정보에 쉽게 접근할 수 있기 때문에 좋은 인상을 줄 것이다.'라는 의미이므로, 접속사 as가 정답이 된다.

어휘 **prospective** 예기되는, 전망이 있는 **access** 접근

5. The manager had already approved the week's work schedule; ------- he accepted Mr. Carton's request for sick leave.
(A) nevertheless
(B) so as
(C) despite
(D) although

해석 부장은 주간 근무 스케줄을 이미 승인했지만, Carton씨의 병가 요청을 받아들였다.

해설 세미콜론과 콤마사이에는 접속부사가 들어가야 한다. '그럼에도 불구하고'하는 의미의 접속부사인 nevertheless 가 정답이며, 의미는 유사하지만 despite는 전치사. although는 접속사이다.

어휘 **approve** 승인하다 **sick leave** 병가

6. ------- he moved into the position of vice president in December, Mr. Clinton has been focusing on spreading Olive's name in the international market.
(A) Since
(B) Unless
(C) Accordingly
(D) Meanwhile

해석 12월에 부사장 직에 오른 이래로 Mr. Clinton는 국제 시장에 Olive의 이름을 퍼뜨리는 데에 주력해 왔다.

해설 문장 내에 두 개의 절이 있으므로 빈칸에는 두 절을 연결해 주는 접속사가 적합하다. '부회장 직에 오른 ------- Mr. Clinton는 국제 시장에 Olive 의 이름을 퍼뜨리는 데에 주력해 왔다'란 문맥에서 빈칸에 적합한 접속사는 (A)의 'since ~한 이래로'이다.

어휘 **since** ~한 이래로 **unless** 만약 ~이 아니라면 **accordingly** 따라서, 그러므로 **meanwhile** 한편, 그 동안 **vice president** 부사장, 부회장 **spread** 퍼뜨리다, 보급시키다 **International market** 국제시장

7. ------- the new shopping center in Atlanta opens, the new bus terminal will not be operational.
(A) During
(B) Rather
(C) Until
(D) By

해석 Atlanta 에 새 쇼핑센터가 개장될 때까지 새 버스터미널은 사용되지 않을 것이다.

해설 ------- 주어+동사~, 주어+동사~ 구조에서 빈칸에는 부사절 접속사만이 가능하다. 따라서 보기 중 유일한 부사절 접속사인 (C)이 정답이다.

어휘 **operational** 조직상의, 운전 중인

8. Most teens start off working in fields ------- pay minimum wage and require little skill.
(A) who
(B) whose
(C) what
(D) that

해석 대부분의 청소년들은 최저임금을 지불하고 최소의 기술을 요하는 곳에서 일을 시작한다.

해설 선행사가 fields 이고 빈칸 뒤에는 동사인 pay 가 있으므로 주격 관계대명사 which 나 that이 적합하다.

어휘 **teen** 10대, 청소년들 **deposit** 보증금, 저축

9. Unfortunately, the person ------- trade skills are needed to solve these problems is off today.
(A) who
(B) whom
(C) whose
(D) that

해석 안타깝게도, 이 문제를 해결하는 데 필요한 업무 능력을 갖추고 있는 사람은 오늘 휴가 중이다.

해설 선행사 the person과 trade skills의 관계를 볼 때 선행사의 소유격 관계대명사가 필요하다. 따라서 빈칸에는 whose가 적합하다.

10. Due to employee complaints, the company has adopted a new benefits program ------- will begin at the end of the fiscal year.
(A) that
(B) such
(C) when
(D) until

해석 종업원 불만 때문에 그 회사는 회계연도 말에 시작될 직원 복지 프로그램을 채택했다.

해설 빈칸 앞에 사물이 선행사로 쓰였고 뒤에 동사가 있으므로 사물에 쓰일 수 있는 주격 관계대명사를 써서 문장을 완성해야 한다.

어휘 due to ~ 때문에 complaint 불평, 불만 adopt 채택하다 benefits program 직원복지계획 fiscal year 회계연도 (= financial year)

B

Questions 11-16 refer to the following magazine review.

Book Review Section: A Guide to Eating Right by Joe Kimberly
Review by Contributor Jeff Montaya

Joe Kimberly's newest book, *A Guide to Eating Right* explores the complexities of the food choices **11.** ------- we encounter every day.

Millions of copies of the book have **12.** ------- sold, and last week it was nominated for the National Literature Award, **13.** ------- is the most prestigious award in the country.

The success of this book is **14.** ------- due to the simplicity of his message. He gives readers straight facts on health and nutrition as well as various tips on **15.** ------- to eat well.

Copies of A Guide to Eating Right by Brent Henley **16.** ------- available at McMaster's Bookstore for $35.00.

서평 부문: A Guide to Eating Right (작가: Joe Kimberly)
기고가 Jeff Montaya 서평

Jce Kimberly의 새 책 A Guide to Eating Right는 우리가 매일 마주치는 음식 선택의 복잡함을 다룹니다. 수백만부의 책이 이미 팔렸고 지난주에 가장 권위 있는 상인 '전국문학상'에 후보로 올랐습니다. 이 책의 성공요인은 그가 전달하고자 하는 메시지의 간결성 때문인 것 같습니다. 작가는 건강과 영양에 대한 정확한 정보와 제대로 먹는 방법에 대한 다양한 방법을 제공합니다. Joe Kimberly의 A Guide to Eating Right는 McMaster 서점에서 35 달러에 구입하실 수 있습니다.

어휘 contributor 기고가, 투고가 encounter 마주치다 nominate 후보로 지명하다, 임명하다 prestigious 일류의, 훌륭한 due to ~에 기인하는, ~때문에

11.
(A) if
(B) that
(C) who
(D) where

해설 명사인 choices와 we encounter이라는 부분을 연결할 수 있는 관계 대명사가 필요한 자리이다. 관계 대명사 자리인지를 쉽게 알 수 있는 것은 we encounter이라는 부분에서 '만나다, 접하다'라는 의미의 타동사(encounter)의 목적어가 보이지 않기 때문이다. 문장의 주요 요소(주어나 동사 등)가 누락되어 있다는 것은 관계 대명사가 도움이 필요하다는 증거라 할 수 있다. 선행사가 사물이기 때문에 which나 that 이 올 수 있다.

12.
(A) yet
(B) hardly
(C) ever
(D) already

해설 수백만부의 책이 이미 팔렸다는 의미로 현재완료의 긍정문과 가장 잘 어울리는 부사는 already이다. ever은 부정문 의문문 조건문에 쓰는 부사이다.

13.
(A) that
(B) what
(C) which
(D) when

해설 적절한 관계 대명사를 선택하는 유형으로, 선행사(award)가 사물이고 주격이라는 것 그리고 콤마(,)가 온 것으로 미루어서 which가 와야 한다. 콤마가 있는 경우에는 that을 사용하지 않는다.

14.
(A) likely
(B) likeness
(C) like
(D) likes

해설 ~ 때문인 것 같다라는 의미로 ~와 같은 이라는 의미로 be 동사와 함께 쓸 수 있는 것은 likely이다.

15.
(A) how
(B) why
(C) what
(D) wherever

해설 전치사(on)와 부정사(to eat well)를 연결하려면 의문부사가 필요하다. 부사인 well의 수식을 받으려면 '방법'을 나타내는 how가 가장 적절하다.

16.
(A) is
(B) are
(C) was
(D) has been

해설 주어가 copies 이므로 복수형 동사 are이 적합하다.

UNIT 16 : 가정법

GRAMMAR PRACTICE   p.185

A

1. should find
2. finish
3. had been
4. could see
5. should change

6. makes
7. were
8. would quit
9. will cancel
10. should have

B
1. (B) 2. (C) 3. (C) 4. (B) 5. (D)

GRAMMAR PRACTICE p.187

A
1. Were it not fo r= If not for = But for
   = Except for = Barring = Without
2. Had it not been for = If not for = But for
   = Except for = Barring = Without
3. unless

B
1. could make
2. Without
3. Providing
4. Barring
5. could be

GRAMMAR PRACTICE p.189

A
1. I wish I had my own car.
2. I wish I had studied harder for the test.
3. Mr. Lee acted as if he were an expert.
4. They sound as if / though they knew each other.
5. She talked as though she had lived in Hawaii.

B
1. providing
2. provided that
3. in case
4. Supposing
5. Given
6. Considering
7. Providing that
8. In case
9. Provided
10. provided that

GRAMMAR IN SENTENCE p.190

1. (If Mr. Smith / had taken / the plane / instead of a train), he / could have arrived / at the meeting / on time.
   ▶ Smith 씨가 / 탔더라면 / 비행기를 / 기차 대신 / 그는 도착할 수 있었을 것이다. / 회의에 / 정시에
   해석 Smith 씨가 기차 대신 비행기를 탔더라면 정시에 회의에 도착할 수 있었을 것이다.

2. (If various types of public transportation were available), they would use their cars much less frequently.
   ▶ (다양한 종류의 대중교통 수단이 이용가능하다면) / 그들은 / 이용할 것이다. / 자동차를 훨씬 덜 빈번하게
   해석 다양한 종류의 대중교통 수단이 있다면 그들은 자동차를 훨씬 덜 이용할 것이다.

3. (if the computer malfunction / had not been reported / quickly) we would not have received the technical support [we needed] this morning.
   ▶ 컴퓨터의 오작동이 / 보고되지 않았다면 / 빨리, 우리는 / 받지 못했을 것이다 / 기술 지원을 [필요했던] / 오늘 아침에
   해석 컴퓨터의 오작동이 빨리 보고되지 않았다면, 우리는 오늘 아침에 필요했던 기술 지원을 받지 못했을 것이다.

4. (If the work / does not comply / with the building codes), it / will have to be removed / or rebuilt.
   ▶ 만약 공사가 (를 할 때) / 준수하지 않으면 / 건축 규정을, 그것은 / 철거되거나 / 재건축되어야 한다.
   해석 만약 공사를 할 때 건축 규정을 준수하지 않으면, 철거되거나 재건축되어야 한다.

5. (If the company / moves / to California), it can easily find highly motivated, qualified and experienced workers [ready to work for the company].
   ▶ (회사가 / 옮긴다면 / 캘리포니아로), 찾기에 수월할 것이다 / 상당히 의욕이 있고 자격과 경력이 있는 사원들을 [회사를 위해 일할 준비가 된]
   해석 회사가 캘리포니아로 옮긴다면, 회사를 위해 일할 준비가 된 상당히 의욕이 있고 자격과 경력이 있는 사원들을 찾기에 수월할 것이다

6. (If you had taken my advice), you could make a lot of money now.
   ▶ (내 충고를 받아들였더라면) 너는 / 벌 텐데 / 큰돈을 / 지금
   해석 내 충고를 받아들였더라면 너는 지금 큰돈을 벌 텐데.

7. (Without air), all living things / could die.
   ▶ (공기가 없으면) 모든 생물은 / 죽을 것이다.
   해석 공기가 없으면 모든 생물은 죽을 것이다.

8. (Providing that you were here / now), I would be happy.
   ▶ (네가 여기 있다면 / 지금) 기쁠 텐데.
   해석 네가 지금 여기 있다면 기쁠 텐데.

9. (Barring your help), I couldn't have finished the report.
▶ (네 도움이 없었더라면) 나는 / 끝내지 못했을 것이다. / 보고서를
해석 네 도움이 없었더라면 나는 보고서를 끝내지 못했을 것이다.

10. (If I had won the lottery), I could be rich now.
▶ (내가 / 당첨되었다면 / 복권에) 나는 지금 부자일 것이다.
해석 내가 복권에 당첨되었다면 나는 지금 부자일 것이다.

UNIT 17 : 비교

GRAMMAR PRACTICE p.193

A
1. diligent
2. well
3. reliable
4. crowded
5. qualified
6. more
7. than
8. less
9. much
10. higher

B
1. Clothes are **more cheaper** than before.
2. O
3. This box is **much** heavier than the other one.
4. O
5. For most people, health and happiness are **much more** important than money.

GRAMMAR PRACTICE p.195

A
1. the tallest
2. the richest
3. the best
4. most
5. the highest
6. the taller
7. warmer
8. higher
9. superior
10. expensive

B
1. It is **the most** delicious food that I have ever eaten.
2. She is the **smartest** girl of all the students.
3. Of the two candidates, Beth Lyon is **the** more qualified for the position.

4. O
5. Cancelations or amendments must be made no later than 5 days **prior to** arrival.

GRAMMAR IN SENTENCE p.196

1. Clothes / are (a lot) cheaper / than before.
▶ 옷이 / (훨씬) / 더 싸다 / 전보다
해석 옷이 전보다 훨씬 더 싸다.

2. The red one / is (far) older / than the blue one.
▶ 빨간 것이 / (훨씬) 더 오래됐다 / 파란 것보다
해석 빨간 것이 파란 것보다 훨씬 더 오래됐다.

3. This box / is (much) heavier / than the other one.
▶ 이 상자는 (훨씬) 무겁다 / 다른 것보다
해석 이 상자는 다른 것보다 무겁다.

4. The demand for the new line of products / is greater / than last year / among teenagers.
▶ 요구는 / 새로운 상품에 대한 / 높아졌다 / 작년에 비해 / 십대들 사이에서
해석 십대들 사이에서 새로운 상품에 대한 요구는 작년에 비해 높아졌다.

5. For most people /, Health and happiness / is (much) more important than / money.
▶ 대부분의 사람들에게 / 건강과 행복이 / (훨씬) 더 중요하다 / 돈보다
해석 대부분의 사람들에게 건강과 행복이 돈보다 더 중요하다.

6. It is / the most delicious food [that I have ever eaten].
▶ 이것이 / 가장 맛있는 음식이다 / [내가 먹어 본 것 중]
해석 이것이 내가 먹어 본 것 중 가장 맛있는 음식이다.

7. She / is the smartest girl / of all the students.
▶ 그녀가 / 가장 똑똑한 소녀이다 / 모든 학생들 중에서
해석 그녀가 모든 학생들 중에서 가장 똑똑하다.

8. Of the two candidates, / Beth Lyon / is the more qualified / for the position.
▶ 두 명의 지원자 중에서, / Beth Lyon이 / 더 적격이다. / 그 직책에
해석 두 명의 지원자 중에서, Beth Lyon이 그 직책에 더 적격이다.

9. This novel of his / is inferior / to the previous one.
▶ 그의 이번 소설은 / 못하다 / 지난번 것보다
해석 그의 이번 소설은 지난번 것보다 못하다.

10. Cancellations or amendments / must be made / no later than 5 days / prior to arrival.
▶ 예약취소나 변경은 / 해야만 한다. 늦어도 5일 이전에 / 도착하기
해석 예약취소나 변경은 도착 5일 이전에 해야만 한다.

UNIT 18 : 강조와 도치

GRAMMAR PRACTICE p.199

A
1. Should you change your mind, just call us to discuss other options.
2. Were I a graduate student, I could apply for the position.
3. Had I won the lottery, I would have called you first.
4. Had you listened to my advice, you would not be in danger now (today).
5. Had I had your phone number, I could have called you last night.

B
1. is 2. are 3. is 4. are 5. is

C
1. Should
2. Had
3. could buy
4. should
5. Had

GRAMMAR PRACTICE p.201

A
1. Jane went to school yesterday, as did David.
2. Laura didn't do her homework last night, nor did Alex.
3. Jane can swim in the sea, as can Tom.

B
1. Never have I seen such a beautiful sunset.
2. Seldom do I have time to read books these days.
3. No sooner had he returned home than it began to rain.

C
1. It was Albert that gave a presentation at the monthly meeting yesterday at 10 am.
2. It was a presentation that Albert gave at the monthly meeting yesterday at 10 am.
3. It was at the monthly meeting that Albert gave a presentation yesterday at 10 am.

GRAMMAR IN SENTENCE p.202

1. Should / anybody / call me, tell them my cell phone number.
▶ 누군가 전화하면, 알려주세요 / 제 휴대폰 전화번호를.
해석 누군가 전화하면, 제 휴대폰 전화번호를 알려주세요.

2. Had / Mr. Simpson / been more careful, he / wouldn't have fallen down / on the street.
▶ Simpson 씨가 조금만 더 주의했더라면 그가 / 넘어지지 않았을 텐데 / 길에서
해석 Simpson 씨가 조금만 더 주의했더라면 길에서 넘어지지 않았을 텐데.

3. I / could buy / you / anything that you want were / I / a billionaire.
▶ 내가 / 사 줄 텐데. / 무엇이든지 네가 원하는 것은 내가 억만장자라면
해석 내가 억만장자라면 네가 원하는 것은 무엇이든지 사 줄 텐데.

4. I will never forgive you should / you / do it / again.
▶ 나는 / 결코 용서하지 않겠어 / 널 네가 / 그런 짓을 하면 또 다시
해석 또 다시 그런 짓을 하면 결코 널 용서하지 않겠어.

5. Had / I / had / no work to do, I / could have come and seen / you / at the party.
▶ 내가 / 없었더라면 / 할 일이 나는 / 가서 / 너를 만날 수 있었을 텐데. / 파티에서
해석 내가 할 일이 없었더라면 파티에 가서 너를 만날 수 있었을 텐데.

6. Jane / was planning / to travel / to Europe, as was David.
▶ Jane은 계획이었다 / 여행 할 / 유럽을, David 가 그렇듯이
해석 Jane은 David와 마찬가지로 유럽으로 여행을 계획하고 있었다.

7. Laura / won't go on a picnic tomorrow, nor will Alex.
▶ Laura는 소풍을 가지 않을 것이고 내일. Alex도 마찬가지다.
해석 Laura는 내일 소풍을 가지 않을 것이고 Alex도 마찬가지다.

8. Seldom / do / I have time / to read books / these days.
▶ 나는 / 거의 없다 / 시간이 책을 읽을 요즘에
해석 나는 요즘에 책을 읽을 시간이 거의 없다.

9. No sooner / had / he returned home / than it began to rain.
▶ 그가 / 돌아오자마자 / 집에 / 비가 오기 시작했다.
해석 그가 집에 돌아오자마자 비가 오기 시작했다.

10. Never / I / thought / one of my friends / would be successful / as a singer.
▶ 나의 친구 중의 한명이 생각해 보지 못했다 / 성공할 줄을 / 가수로
해석 나의 친구 중의 한명이 가수로 성공할 줄은 꿈에도 몰랐다.

ACTUAL TEST 5

p.204-205

A
1. (D) 2. (C) 3. (D) 4. (A) 5. (A) 6. (A)
7. (B) 8. (D) 9. (C) 10. (A)

B
11. (D) 12. (A) 13. (D) 14. (B) 15. (C) 16. (C)

A

1. If she ------- up earlier than usual not to miss the plane, Hillary could have participated in the annual conference in New York.
(A) wake
(B) woke
(C) has waken
(D) had woken

해석 만약 비행기를 놓치지 않기 위해서 평소보다 일찍 일어났더라면, Hillary는 뉴욕에서 열리는 연례 컨퍼런스에 참석할 수 있었을 텐데.

해설 가정법 과거 완료는 과거의 일을 가정할 때 사용하며, <If+주어+had +p.p., 주어+would / could / might / should+have+p.p.>의 공식으로 표현된다. 따라서 주절의 동사부가 could have gone인 것으로 보아 빈칸에는 had woken이 들어가야 함을 알 수 있다.

2. Read the operation manual carefully and then call the customer service representative ------- you experience any problems with Philips shaver.
(A) had
(B) will
(C) should
(D) has

해석 Philips Shaver를 사용하다 어떠한 문제라도 겪게 되면, 사용 안내서를 읽어보고 나서 고객 서비스 직원에게 연락하세요.

해설 Read the operation manual carefully and then call the customer service representative if you should experience any problems with Philips Shaver. 의 도치된 형태이므로, 빈칸에는 Should가 적합하다.

3. If the drinking water ------- the standard, this water can be associated with little of this risk and be considered safe.
(A) meet
(B) to meet
(C) had meet
(D) meets

해석 식수가 기준에 맞는다면 이 물은 이 위험성과는 거의 관련이 없어서 안전하다고 생각할 수 있다.

해설 빈칸에 알맞은 동사를 고르는 문제로, 가정법 현재 문장이다. 가정법 현재는 <If+주어+현재 동사, 주어+will / can / may+동사원형>으로 쓴다. 주어가 drinking water이므로 단수형 동사 meets가 적합하다.

어휘 **be associated with** ~과 관련이 있다

4. I would have picked you up at the airport ------- you notified me of your arrival in Chicago in advance
(A) had
(B) have
(C) if
(D) provided

해석 시카고에 도착한다는 것을 미리 나에게 알려 주었더라면, 내가 공항에 마중 나갈 수 있었을 텐데.

해설 가정법 과거 완료 구문 I would have picked you up at the airport if you had notified me of your arrival in Chicago in advance의 도치된 형태이다. 따라서 빈칸에는 had가 들어가야 된다.

어휘 **pick up** 마중가다 **in advance** 미리

5. ------- I known you invited family members and friends for my birthday party, I would have cooked dinner and cleaned my room.
(A) had
(B) have
(C) if
(D) provided

해석 내 생일을 위해서 친지들과 친구들을 당신이 초대했다는 것을 알았더라면, 요리도 하고, 내 방을 청소도 해 놓았을 텐데.

해설 가정법 과거 완료 구문 If I had known you invited family members and friends for my birthday party, I would have cooked dinner and cleaned my room. 의 도치된 형태이다. 따라서 빈칸에는 had가 들어가야 된다.

6. ------- had the vice president left the office than his employees started talking about him.
(A) No sooner
(B) As soon as
(C) No longer
(D) No later than

해석 부사장이 사무실을 나서자마자 직원들은 그녀에 대해 이야기하기 시작했다.

해설 도치된 구문으로 '~하자마자 ~하다'는 'no sooner ~ than'이다.

7. As the best salesperson this year, William Rutherford received ------- bonus among the employees in the company.
(A) the higher
(B) the highest
(C) high
(D) highly

해석 올해의 최고 영업사원인 William Rutherford는 그 회사 직원들 가운데 최고 보너스를 받았다.

해설 의미상 '전 직원들 사이에서 최고의 보너스를 받았다'는 뜻이므로 최상급인 the highest가 적합하다.

8. Under the new rules, pizza will be served with less sodium, and more whole grains and a ------- selection of fruits and vegetables will be available.

(A) widen
(B) widest
(C) widely
(D) wider

해석 새로운 제도 하에, 피자는 나트륨을 줄여 제공하고 더 많은 통곡물, 과일, 야채가 마련될 예정입니다.

해설 모두 비교급으로 구성되어 and 로 연결되어 있으므로 빈칸은 형용사의 비교급 형태인 wider이 적합하다.

어휘 **sodium** 나트륨   **whole grain** 통곡물

9. Ms. Frazier prefers to travel around the world by herself rather ------- with a tour group.

(A) to
(B) as
(C) than
(D) among

해석 Frazier 여사는 관광 단체와 함께 세계를 여행하는 것 보다는 홀로 여행하는 것을 선호한다.

해설 ~보다라는 표현으로 rather than 이 적합하다. than이 문장 중에 사용되면 어딘가에 무조건 비교급이 사용되어야만 하지만 rather than은 반드시 그렇지는 않다. 비교급에서 than의 강조형으로도 사용할 수도 있지만 비교의 내용 없이 instead of의 의미로, 얼마든지 독립적으로 사용할 수 있다.

어휘 **prefer** 선호하다   **by oneself** 혼자서   **rather than** ~보다는

10. One of the possible conclusions is that the success of today's insurance companies depends much ------- on the business strategies.

(A) more
(B) many
(C) well
(D) than

해석 하나의 가능한 결론은 오늘날 보험회사들의 성공은 사업전략에 훨씬 더 좌우된다는 것이다.

해설 much 의 수식을 받으려면 비교급이 가장 적합하다. 그러므로 정답은 (A) more이다.

어휘 **insurance company** 보험회사   **depend on** ~에 좌우되다   **much more** 훨씬 더   **business strategy** 사업전략

B

Questions 11-16 refer to the following news article.

The next time your baby or toddler comes down with a cold, there will be **11.** ------- relief available **12.** ------- far as medicine goes. The government has warned parents that over-the-counter cough and cold products should not be used to treat children **13.** ------- than 2 years of age. Serious and potentially life-threatening side effects such as death and rapid heart rates **14.** ------- on rare occasions.

The Food and Drug Administration stated that the medicines have not proven to be safe or **15.** ------- in children under 2.

Officials are now evaluating the risks of use by kids aged 2 to 11 and should have their decision by spring. Parents are asked to be **16.** ------- more careful when choosing cold products for their babies.

다음부터 당신의 아기 혹은 아주 어린자녀가 감기에 걸린다면, 치료약에 관한한 별다른 방법이 없을 것입니다. 정부는 처방전 없이 파는 기침 감기약을 2살 미만의 어린이들이 먹어서는 안된다고 부모들에게 경고합니다. 심각하고 잠재적으로는 생명까지 위협하는 죽음이나 빠른 심장 박동 같은 부작용이 드물게 보고되어 왔습니다. 식품의약청은 그 약들이 2살 미만의 아이들에게 안전하거나 효과적이라고 증명되지 않았다고 보고했습니다. 현재 당국자들은 2살에서 11살까지의 아이들이 복용 시 있을 수 있는 위험성을 평가하고 있고 봄까지 결정을 내려야만 합니다. 부모들은 아기가 먹을 감기약을 고를 때 훨씬 더 신중해야 합니다.

어휘 **toddler** 유아   **relief** 고통의 경감, 안도, 안심   **as far as S(주어) go / goes** 그 일에 관한 한, 어떤 범위 내에서는   **medicine** 치료약   **over-the-counter** (약을 살 때) 처방전 없이   **side effect** 부작용   **The Food and Drug Administration** 식품의약청

11.
(A) few
(B) many
(C) various
(D) little

해설 ------- relief 에서 relief 가 셀 수 없는 명사임을 알 수 있으므로 little 이 적합하다.

12.
(A) as
(B) much
(C) how
(D) very

해설 빈칸 뒤에 나온(far as medicine goes) 부분을 완성시킬 수 있는 단어가 필요한데 '~하는 한'이란 의미를 지닌 as far as를 알고 있다면 쉽게 풀리는 문제이다. 동등비교를 나타내는 관용어구들 중 대표적인 것이므로 잘 암기해 두어야 한다.

13.
(A) as
(B) more
(C) most
(D) less

해설 비교를 나타내는 접속사 than과 어울리는 부사를 찾는 문제로, more 나 less 중 하나를 선택해야 한다. as나 most는 than과 함께 사용하지 않는다. 문맥상 아주 어린 아이들에 대한 내용이기 때문에 more 보다는 less가 어울린다.

14.
(A) have reported
(B) have been reported
(C) has been reported
(D) has reported

해설 주어가 side effects 로 복수 명사이므로 have를 써야 하고, 빈칸 뒤에 목적어가 없으므로 수동형이 적합하다.

15.
(A) effect
(B) effected
(C) effective
(D) effectively

해설 the medicines have not proven to be safe or ------- 에서 be safe 에 동일한 위치에 와야하는 병렬 구조이므로 effective 가 적합하다.

16.
(A) best
(B) lots
(C) much
(D) very

해설 비교급을 수식하는 부사에 대한 문제로, much가 적절하다. 비교급을 강조하는 부사들 가운데는 even, still, far, a lot 등이 있다. 관용적으로 흔히 쓰이는 a lot better, a lot worse, a lot more 등을 기억해 둔다.

MINI TEST 3   p.206-209

A
1. (B)   2. (C)   3. (A)   4. (C)   5. (B)   6. (A)
7. (B)   8. (A)   9. (B)   10. (B)

B
1. (C)   2. (B)   3. (C)   4. (B)   5. (A)   6. (D)
7. (C)   8. (C)   9. (A)   10. (C)

C
1. (D)   2. (C)   3. (B)   4. (A)   5. (D)   6. (A)
7. (B)   8. (D)   9. (A)   10. (C)   11. (D)   12. (C)

A

1. We give you three options for delivery on most items unless they're either heavy ------- fragile.
(A) both
(B) or
(C) neither
(D) but

해석 저희는 배달될 물품이 무겁거나 깨지기 쉬운 물건이 아닌 한 대부분 물품의 배달 방법으로 세 가지 선택 사항을 드립니다.

해설 '무겁거나 깨지기 쉬운'이라는 의미가 되어야 하므로 선택의 접속사 or 가 정답이 된다.

어휘 fragile 깨지기 쉬운

2. ------- I had some trouble at the airport understanding the immigration official, my trip to Italy was pleasant.
(A) Despite
(B) In spite of
(C) Although
(D) Even

해석 공항에서 이민국 관리의 말을 이해하는 데 약간의 어려움이 있긴 했지만, 이탈리아의 내 여행은 즐거웠다.

해설 보기의 단어는 모두 뜻이 유사하다. despite 와 in spite of 는 전치사이며, even '~조차도'라는 의미의 부사이다. 보기 중 절과 절을 연결하는 접속사는 although이다.

어휘 immigration 이민, 이주

3. Now, the online system can track sales records far ------- than a printed list.
(A) more easily
(B) easiest
(C) easy
(D) easier

해석 이제 온라인 시스템은 영업 기록을 출력된 명부보다 훨씬 더 쉽게 찾을 수 있게 한다.

해설 far는 비교급을 수식하는 부사로 '훨씬'이란 뜻이다. 빈칸 뒤에 than 이 있는 것으로 보아 비교급이 사용되어야 하므로 원급인 (C)와 최상급인 (B)는 답이 될 수 없다. 동사 track을 수식하여야 하므로 부사의 비교급이어야 하므로 형용사의 비교급인 (D)도 오답이다.

어휘 track 추적하다   printed 인쇄된

4. This new device is ------- as reliable as the current one, so don't worry about the malfunctioning of the system.
(A) much
(B) far
(C) just
(D) a lot

해석 이 새로운 장치는 지금 있는 것처럼 믿을 만하니 시스템의 오작동에 대해 걱정할 필요가 없습니다.

해설 원급비교를 강조하는 부사로는 just와 nearly 등이 있다.

어휘 malfunction 오작동

5. The recent survey results indicated that ------- competition had lea to higher ticket prices and reduced choices among airlines during the past 15 years.

(A) least
(B) less
(C) fewer
(D) a few

해석 최근 조사결과에 따르면 줄어든 경쟁(경쟁의 감소)이 지난 15년간 항공권 가격 상승과 항공사 선택폭 감소의 원인이 되고 있다.

해설 more는 가산명사, 불가산명사 모두의 앞에서 쓸 수 있지만, competition이 셀 수 없는 명사이므로 셀 수 없는 명사와 같이 쓰여 '덜', '더 적은'이란 의미로 사용되는 less를 골라 써야 한다.

어휘 **survey** 설문조사 **indicate** 나타내다, 지시하다 **reduced** 감소된 **lead to ~** ~의 원인이 되다

6. Of these two applicants, Mr. Luke is the ------- qualified to work on our confidential project.

(A) better
(B) much
(C) too
(D) very

해석 두 명의 지원자 중 루크가 우리의 비밀 프로젝트에서 일하기에 더 적격이다.

해설 of the two applicants가 비교 대상이 둘임을 명시하므로 than이 필요 없다. 비교급이라도 비교대상의 둘 인 경우에는 정관사를 사용한다. the가 있으므로 최상급을 성급히 고르지 않도록 한다.

어휘 **applicant** 지원/신청/후보자 **qualified** 자격 있는 **confidential** 비밀의

7. Employees ------- would like to contribute to the public charity drive are invited to place their donations in the charity box in Ms. Lee's office.

(A) if
(B) that
(C) whom
(D) whose

해석 공공 자선 운동에 기여하고자 하는 직원은 누구나 Ms. Lee의 사무실에 있는 자선 운동에 기부를 하도록 초대됩니다.

해설 Employees ------- would like to~에서 빈칸에는 employees를 선행사로 취하는 관계대명사 자리이다. 그러므로 주격관계대명사인 who 또는 that이 가장 적합하다.

어휘 **contribute** 기부, 기여하다 **donation** 기증, 증여 **charity** 자애, 박애, 자선

8. The new bathroom fixtures will be installed next Wednesday ------- the old ones are removed this week.

(A) after
(B) although
(C) because
(D) since

해석 오래된 설비들이 이번 주에 제거 된 후에 새로운 욕실 설비가 다음 주 수요일에 설치 될 것이다.

해설 오래된 설비들이 제거 된 후에 새로운 욕실 설비가 설치 될 것이므로 해석 상 after 이 가장 적합하다.

어휘 **fixture** 정착물, 내부시설 **remove** 제거하다

9. ------- the weather improves this afternoon, we will have to cancel the workshop and the seminar.

(A) Without
(B) Unless
(C) As a result of
(D) While

해석 날씨가 오늘 오후에 좋아지지 않는다면, 우리는 워크샵과 세미나를 취소해야 할 것이다.

해설 빈칸은 절을 이끄는 접속사 자리이다. 문맥상 '만약 ~이 아니면'의 의미를 지닌 접속사 unless가 정답으로 가장 적절하다.

10. ------- the artists of the sculptures in the exhibition may be, they certainly have a keen sense of beauty.

(A) Who
(B) Whoever
(C) What
(D) Whatever

해석 전시회에서 조각가가 누구이든지 그는 미에 대한 날카로운 감각이 있다.

해설 ------- the artists of sculpture in the exhibition may be은 부사절 역할을 해야 하며, be 동사의 보어가 없다. 불완전한 절이면서, 접속사, 선행사를 모두 포함하는 복합관계대명사 whoever이 적합하다.

어휘 **sculpture** 조각 **keen** 예리한 날카로운

B

1. All special (A)[orders] must (B)[be] approved, completed, and (C)[delivered] by a shift member (D)[within] 48 hours of receiving the order.

정답 (C) deliver → delivered

해석 모든 특별 주문은 주문을 받은 후로부터 48시간 이내에 교대 직원들에 의해 승인, 완료되어 배달되어야 한다.

해설 주문은 승인되어지고, 배달되어지고 완료되어져야 하므로 수동태가 쓰여야 한다. 또한 A, B, and C 의 형태가 동일해야 함을 참고하자.

2. Many tourists recommend stopping (A)[at] beautiful Albert Park, (B)[which] one can get some rest and (C)[enjoy] a picnic (D)[with] family members.

정답 (B) which → where

해석 많은 관광객들은 아름다운 알버트 공원에 멈추기를 추천하는데 그곳에서 사람들은 휴식을 취할 수 있고 가족들과 함께 피크닉을 즐길 수 있다.

해설 앞의 선행사가 장소이므로 관계부사 which 가 아닌 where가 와야 한다.

3. The UN's World Health Organization's job (A)[is] (B)[to] make the world a (C)[healthiest] place to live (D)[in].

정답 (C) healthiest → healthier

해석 유엔 세계 보건기구는 세상을 보다 살기에 건강한 곳으로 만드는 일을 한다.

해설 문맥상 비교급이 올 자리이다. 따라서 최상급 healthiest를 healthier로 바꾼다.

4. (A)[Nationally], (B)[while] the past two years, (C)[the rate] of increase of the average full-professor salary comparted to (D)[that of] the average assistant professor decreased substantially.

정답 (B) while → during

해설 전국적으로 지난 2년 동안 정교수의 평균 봉급 인상률은 사실상 조교수들의 평균 봉급보다 줄었다.

해설 전치사와 접속사의 비교 문제로 during은 명사구를 받는 전치사이며, while은 절을 받는 접속사이다.

5. The factory supervisors believe (A)[there it is] every (B)[indication] (C)[that] products have (D)[been manufactured] at the highest level of quality.

정답 (A) there it is → there is

해설 공장 감독들은 제품이 최고 수준의 품질로 제조되었다는 징후가 있다고 믿는다.

해설 '~이 있다'는 의미로 유도부사 there와 be동사를 쓰므로, there와 is 사이에 it을 삭제해야 한다.

6. (A)[For] his convenience, Mr. Lee decided (B)[to rent] a house (C)[in] the city (D)[rather buying] a house in the country.

정답 (D) rather buying → rather than buy

해설 편의를 위해, Lee씨는 외곽에 집을 사기 보다는 시내에 집을 빌리기로 결정했다.

해설 '~보다 차라리'의 의미로 rather than을 쓰는데 decided to rent처럼 병렬구조를 이루기 때문에 rather than buy로 고쳐야 한다.

7. Ms. Lambert will (A)[receive] an award (B)[for creating] a business plan (C)[considers] original, innovative (D)[and] unique with good ideas for the future of the company.

정답 (C) considers → which considers

해설 Lambert씨는 회사 미래에 대한 독창적이며, 혁신적이며, 독특한 아이디어를 고려하는 사업계획을 기획한 것에 대하여 상을 받을 것이다.

해설 문장에 동사가 두개이므로 이 문장에서는 a business plan을 선행사로 하는 관계사 절로 만들어야 한다.

8. Buyers (A)[who] will stay for a week (B)[may] stay at the hotel outside the city, (C)[except] they (D)[request] accommodations downtown.

정답 (C) except → unless

해설 일주일 동안 머무를 바이어들이 도심지에 있는 숙박 시설을 요청하지 않는다면, 도시 외곽지역에 있는 호텔에 머무를 것이다.

해설 전치사 except 다음에 절(주어+동사)이 나왔으므로, 접속사 unless로 바꿔야 한다.

9. (A)[In addition to] both (B)[candidates] have the (C)[required] educational backgrounds, Ms. Johnson has (D)[far] more experience.

정답 (A) in addition to → Although

해설 두 명의 지원자 모두 요구된 학력의 소유자이지만 Johnson씨는 훨씬 더 경험이 많다.

해설 뒤에 주어+동사 구문이 나오므로 전치사인 in addition to를 접속사 although로 바꿔야 한다.

10. Ms. Brown is going to (A)[study] in the office (B)[until] late at night (C)[due to] she has a test for (D)[promotion] tomorrow.

정답 (C) due to → because

해설 Brown씨는 승진 시험이 내일 있기 때문에 밤늦게까지 사무실에서 공부를 할 예정이다.

해설 due to 다음에 절이 왔으므로, 접속사 because로 바꿔야 한다.

C

Questions 1-6 refer to the following article.

School has always been **1.** ------- important means of **2.** ------- the wealth of tradition from one generation to the next. This applies today to an even **3.** ------- degree than in former times. **4.** ------- modern development of economic life, the family as bearer of tradition and education **5.** -------. The continuance and health of human society are therefore in a **6.** ------- higher degree dependent on the school than formerly.

학교는 언제나 풍부한 전통을 한 세대에서 다음 세대로 전하는 중요한 수단이었다. 이것은 이전 시대보다 오늘날 더 크게 적용된다. 현대 경제 생활의 발달로 인해, 전통과 교육의 역할을 담당하는 가족의 기능이 약화되었다. 따라서 인간 사회의 지속성과 건강은 전보다 훨씬 더 학교에 의존하고 있다.

어휘 **means** 수단, 방법 **transfer** 전달하다 **the wealth of tradition** 풍부한 전통 **generation** 세대 **apply** 적용되다, 알맞다 **in an even higher degree** 훨씬 더 크게 **bearer** 전하는 사람 **weaken** 약화시키다 **continuance** 지속, 존속, 연속 **dependent on** ~에 의존하는 **formerly** 전에, 이전에

1.
(A) much
(B) little
(C) most
(D) the most

해설 문맥상 ------- important means는 '가장 중요한 수단'이라는 의미가 되어야 하므로, 최상급을 나타내는 the most가 적합하다.

2.
(A) transfer
(B) transfers
(C) transferring
(D) transferred

해설 of ------- the wealth 에서 전치사 동명사 명사의 구조이므로 transferring 이 적합하다.

3.
(A) high
(B) higher
(C) highest
(D) highly

해설 뒤의 than과 짝을 이룰 수 있는 비교급이 필요하므로 (B) higher가 정답이다. 빈칸 앞의 even은 '훨씬'이란 뜻으로 higher를 강조하고 있다.

4.
(A) Through
(B) Without
(C) In
(D) Along

해설 '현대 경제생활의 발달로 인하여'라는 의미로 through 가 가장 적합하다.

5.
(A) have weakened
(B) have been weakened
(C) has weakened
(D) has been weakened

해설 빈칸 뒤에 목적어가 없으므로, '해지고 있다'라는 의미로 현재완료 수동을 써야한다. 주어가 family 이므로 단수동사인 has been weakened 가 적합하다.

6.
(A) still
(B) many
(C) more
(D) further

해설 비교급을 강조하는 부사로는 much, far, even, still, a lot 등이 있다. 그러므로 빈칸에는 still이 적합하다.

Questions 7-12 refer to the following e-mail.

To: steve.taylor@email.com
Subject: Board Meeting on February 28

Steve, is there any possibility **7.** ------- you could reschedule the regular board meeting? I have just received an invitation to attend a conference in Shanghai during the last week of February. The Shanghai conference is sponsored by the Hong Kong Spindle Corporation. It is our **8.** ------- customer in Asia and purchases many of our components for its automated spindle monitoring systems. Managers from other companies **9.** ------- may be interested in our products will be attending the conference. It's too good an opportunity **10.** -------. Please let me know **11.** ------- you can help in this matter.
I am available during the third week of February and the first week in March. If you tell me you can't reschedule, then I'll try to figure out **12.** ------- I can do about the meeting.

Steve씨, 정기 이사회 시간을 재조정해주실 수 있습니까? 저는 2월 마지막 주 동안 상하이에서 열리는 회의 참석 초대장을 받았습니다. 상하이 회의는 홍콩 Spindle 회사가 후원합니다. Spindle 회사는 아시아에서 최고의 고객이고 자동 스핀들 모니터링 시스템에 필요한 우리의 부품들을 대량 구매합니다. 우리 제품에 관심 있는 다른 회사의 매니저들도 회의에 참석할 것입니다. 놓치기에는 너무 아까운 좋은 기회입니다. 이 일에 대해 도움을 주실 수 있는지 알려주세요. 저는 2월 셋째 주와 3월 첫째 주에 시간이 있습니다. 이사회 시간을 재조정할 수 없다고 하시면 제가 할 수 있는 것이 무엇이 있을지 찾아보도록 하겠습니다.

어휘 **reschedule** (행사, 계획 등의) 예정을 다시 세우다
conference 회의 **sponsor** 후원하다 **purchase** 구매하다
component 부품, 성분 **automated** 자동화된, 자동의
spindle 물렛가락, 축, 굴대 **pass up** 놓치다, 포기하다, 거절하다
figure out ~을 생각해내다

7.
(A) who
(B) that
(C) which
(D) what

해설 빈칸 뒤에 나온 문장과 possibility를 연결하는 단어를 찾는 유형이다. 빈칸 뒤에 나온 문장에 빠진 요소가 없다는 것이 중요한 힌트가 된다. 관계 대명사로 연결되는 문장은 불완전하기 때문에 일단 관계 대명사는 정답 후보에서 제외된다. 결국 possibility의 내용을 설명하는 '동격절'을 연결하려면 that 이 필요하다.

8.
(A) well
(B) better
(C) more
(D) best

해설 in Asia 라는 범위를 정해주면서, our 이라는 소유격이 빈칸 앞에 있으므로 최상급을 나타내는 best 가 적합하다.

9.
(A) that
(B) whom
(C) which
(D) whose

해설 Managers from other companies ------- may be interested in our products에서 선행사가 managers 인 주격관계대명사 자리이다.

10.
(A) passed up
(B) to passing up
(C) to pass up
(D) passing up

해설 빈칸 앞에 위치한 opportunity를 수식하는 to 부정사의 형용사적 용법이다.

11.
(A) although
(B) because
(C) since
(D) whether

해설 타동사인 know는 목적어가 필요한데 빈칸 뒤를 보면 하나의 문장이 나와 있다. 네 개의 선택지 모두 각각의 의미를 따져보면 모두 정답 후보가 될 수 있지만, 지문의 내용을 따져서 정답을 찾아야 한다. 일정 변경에 대한 도움을 줄 수 있는지에 대한 물음을 하는 것이기 때문에 명사절을 이끄는 whether가 가장 적당하다.

12.
(A) which
(B) that
(C) what
(D) who

해설 타동사구인 figure out의 목적어를 완성시키기 위해서는 what(the thing which)이 필요하다. 나머지 선택지는 모두 관계 대명사이기 때문에 어색하다. 선행사가 보이지 않기 때문이다. what이 관계 대명사로 쓰이면 선행사를 포함하고 있기 때문에 별도의 선행사를 필요로 하지 않는다.

실전 FINAL TEST p.210-213

A
1. (B) 2. (C) 3. (B) 4. (B) 5. (D) 6. (C)
7. (B) 8. (A) 9. (B) 10. (C)

B
1. (C) 2. (C) 3. (A) 4. (B) 5. (C) 6. (B)
7. (C) 8. (A) 9. (D) 10. (B)

C
1. (B) 2. (D) 3. (C) 4. (B) 5. (A) 6. (A)
7. (B) 8. (D) 9. (B) 10. (C) 11. (C) 12. (A)

A

1. Access to the Children's Memorial Hospital may be difficult for the next few months because the parking lot -------.
(A) is renovating
(B) is being renovated
(C) has been renovating
(D) renovated

해설 메모리얼 아동 병원은 주차장 보수 때문에 향후 몇 개월간 출입이 어려울 것이다.

해설 시간부사와 의미를 통해 적절한 동사의 시제를 결정하는 유형이다. 현재 공사가 진행 중 이라는 진행형이 필요하며 주차장이 주어로 사용되고 있으므로 동시에 수동태 구조가 필요하다. 현재진행형의 수동형은 am / is / are+being+p.p. 의 형태임을 기억해야 한다.

어휘 access to ~로의 진입/출입/접근/이용

2. When making a nomination for the service award, please consider organizations ------- programs primarily benefit women and children in need.
(A) which
(B) what
(C) whose
(D) who

해설 서비스상의 후보를 정할 때 프로그램이 무엇보다도 도움이 필요한 여자와 아이들에게 이로운 단체를 고려해 주십시오.

해설 빈칸 뒤의 문장은 주어 동사 목적어가 완벽하므로 주격, 목적격 관계대명사가 들어갈 수 없는 상황이다. 빈칸 뒤의 명사 programs와 선행사 organizations 사이에는 organizations' programs의 소유관계가 성립하므로 소유격 관계대명사 whose가 적당하다.

어휘 nomination 지명, 추천 award 상 consider 참작하다, 고려하다 primarily 우선적으로 benefit 이롭게 하다, 혜택을 주다 in need 도움이 필요한

3. In addition to holiday specials, customers can purchase ------- they are looking for with ease.
(A) that
(B) what
(C) who
(D) which

해설 고객들은 크리스마스 특별 할인 품목 외에도 그들이 찾고 있는 것을 쉽게 구입할 수 있다.

해설 ------- they are looking for는 타동사 purchase의 명사절로, '그들이 찾고 있는 것'이란 의미가 되어야 문맥이 통하므로 '~하는 것'이란 의미의 관계대명사 what이 적합하다.

어휘 with ease 쉽게, 손쉽게

4. Carl McGuire is a vice president for New York Telephone, ------- he has worked for 30 years.
(A) which
(B) where
(C) who
(D) that

해설 Carl McGuire은 New York Telephone 사의 부사장인데, 그는 그곳에서 30년 동안 일했다.

해설 선행사는 New York Telephone이고, 빈칸 이하인 he has worked for 30 years는 완전한 절이므로 빈칸에는 관계부사 where가 적합하다.

5. Tommy Electronics, Inc. provides innovative products ------- revolutionize business operations for our customers worldwide.
(A) who
(B) whom
(C) whose
(D) that

해설 Tommy 전자는 전 세계의 고객들에게 사업 운영을 급격히 변하게 하는 혁신적인 제품을 제공한다.

해설 innovate products 가 선행사이므로 which 또는 that 이 가장 적합하다.

어휘 revolutionize 혁명(대변혁)을 일으키다

6. All the money Mr. Fetzer earns each month in commissions on sales ------- to his account 30 days after the last day of the month.
(A) credited
(B) are credited
(C) is credited
(D) credits

해석 Fetzer 씨가 이달에 판매 수수료로 벌어들인 돈은 이달 말일로부터 30일 후에 그의 계좌로 들어간다.
해설 주어인 money는 셀 수 없는 명사이므로 단수 동사를 써야 한다. 또한 credit은 타동사이나 목적어가 없는 형태이므로 수동형이 적합하다.
어휘 commission 수수료 credit ~의 대변에 기입하다, ~을 믿다, 신용하다 account 계좌

7. After the inspection -------, all the management of our factory was pleased to get a good result.
(A) had completed
(B) had been completed
(C) will be completed
(D) is completing

해석 검사가 끝난 후, 우리 공장의 경영진은 좋은 결과를 받은 것에 기뻐했다.
해설 빈칸은 동사 자리이며, after 이하가 먼저 있었던 일이며, complete은 타동사인데 목적어가 없으므로, 과거완료시제의 수동형을 써야 한다. 그러므로 정답은 (B) had been completed이다.
어휘 inspect 검사하다 inspection 검열, 조사 complete 완성하다 management 경영진 factory 공장 result 결과

8. The new sales plan ------- after receiving the analysis of the customer survey responses.
(A) has been modified
(B) has modified
(C) modified
(D) were modified

해석 새로운 판매 기획은 소비자 조사 반응 분석을 받고 나서 수정되었다.
해설 modify는 타동사이므로 뒤에 목적어가 없으면 수동형으로 써야 한다.
어휘 modify 수정하다 analysis 분석

9. Please ask your customers to confirm their billing addresses before receiving their ------- by credit card.
(A) paying
(B) payment
(C) payable
(D) paid

해석 신용카드로 대금을 받기 이 전에, 고객들에게 그들의 계산서가 발송되는 주소를 확인하도록 요구해라.
해설 정관사 the 뒤에는 명사가 와야 한다.
어휘 confirm 확인하다 billing 청구서 작성 발송

10. If the computer malfunction had not been reported quickly, we ------- the technical support we needed today.
(A) will not receive
(B) cannot receive
(C) would not have received
(D) had received

해석 컴퓨터의 오작동이 빨리 보고되지 않았다면, 우리는 오늘 필요했던 기술 지원을 받지 못했을 것이다.
해설 if절의 동사 형태에 주목하자. had not been reported의 형태는 '가정법 과거완료'로 이미 완료된 사건에 대한 반대 상황을 가정할 때 사용된다. 주절 형태는 '조동사(would / should / could)+have+과거분사'의 형태를 취해야 한다.

B

1. (A)[After] the new employees (B)[have completed] (C)[them] orientation and training, they will (D)[be assigned to] their respective departments.

정답 (C) them → their
해석 새로운 직원들이 오리엔테이션과 훈련을 마치면 각각 특기 부서로 배치 될 것이다.
해설 'orientation~' 앞에는 대명사 목적격이 아닌 명사를 받는 소유격이 필요하므로 them을 their로 수정해야 한다.

2. All (A)[the] money Mr. Robinson (B)[earns] each month in commissions on sales (C)[are credited] (D)[to] his account 45 days after the last day of the month.

정답 (C) are credited → is credited
해석 Robinson씨가 이달에 영업 수당으로 벌어들인 돈은 이달 마지막 날로부터 45일 후에 그의 계좌로 들어간다.
해설 money는 셀 수 없는 명사이므로 복수 동사인 are와 같이 나올 수 없다.

3. According (A)[to a recent] survey, online (B)[shoppers] buy (C)[from] small and large e-businesses (D)[alike].

정답 (A) to recent → to a recent
해석 최근 조사에 따르면, 온라인 구매자들은 인터넷 쇼핑몰의 크기에 관계없이 물품을 구입한다.
해설 survey는 셀 수 있는 명사이므로 관사 a를 앞에 붙여야 한다.

4. Joseph's films (A)[have] received (B)[highly] praise for (C)[his] portrayals of multidimensional characters (D)[and] funny, true-to-life human interactions.

정답 (B) highly → high
해설 Joseph의 영화들은 다중인격체들과 재미있고 진솔한 삶을 사는 인간 관계를 표현한 것으로 높은 칭송을 받아왔다.
해설 명사를 수식하는 것은 형용사이다. 따라서 부사 highly를 형용사 high로 바꿔야 한다.

5. (A)[Thousands of] high school students (B)[are held] back every year, mainly (C)[so] they need (D)[help with] developing ideas for reading or writing as well as analyzing an extended essay.

정답 (C) so → because
해설 수천 명의 학생들이 매년 뒤처지고 있고 주로 그들이 쓰기와 읽기에 있어서 의식을 진전시키고 보통수준의 수필을 분석하는데 도움을 필요로 하기 때문이다.

해설 앞 문장에 대한 이유를 뒤 문장이 설명하고 있으므로 이유나 원인을 나타내는 접속사 because나 since로 고쳐야 한다.

6. The Public Relations Department (A)[has received] a couple of (B)[e-mails which] customers (C)[complain about] the poor customer service (D)[at] our movie theater.

정답 (B) e-mails which → e-mails where

해설 홍보 부서는 우리 영화관의 형편없는 고객 서비스에 대한 고객들의 불만사항이 담긴 두 통의 이메일을 받았다.

해설 전치사 in이 포함된 관계부사가 올 자리이다. 따라서 which를 where로 바꿔야 한다.

7. (A)[A wide range] of skiing opportunities exist (B)[within] a short (C)[distant] (D)[of] the Hampshire campus.

정답 (C) distant → distance

해설 폭 넓은 스키의 기회가 Hampshire 캠퍼스에서 가까운 거리 내에 산재해 있다.

해설 '가까운 거리 내에'라는 의미를 가진 숙어로 'within a short distance'를 쓴다.

8. I should inform (A)[to you] that our store policy (B)[prohibits] (C)[refunds] or exchanges (D)[on] sale items.

정답 (A) to you → you

해설 저희 가게 정책은 할인 품목에 대해서는 환불 또는 교환을 금지하고 있습니다.

해설 inform은 타동사이므로 to를 삭제해야 한다.

9. Before (A)[retiring] from NJT today, Benjamin (B)[was] a manager for New Jersey Telephone, (C)[where] he worked (D)[since] 40 years.

정답 (D) since → for

해설 오늘 New Jersey 전화회사로부터 퇴직하기 전에 Benjamin은 New Jersey 전화회사의 부장이었고 그곳에서 40년동안 일했다.

해설 기간을 나타내는 전치사 for가 사용되어야 하며 since는 ~이래로 라는 뜻으로 현재완료와 함께 주로 쓰인다.

10. Mr. Smith will (A)[be reprimanded] for having given (B)[inaccurately] and questionable (C)[information] to overseas buyers (D)[at the] last conference.

정답 (B) inaccurately → inaccurate

해설 Smith씨는 지난번 회의에서 해외 바이어들에게 부정확하고 의문이 가는 정보를 준 것으로 질책 받을 것이다.

해설 형용사 questionable과 and로 대구를 이루며 부사인 inaccurately를 형용사 inaccurate로 바꿔야 한다.

C

Questions 1-6 refer to the following letter.

April 10th

Family Medical Services
1649 East Lake Avenue
Brookings, NY 84325

To **1.** ------- It May Concern:

Recently, I **2.** ------- another notice for payment from your Billing Department.

I **3.** ------- you a copy of the statement from my credit card company showing the amount of $30 for my blood tests once again. Please note that this charge **4.** ------- on March 15; my balance **5.** ------- on March 30.

Please **6.** ------- to this letter by calling me at (815)-881-5595.

Sincerely,
Ann Lauren

4월 10일

가족 의료 서비스
1649 이스트 레이크 애버뉴
브룩킹스, 뉴욕 84325

담당자 귀하,
최근에 저는 귀사의 청구 담당 부서로부터 다시 공지를 받았습니다. 혈액 검사에 대하여 30달러를 지불했다는 증명서 사본을 신용카드 회사에서 받아서 다시 보내 드립니다.
이것은 3월 15일에 청구된 것이며 3월 30일에 지불되었다는 것을 숙지하여 주시기 바랍니다. 이 편지를 받으시면 (815)-881-5595로 저에게 전화 주시면 감사하겠습니다.

Ann Lauren 드림

어휘 **billing department** 청구서 발송부   **statement** 명세서
charge 요금   **balance** 잔고, 잔여, 나머지

1.
(A) Who
(B) Whom
(C) What
(D) That

해설 관계자 분에게 라는 관용적인 표현으로 To Whom It May Concern을 기억해 두자. Whom은 전치사 To의 목적격으로 쓰였다.

2.
(A) am receiving
(B) will receive
(C) receive
(D) have received

해설 recently는 현재 완료형 또는 과거형과 함께 쓴다.

3.
(A) have been sent
(B) was being sent
(C) am sending
(D) was sent

해설 지금 현재 쓰고 있는 편지와 함께 보내고 있으므로 현재진행형이 가장 적합하다.

4.
(A) will be made
(B) was made
(C) have made
(D) was making

해설 Part 6에는 날짜를 비교하여 시제를 찾는 문제가 자주 등장한다. 편지를 쓴 날짜는 April 10,이고 본문에서 on March 15는 과거의 일이므로 과거시제가 가장 적합하다.

5.
(A) was paid
(B) paid
(C) is paying
(D) has paid

해설 빈칸 뒤에 목적어가 없이 전치사 on 만 있으므로 수동형이 적합하다.

6.
(A) respond
(B) contact
(C) call
(D) answer

해설 빈칸 뒤에 전치사 to 가 있으므로 자동사인 respond 가 적합하다.

Questions 7-12 refer to the following notice.

O'Hare International Airport Security Update

Due to increased security **7.** ------- at O'Hare International Airport, be aware of the following precautionary measures.

All non-ticketed individuals will **8.** ------- from passing the security barriers. All ticketed passengers may be subject to: Hand search of all carry-on items. Passengers will be asked for their cooperation; passengers not approach, touch, or in any way interfere with the security agent **9.** ------- the search. If any **10.** ------- occurs, agents may be asked to escort passengers to a Security Office.

There may be pat-down and sensor-wanding by same-gender security agents if there is a need as **11.** ------- by metal detector sensors.

For a complete **12.** ------- of passenger regulations and rights, please visit us online at www.bghairport.com or contact your local airline branch or travel agency.

오헤어 국제공항 보안 업데이트

오헤어 국제공항의 보안 기준이 강화됨에 따라 다음과 같은 예방책을 주지하여 주시기 바랍니다.

탑승권을 소지하지 않으면 보안 검색대를 통과할 수 없습니다. 탑승권을 소지한 승객은 다음 절차를 거치게 됩니다.

소지한 물품의 검색. 승객들의 협조가 요구됩니다. 승객들은 검색 중에 보안 요원에게 접근하거나 손을 대는 등 어떠한 방해도 해서는 안 됩니다. 이러한 방해가 발생하면 승객은 보안 사무국으로의 호송이 요청될 것입니다. 금속 탐지기 센서가 작동하는 등 필요한 경우에는 같은 성별의 보안 요원에 의해 몸수색과 막대 탐지기 수색을 하게 됩니다.

승객 규정과 권리에 대한 리스트를 원하시면 www.bghairport.com 으로 방문해 주시거나 지역 항공사 또는 여행사에 연락해 주십시오.

어휘 **standard** 기준 **be aware of** ~을 알아차리다, ~을 알다
precautionary 예방   **bar A from B** A가 B하는 것을 금지하다, 막다 **be subject to** ~을 조건으로 하다, ~을 필요로 하다
carry-on (항공기 내에) 들고 들어갈 수 있는, 휴대할 수 있는
interfere with 방해하다   **pat-down** 몸수색 **sensor-wanding** 센서 막대로 몸을 훑기

7.
(A) standard
(B) standards
(C) standardize
(D) standardized

해설 '보안 기준'이라는 의미의 복합명사 자리이다. 가산 명사는 관사 a나 the와 함께 쓰지 않을 때는 복수형을 써야 한다. 그러므로 standards 가 적합하다.

8.
(A) bar
(B) have barred
(C) be barring
(D) be barred

해설 조동사 will 다음에 동사원형을 써서, '금지 되어지다'라는 의미로 수동형인 be barred 가 적합하다.

9.
(A) throughout
(B) during
(C) along
(D) with

해설 '수색하는 동안'이라는 의미 특정 명사 앞에는 during을 쓴다.

10.
(A) interfere
(B) interfered
(C) interference
(D) interfering

해설 부사절 접속사 if 뒤의 any는 형용사이며 빈칸은 형용사 뒤에 오는 명사 자리이며 동시에 주어 역할을 해야 한다. 그러므로 interference 가 가장 적합하다.

11.
(A) display
(B) displaying
(C) displayed
(D) displays

해설 as 다음에 분사가 필요한 자리이며 뒤에 목적어가 없으므로 수동형인 과거분사 displayed 가 적합하다.

12.
(A) list
(B) lists
(C) listing
(D) listed

해설 부정관사 a 뒤에는 반드시 가산 명사의 단수형이 와야 한다. 형용사 complete의 수식을 받는 가산 단수 명사는 list이다.

불규칙 변화 동사표

현재	과거	과거분사	뜻
be	was / were	been	~이다, 있다
become	became	become	되다
begin	began	begun	시작하다
bend	bent	bent	구부리다
bet	bet	bet	내기하다
bite	bit	bitten	물다
bleed	bled	bled	피 흘리다
blow	blew	blown	불다
break	broke	broken	깨다
bring	brought	brought	가져오다
build	built	built	세우다
burst	burst	burst	터지다
buy	bought	bought	사다
catch	caught	caught	잡다
choose	chose	chosen	선택하다
come	came	come	오다
cost	cost	cost	비용이 들다
creep	crept	crept	기다
cut	cut	cut	자르다
deal	dealt	dealt	다루다
do	did	done	하다
draw	drew	drawn	그리다
drink	drank	drunk	마시다
drive	drove	driven	운전하다
eat	ate	eaten	먹다
fall	fell	fallen	떨어지다
feed	fed	fed	먹이다
feel	felt	felt	느끼다
fight	fought	fought	싸우다
find	found	found	발견하다
fit	fit	fit	꼭 맞다
fly	flew	flown	날다
forget	forgot	forgotten	잊다
forgive	forgave	forgiven	용서하다
freeze	froze	frozen	얼다

현재	과거	과거분사	뜻
get	got	gotten	얻다
give	gave	given	가지다
go	went	gone	가다
grow	grew	grown	성장하다
hang	hung	hung	자라다
have	had	had	가지다
hear	heard	heard	듣다
hide	hid	hidden	숨기다
hit	hit	hit	치다
hold	held	held	잡다
hurt	hurt	hurt	다치게 하다
keep	kept	kept	유지하다
know	knew	known	알다
lay	laid	laid	놓다
lead	led	led	이끌다
leave	left	left	떠나다
lend	lent	lent	빌려주다
let	let	let	시키다
lie	lay	lain	눕다
lose	lost	lost	잃다
make	made	made	만들다
mean	meant	meant	뜻하다
meet	met	met	만나다
pay	paid	paid	지불하다
put	put	put	놓다, 두다
quit	quit	quit	그만두다
read	read[red]	read[red]	읽다
ride	rode	ridden	올라타다
ring	rang	rung	(소리) 울리다
run	ran	run	달리다
say	said	said	말하다
see	saw	seen	보다
seek	sought	sought	찾다
sell	sold	sold	팔다
send	sent	sent	보내다

Memo

Memo

https://books.english.co.kr